BOSTON COLLEGE, CONNECTICUT, GEORGETOWN, PITTSBURGH, PROVIDENCE, SETON HALL, ST. JOHN'S, SYRACUSE, VILLANOVA

Ten short years ago, the only common thread among these nine schools was cumulative basketball identity crisis. Though several teams within the group were of high caliber, the lack of an identifiable nucleus left them with little media coverage and even less noteriety.

How things have changed for the Big East.

Big-name coaches like John Thompson, Jim Boeheim, and Lou Carnesecca have given it indisputable distinction. Big-talent players like Patrick Ewing, Chris Mullin, and Mark Jackson have made the action as fast-paced and climactic as pro ball. Big-money media attention has made the Big East the most glamorous and most watched college basketball conference in the United States.

Now BIG HOOPS takes you behind the scenes for a close-up look at the plays and personalities that make the Big East the most thrilling conference in the NCAA. . . .

"REYNOLDS CAPTURES THE ESSENCE OF COLLEGE BASKETBALL . . . his love for the sport is evident."—*Publishers Weekly*

BIG HOOPS

A Season in the Big East Conference

by

Bill Reynolds

A SIGNET BOOK

SIGNET
Published by the Penguin Group
Penguin Books USA Inc., 375 Hudson Street,
New York, New York 10014, U.S.A.
Penguin Books Ltd, 27 Wrights Lane,
London W8 5TZ, England
Penguin Books Australia Ltd, Ringwood,
Victoria, Australia
Penguin Books Canada Ltd, 2801 John Street,
Markham, Ontario, Canada L3R 1B4
Penguin Books (N.Z.) Ltd, 182–190 Wairau Road,
Auckland 10, New Zealand

Penguin Books Ltd, Registered Offices:
Harmondsworth, Middlesex, England

Published by Signet, an imprint of New American Library, a division of
Penguin Books USA Inc. This book previously appeared in an NAL Books edition.

First Signet Printing, November, 1990
10 9 8 7 6 5 4 3 2 1

 REGISTERED TRADEMARK—MARCA REGISTRADA

PRINTED IN THE UNITED STATES OF AMERICA

To my brother, Geoff, and my sister, Polly, both of whom grew up listening to the thump of the ball on the driveway. And to CZ, who believed when no one else did.

ACKNOWLEDGMENTS

A lot of people contribute to the making of a book. At the risk of leaving some people out, here are some special ones: David Vigliano, a great agent who believed in the idea from the beginning, and Kevin Mulroy who supported it. Both have my gratitude and enduring thanks.

Thanks to Michael Wilbon, David Ramsey, Bob Snyder, Steve Halvonik, Randy Smith, Phil Chardis, Pat Drewry, Mike Gorman, Dick Weiss, Charlie Pierce, Rich Chvotkin, Chuck Wilson, Bill Raftery, Ron Perry, Tom McElroy, Dee Rowe, Linda Bruno, Teri Schindler, and Ray Perry: all gave their insight.

Also to Gregg Burke, Tim Tolikan, Reid Oslin, John Paquette, Larry Kimball, Bill Shapland, Craig Miller, pros all. And thanks to John Paine, who can play on my team anytime; to Ken Ford, Liz Abbott, Jim Cox, Ed Shein, and Karen Anderson for helping me keep it in perspective; and to Greg Donaldson, Rick Landau, Mike Fahey, and John Mogulescu, friends forever.

Special thanks to Chris Plonsky, who repeatedly went out of her way, and to Dave Reid and Dave Bloss of the *Providence Journal*, two of the greatest bosses anyone could ever have.

CONTENTS

BIG
HOOPS

INTRODUCTION

One day in the mid-seventies I walked into the sports information office at Providence College. I was trying to eke out a living as a free-lance writer at the time, and one of the things I did then was some work—writing game programs, feature stories on the players—for Mike Tranghese, then the Providence sports information director.

"Dave Gavitt has a great idea. What do you think of a league in the East?" Tranghese asked.

"What kind of a league?"

"A good one."

I wasn't sure about a league, but I knew better than to underestimate Dave Gavitt. Back then he was the coach and athletic director at Providence, but our paths had crossed before. He had been the coach at Dartmouth when I had played for Brown in the late sixties. More important, he had been an assistant coach at Worcester Academy, a Massachusetts prep school, the year before I went there. He had worked there for Dee Rowe, who later coached at Connecticut, and basketball at Worcester Academy was a way of life.

Gavitt is now often called the most important man in college basketball. But the roots of his Big East Conference go back to a different time, a time of long bus rides on cold, winter nights, cramped gyms, and locker rooms that never seemed to have enough hot water. It was a basketball world so different from the one he inhabits now.

But I wasn't thinking about any of that on that afternoon long ago when I walked into Tranghese's office. A new league in the East? Just what exactly did that mean?

Tranghese talked that day about the advantages of a new league, but it all seemed fuzzy. And why would Providence College want to be in a league? Weren't they drawing well enough? Weren't they invariably going to a post-season tournament? What did they need a league for?

College basketball was different in the mid-seventies. Few games were on television. Few colleges had big arenas, especially in the Northeast. Yes, Providence played in a new downtown civic center, but that was rare. Boston College played in Roberts Center, their cramped gym on campus. Connecticut, Villanova, St. John's, Seton Hall, all played in small, dark gyms on campus. As for Georgetown or Syracuse? I had no idea. Providence rarely played them in those days.

I was surprised when Tranghese left Providence College to go to work for this new Big East Conference. There wasn't even a conference office that first year, not really. Tranghese and his secretary, Diane Woods, shared a cubbyhole of a room in the back of the Providence advertising firm of Duffy & Shanley. Gavitt was still the athletic director at Providence College, so he was rarely around. There was no sign, no receptionist, and to get to Tranghese's desk you had to walk through the middle of the advertising agency, past desks and people who had no clue who you were or where you were going.

One of Tranghese's jobs that first year was to sell the conference, to make sure, as he used to say, that by the end of that first year people would not confuse the Big East with some new taste treat from McDonald's. My role was to help write a weekly newsletter. A house organ full of stats and feature stories, it was sent to newspapers and various subscribers around the league, intended to educate people to what this new league was.

There was an innocence to the Big East then. With the exception of John Thompson, the coaches were accessible. I could call them on the phone and get what I wanted easily enough. The players had not yet been flooded with media demands. The coaches had not yet started to make the kind of money that has since made them celebrities.

This was before John Thompson had become a national figure. He was just somebody who didn't return phone calls then, someone I remembered from growing up in Rhode Island and seeing play for Providence College in the early sixties. Rollie Massimino and Jim Boeheim were known only to the most ardent of basketball aficionados. The most famous coach was Looie Carnesecca.

In a sense I watched the Big East grow up.

Not that I was aware of it at the time. That changed a few years ago when I became a sports writer. The first Final Four tournament I ever covered, fittingly enough, was in Lexington, Kentucky, in 1985, the year Villanova won. That was the year that three Big East teams made the Final Four: the Wildcats, Georgetown, and St. John's. Shortly before the semifinals started, the chant of "Big East, Big East" reverberated through the building. I saw Tranghese two days later, on the afternoon of the national championship game between Villanova and Georgetown. The Big East would have their first national champion. Tranghese just shrugged. Then he smiled. What was there to say? Seven years before he had been sitting in the back of the Providence advertising firm, and he remembered.

Dick Weiss of the Philadelphia *Daily News* says that to understand college basketball you had to be around in the late 1950s and 1960s. It's easy to forget that. We see the games on television, and it's only natural to think that college basketball began with the Carrier Dome and the Big East. It didn't. And if the Big East has now come to define college basketball in the East, to fully appreciate it it's important to understand what it evolved out of.

Big Hoops tries to capture some of the subculture that is college basketball, and to provide an understanding of the Conference that television cameras can't. *Big Hoops* is more than just the games. It covers the coaches, the players, the pressure, the effect of celebrity, the phenomenon that is the Big East Conference. But most of all it's about the culture of basketball, viewed from the perspective of someone who remembers when a basketball conference in the East was just an idea floating around in Dave Gavitt's head.

PROLOGUE

It is media day in the media league.

The setting is the ballroom of the Grand Hyatt Hotel on 42nd Street in Manhattan, and over three hundred reporters, including Billy Packer of CBS, Dick Schaap of NBC, and Dick Vitale and Billy Raftery of ESPN, have gathered in the large, mirrored ballroom. On a raised dais the nine coaches of the Big East sit at small tables. In an adjacent ballroom are an assortment of players from each school, many of the league's glamour players. A decade ago Big East media day was little more than a public-relations ploy to get the league some November publicity. Now it's become an event.

Hovering in the air is the feeling that this is going to be a big year for the Big East. In addition to being the league's 10th anniversary, it figures to be a season in which the Big East reestablishes its claim as the best college basketball conference in the country. Four league teams are ranked in the top 20: Georgetown, Syracuse, Villanova, and Connecticut. The Big East recruited the two best high-school players in the country last year in Georgetown's Alonzo Mourning from Chesapeake, Virginia, and Syracuse's Billy Owens from

Carlisle, Pennsylvania. They are the cornerstone of a recruiting class that's being touted as the best since the Patrick Ewing–Chris Mullin–Ed Pinckney class that came into the league in September 1981.

It's all a media smorgasbord, reporters moving from coach to coach like it's a trip to the salad bar. It also doesn't take the coaches long to realize just where they fall in the Big East pecking order, since there's a direct relationship between success of the coach and the number of writers who surround his table. Jim Boeheim of Syracuse, Rollie Massimino of Villanova, Lou Carnesecca of St. John's: they are the heavyweights and are continually mobbed. Paul Evans of Pittsburgh, P. J. Carlesimo of Seton Hall, and Jim Calhoun are the contenders. Jim O'Brien of Boston College and Rick Barnes of Providence are the lightweights, coaches of the two teams expected to finish eighth and ninth in the league and play in the qualifying game in the Big East Tournament next March, the Big East's so-called "game of shame."

And John Thompson?

On this morning in New York he is in a class by himself.

These are strange times for Thompson—"Large Father," as he's called around the league. On one hand he's become larger than life, one of the most famous coaches, certainly the most recognizable black coach, in all of basketball. He has a sneaker contract from Nike that pays him $200,000 a year, the highest in the country. He has a salary at Georgetown that pays him in the vicinity of $400,000 a year. He does national ads for Transamerica Life and Digital. He is represented by Pro-Serve of Washington, the only coach among the roughly one hundred celebrities Pro-Serve represents. He lives in a house provided for him by Georgetown alumni. By any standard of measurement he's at the pinnacle of his profession.

But earlier in the fall his United States Olympic basketball team lost to the Russians in the semifinals, 82–76, a game in which not only Thompson's method in selecting his team but also his coaching had come into question. There were rumors of players chafing under his strong hand. Others said that Thompson had recreated a Georgetown environment, complete with closed practices and minimal contact with the media. Hoya Paranoia cloaked in the American flag. The joke around the Olympic Village was that the Soviets were more accessible than the Americans.

From the time he had selected the team, Thompson had been criticized for his choices. Dana Barros, who had led the Big East in scoring, originally wasn't even invited to the trials, though John Turner, a Georgetown transfer from Allegany Junior College, was. Sherman Douglas, considered by many to be among the elite point guards in the country, didn't make the first cut. There were other examples, and the consensus was that Thompson was trying to replicate a Georgetown team, emphasizing pressure defense at the expense of scoring ability.

But on this morning he is being downright charming, another evidence of the theory that he turns on the charm in direct proportion to how much he feels he's under attack. No one ever said John Thompson isn't complicated.

"How tired are you now?" he is asked. It is a reference to the punishing schedule he has had the past two years, a schedule that began when he spent the summer of 1987 scouting international teams.

"I'm tired of people asking how tired I am," he says, patting his side in mock horror. "I feel like I have leprosy."

Next to Thompson is Pittsburgh's Paul Evans. Two years ago he was one of the hottest coaches in the country, someone who made his players into overacheivers. He had led a Navy team featuring David Robinson into the Eastern Regionals, then jumped to Pittsburgh for the big bucks and the Big East's big stage. At the time Pitt was the Big East's mystery guest, the football school that had gotten into the Big East in 1982 only to become a study in underachievement. Last year he was 24–7, but the year had ended badly. Pittsburgh had lost to Vanderbilt in the second round of the NCAA tournament, amid charges by some players that Evans and the coaching staff had unraveled in the closing seconds.

Evans's personal life-style was also under scrutiny. Divorced three times, he had a tendency to be all too visible in the city's singles bars. The cumulative effect was that for all the victories, some of the luster had come off Evans in his two years at Pitt.

There's a certain irony in Evans sitting next to Thompson. After losing a close game in the Capital Centre to Georgetown the year before, a game marred by a bench-clearing brawl, Evans had angrily ripped Georgetown: "They let John Thompson run everything at the school. He's more powerful than the athletic director and the president."

It was not Evans's first clash with the coaching hierarchy in the Big East, the old guard that includes Thompson, Massimino, Boeheim, and Carnesecca. They are the four most successful Big East coaches, the four that have become national figures. They are also the only four who have essentially been in the league since the beginning in 1979, although Massimino and Villanova joined the following year. The five others are the understudies. So there have been times when there's been subtle pressure for the other five to acquiesce to the kings.

Not Evans.

On the other side of Evans is Rick Barnes of Providence, the new coach in the Big East. At 34, he looks as youthful as a former college kid on his first job out of college, and he's the first coach in Big East history with a Southern accent. A year ago he was at George Mason in Fairfax, Virginia, in his first year as a head coach. Now he's taking over a Providence team that had been riddled with dissension the previous year and universally picked to finish ninth in the conference this year.

"I think a lot of people in this room are taking this a whole lot more seriously than I am," he says, looking around the room.

To Thompson's right is Jim Calhoun of Connecticut, a big man in his mid-forties. About to begin his third season at Connecticut, he has come direct from winning the National Invitational Tournament, the shining moment of Connecticut basketball. Two years ago he was a highly successful, if obscure, coach at Northeastern. His teams had played in relative anonymity, but when it all unraveled for Dom Perno at Connecticut, the school had come wooing Calhoun, giving him a seven-year contract for more money than he had ever dreamed of. All of a sudden the anonymous coach was in a media spotlight, covered by a press horde from 14 daily newspapers, the biggest in college basketball. Calhoun loved it. He took to the attention like a moth to light.

Now his Huskies have already been ranked as high as 12th in the country in one preseason poll. His first two years have been a coaching honeymoon, but now he's expected to win.

Next to him is Jim O'Brien of Boston College. Besides Thompson, he is the only Big East coach who played in the pros. After starring on good Boston College teams in the late sixties, O'Brien played several years in the ABA. Now he's in his third year at Boston College. Last year, with inferior talent and expected to finish last, the Eagles won six Big East games. Then they went to the semifinals of the NIT, ending the year on a high note. Some people thought O'Brien did the best coaching job in the conference, having done the most with the least.

On one side of the room, at tables on a raised dais, are Massimino, Boeheim, Carlesimo, and Carnesecca.

Four years ago Massimino was the coaching story in the country. His Wildcats, the Cinderella team of the 1985 NCAA tournament, beat Georgetown in one of the most exciting finals in tournament history. The classic underdogs, Villanova was a team the entire country had fallen in love with, led by the rumpled coach on the sidelines whose emotions were etched all over his face: "Daddy Mass." Add in wheelchair-bound Jake Nevin, Villanova's long-time trainer who was dying of Lou Gehrig's disease on the bench, and it was one of the great stories in all of sports, the kind of heart-warming human-interest story that college basketball seems to have a patent on.

Last year Massimino's Villanova team finished 24–13 and went to the finals of the Southeast Regional before getting beaten by Oklahoma. It was the furthest any Big East team advanced in the tournament. Now he's back with a senior-dominated team, one that's already drawing comparisons to the '85 team.

Next to Massimino is Boeheim, a tall, angular man with a high forehead who looks like a prep-school history teacher. A former Syracuse player (his backcourt partner was the great Dave Bing), Boeheim has long been used to the pressure that comes with coaching at Syracuse, one of the places where no matter what you do it's never enough. He's routinely criticized in Syracuse, even though his winning percentage is .756, fourth best among active coaches, behind Jerry Tarkanian, John Cheney, and Dean Smith. He's also taken the Orangemen to a postseason tournament in each of his 12 seasons.

By the first of the year he will already have won 300 games, one of the quickest ever to do so, but even then the perception of him will be that he's someone who wins because of his players' talent, not for his coaching ability. That's the monkey that always seems to be on Boeheim's back. The one thing that will take it off is winning the national championship. Two years ago in New Orleans he came close, losing to Indiana at the buzzer, and last year the Orangemen went 26–5. Most coaches would mortgage their mothers for that, but at Syracuse it's not enough. They lost to underdog Rhode Island in the second round of the NCAA tournament, and another season had ended in disappointment and finger-pointing. No wonder Boeheim's public image is of a man who's always tasting something sour.

Now, once again, he's faced with unbelievably high expectations. The Orangemen have been picked as high as fifth in the country.

P. J. Carlesimo is fortunate to be here at all.

Last February he was all but gone as the coach at Seton Hall. The Pirates were last in the league, and booing at home games had become as much a part of the pregame ritual as layup drills and the National Anthem. Rumors were everywhere that Carlesimo, in the last year of his contract, would not be renewed. The best-liked coach in the conference, it hadn't happened for P. J. at Seton Hall.

When he had gotten the job in 1982, the Hall had been awful. Though the talent steadily improved, the Hall remained a Big East patsy. Then in February, a front-page article in the student newspaper said that the student senate had asked for Carlesimo's resignation. He never reacted, seemingly oblivious to the controversy that swirled around him, trying to prevent his impending fate from being a distraction to his team, while everyone knew the firing squad was all lined up, guns loaded, about to pull the triggers.

But the Hall won six of their last seven and reached 20 wins for the first time in over 30 years. They also got their first NCAA bid ever, and Carlesimo was named the Big East coach of the year. He also got a new five-year contract.

And it was only afterward that he publicly showed the emotion that he'd been hiding all year. He accepted the Big East coach-of-the-year trophy with tears in his eyes. He broke down at the Pirates' postseason banquet, an event that even the Seton Hall chancellor said, only half in jest, came close to "being a testimonial."

Next to Carlesimo is Carnesecca, as New York as an egg cream. He is short, he wears glasses, he has brown hair that falls across his forehead. The rumpled, lovable master of the malapropism, Carnesecca has long been one of New York City's icons, college basketball's version of Casey Stengel. He runs up and down the sidelines like some marionette on amphetamines, dying a thousand deaths, his emotions stamped all over his face.

But the past few years the snipers have been taking their shots. He's been criticized for his propensity to make playground players walk the ball up the court, essentially robbing them of their individual games. Last year Pat Riley said that Willie Glass, a former Carnesecca player in training camp with the Lakers, was the least fundamentally sound player he'd ever seen.

Last year when Chris Mullin, Carnesecca's all-time pet, admitted his alcohol problem had begun at St. John's, the coach said he had known nothing about it. This started Peter Vecsey of the New York *Post* making constant references to Looie's blinders. Now whenever something happens that is painfully obvious, Vecsey writes that "everyone knew except Looie Carnesecca."

They are nine different personalities, all with their own

pressures. They are also coaching in an era that's very different from what it used to be. Unlike the pros, college basketball has become a coach's game. The coaches are the recognizable names. The average fan sitting out there in TV land might not know who makes up the starting Villanova backcourt, but he knows Rollie Massimino is the coach. He knows Carnesecca is the coach at St. John's and that Jim Boeheim is the one standing on the sidelines in the Carrier Dome, no matter who is slam-dunking. The coaches have become the stars.

Reporters lift their heads as Dave Gavitt, the commissioner and founder of the Big East, takes the podium in the front of the room.

He is 51, the former coach of Providence and the coach of the ill-fated 1980 Olympic team. Some have called him the most powerful man in college basketball. Certainly he is one of the most respected. A few weeks ago he was named the president of the United States of America Amateur Basketball Association.

The results of the coaches' preseason voting are announced: Syracuse and Georgetown tied for first, Villanova third, Pittsburgh and UConn tied for fourth. Then St. John's, Seton Hall, Boston College, and Providence.

The preseason first guards are both seniors, Sherman Douglas of Syracuse and Boston College's Dana Barros. The other three are Cliff Robinson, a 6-11 senior from the University of Connecticut; Derrick Coleman, a 6-9 Syracuse junior; and Doug West, a 6-5 senior from Villanova. The second team features Georgetown guard Charlie Smith, the point guard on the Olympic team; Villanova senior point guard Kenny Wilson; Syracuse junior swingman Stevie Thompson; Tom Greis, the 7-2 junior center from Villanova; and Ramon Ramos, a 6-8 senior from Seton Hall who played on the Puerto Rican Olympic team.

The preseason freshman of the year is Mourning.

Mike Tranghese, Gavitt's right-hand man, stands in the front of the room, thinking aloud about the first Big East media day, and how far this conference has come in nine years.

"That first year no one knew who we were," he says. "I would say I was with the Big East and get met with this blank stare. That first year Dave and I went to every Big East city, but by the second year we knew we had to have some kind of media day to spread the name around. We went to the Meadowlands that year, brought in all the coaches and had about 70 or so media people. But we had the key people. I knew I had to have a Dickie Weiss from Philadelphia, a Mike Madden from Boston. I sent people notes. I made phone calls. We felt we had to educate everyone to what a conference was, because no one had played in a conference before. For example, we had to make the people in Philadelphia know that from now on Villanova playing Georgetown was a bigger game than Villanova playing Temple. The other thing we did that second year was run it like a trade show, with the coaches at different tables. The third year we brought the kids in too."

Now Big East media day is the unofficial start of the college basketball season in the East.

All presided over by Gavitt, who sits at the platform at the head of the room, the king of all he surveys.

"See all these coaches?" says Rod Baker, an assistant coach at Seton Hall. "They should all get down on their knees and kiss his ring."

He turns and walks down the hallway toward the TV room, where the league's top players are taking star turns. Pointing the several reporters who are fighting to angle themselves into position to hear what some of the players are saying, he notes, "People are hanging on the words of kids who didn't score 700 on their SATs." He shakes his head at the incongruity of it all.

Rod Baker doesn't know it yet, but lowly Seton Hall will by the end of the year be in the glare of the bright Kleig lights themselves. In this 1988–89 season, which will see Providence rocket upward and Villanova head in quite a different direction, the boys from South Orange, New Jersey, will rise above Georgetown, above Syracuse, all the way to the lofty heights of the NCAA Championship game.

Yes, this season in the Big East will be filled with surprises.

1

THE TRADITIONAL POWERS

If April is the cruellest month, then December must be the kindest, at least for the powerhouses in college basketball. This time of year has become little more than a glorified layup drill as Big East teams fatten up their records with a succession of post-Thanksgiving turkeys. In a league as competitive as the Big East, no coach wants to risk too many losses outside of league play. Most of the top schools in the country use December as an opportunity to win some easy games and get their teams ready for upcoming league play in January. Take Georgetown, an obvious example. Their December schedule is littered with such formidable opponents as St. Leo's, Shenandoah, Oral Roberts, and appearances in the South Florida Tournament and the Hawaii-Loa Classic. They play only two significant games in December, both at home, against Virginia Tech and DePaul.

There are two reasons for this. The first is obvious: an easy schedule allows a coach the latitude to develop his team slowly. The second? It is a practice that's rewarded at the end of the year when the NCAA Tournament Committee picks the teams to fill the tournament. Not that anyone admits this. The party line is that strength of schedule is more impressive to the Tournament Committee than some easy wins. Not true. Playing in the Big East Conference gives Big East teams a strenuous schedule, and so at the end of the year Big East teams are usually selected by overall wins. No Big East team that's won 18 games has ever failed to make the NCAA Tournament. A coach would be crazy not to stockpile December wins.

The exception to this practice is an appearance in a prestigious tournament, like the Big Apple NIT or the Great Alaska Shootout, or else showcase games with quality intersectional opponents, designed for national television. Even then, Big East teams often sandwich easy games around competitive ones. So Syracuse, which will play this season in the Big Apple NIT, also has Kentucky State and U.S. International on the December schedule.

This year the Big East team with the toughest December schedule is Seton Hall. They have elected to play in both the Great Alaska Shootout and the Sugar Bowl Tournament. They feel they have something to prove.

On the flip side, a bad December can put a Big East team in immediate jeopardy. The case in point this season is Villanova. With a veteran team returning, the Wildcats will lose December games to Southern Illinois, Penn, and LaSalle, and they will be haunted all year by these losses.

As the season starts, let's look at each individual team in turn and meet the students who will be supplying so many thrills all season. And who is the first team we should pick? Why, that's as easy as beating a December patsy.

GEORGETOWN

In northwest Washington, D.C., lies Georgetown, one of the most prestigious addresses in the District, marked by high-priced townhouses, shady streets, and trendy shops. Georgetown University is the oldest Catholic college in the country, full of Gothic gray-stone buildings. McDonough Gym, the school's monument to a different era, is down behind the main campus. A red brick structure, it is an old-

style campus gym. In the lobby, pictures of past Hoya
players stare down from the walls. This is where the Hoyas
used to play until the arrival of Patrick Ewing and the move
to the Capital Centre in suburban Maryland, half an hour
away. Even now, eight years later, it's not a unanimously
popular decision, to the point that Georgetown students
have boycotted many December games against the St. Leo's
of the world. But there was really no other choice. The
program had long ago outgrown McDonough, and there is
no facility in the District large enough.

Once upon a time McDonough was certainly big enough.
Go back thirty years and the Hoyas were coached by white
men with Irish-Catholic surnames: Nolan, O'Keefe, Magee.
They played a regional schedule—schools in the D.C. area,
Catholic schools in the Northeast—all without much success.

"When they played on Saturday nights there might have
been a hundred people there in tuxedos and evening gowns,"
remembers Jim Cox, who went to graduate school at Georgetown in the mid-sixties. "It was the thing to do on a Saturday
night. Go to the game before going somewhere in D.C. to a
party. It was like an Ivy League game. The players were all
white, and many of them came from New York and New
Jersey, where they had gone to Catholic high schools. They
didn't have any D.C. kids. It was like they always wanted to
have a good team because it was a social thing, but they
didn't know how to go about it."

Enter John Thompson.

He had been a local high-school coach who was inheriting
a Georgetown basketball team that had gone 3–23 the year
before. From the beginning he began recruiting inner-city
black kids to a prestigious school that was predominantly
lily-white. He stressed education. He kept a deflated basketball on his desk, a symbol to his kids that one day the ball
wasn't going to bounce anymore. He hired Mary Fenlon, a
former nun he had known at nearby St. Anthony's High
School, and made her the overseer of the players' academic
progress. He called her the "conscience of the program." In
a college game that was becoming more pressurized and
cutthroat, Thompson's approach was refreshing.

As soon as Thompson became successful at Georgetown, focusing national attention on both himself and the unique way things were done at Georgetown, the perception became more complicated.

Then Thompson recruited Patrick Ewing and everything escalated. Ewing became the cornerstone of Thompson's defensive philosophy, which relied on aggressiveness and intimidation. The Hoyas became the Oakland Raiders of college basketball, replete with their black and gray uniforms, and they gained a reputation for coming off the bench en masse the moment a Georgetown player got into any kind of altercation. Soon they were the most hated college team in the country, an antipathy Thompson seemed to feed off of. He seemed to thrive on this "us versus them" theme, circling the wagons, creating the image that it was Georgetown against the world.

In 1984, the year he won the national title, the bunker mentality was well established. He said that year that he had long before stopped worrying what people thought about him. After he won the NCAA title he said, "If Hoya Paranoia makes us the way we are, somebody else better catch it."

He was infamous for sequestering his players far away from tournament sites. When Georgetown played in the Final Four in New Orleans in '82, he stashed them in Biloxi, Mississippi, an hour away. Player interviews were doled out infrequently. The postgame locker room was closely monitored by Mary Fenlon, who stood at the doorway counting out the minutes. Thompson seemed to revel in the mystique that surrounded both himself and his team. Former player Derrick Jackson was quoted as saying Thompson was a man "big with intimidation."

It also became apparent that Thompson was going to do things his way. If blacks were accused of "playground ball," his team would be under control. If blacks were accused of being undisciplined, his team would be more disciplined than one designed by General Patton.

For the delicate issue of race always hovers over the Georgetown program. The last white player who saw an appreciable amount of playing time was Jeff Bullis, back

before the Big East started. The last recruited white player
was David Dunn, who later transferred to Georgia. The
past few years there was one white player on the bench, and
he was a walk-on, the son of Georgetown assistant AD
(athletic director) Joe Lang. This year there are none.
Thompson's standard response to this is that it's not racial,
that he only gets involved with the kids his assistants identify
for him.

In a sense he's become as controversial as Indiana's Bobby
Knight.

In a 1984 article in *Sports Illustrated*, writer Curry
Kirkpatrick discussed the Hoyas' national image in a story
about their Big East Tournament title. "In New York the
Hoyas MO was that familiar mix of public non-relations,
suspicion and silly security precautions—now known as Hoya
Paranoia—and intense play." Kirkpatrick went on to say
how Thompson had sequestered the team in Harlem a long
cab ride from the Garden, and that the Hoyas had been the
last team to arrive at the Big East luncheon, "as usual."

Then, after saying that Thompson is a surpassingly bright,
deep, discerning, and articulate fellow who genuinely cares
about his players' academic attainments, he wrote that upon
occasion, "Thompson plays the tough-guy role to the hilt,
complete with such witty repartee as 'get outta my face.'
More often than not, his team, along with its leather-jackets-
and-chains image, appears precisely to slip into the same
character. But, of course, that's the point."

Kirkpatrick described how the Georgetown-Syracuse final
that year was marred by the Hoyas' Michael Graham pushing
Syracuse's Andre Hawkins to the floor and then taking a
wild swing at him with his left hand. Then he went on to say
that "still another Georgetown game had been spoiled by an
ugly incident, the inevitable result of the preposterous
paramilitary atmosphere surrounding the team."

After a game against Pittsburgh last year, a game marked
by another fight, Thompson had been taken to task by Billy
Raftery, a former Seton Hall coach who was doing the
game for CBS. After watching the replay, which clearly
showed that the Hoyas' Perry McDonald had started the

fight, Raftery claimed that fights happen all too frequently in Georgetown games and that it was Thompson's responsibility to control the problem. That night, on his TV show in Washington, Thompson attacked Raftery, essentially saying he had no right to say what he had, since he had been a failure as a coach at Seton Hall.

This was untrue. Raftery had had a winning record at Seton Hall, during an era when Seton Hall basketball had enjoyed very little support. Raftery had also been one of the genuinely nice people in college coaching, friendly, accessible, liked by everyone. It was an example of Thompson at his worst: thin-skinned, overly defensive, a bully when he feels cornered.

He certainly is a large bear of a man at 6-10, weighing at least a hundred pounds more than when he was Bill Russell's backup center on the Boston Celtics in the mid-sixties. Everything about him seems larger than life, from his mystique to his glare along the sidelines during games. Other coaches have long thought Thompson's overbearing size works to his advantage in intimidating officials during games.

A coach can only do so much on the sidelines, though. He needs top players, and in 1988 Thompson has once again compiled a strong group of players. Of course, with all the hype about his celebrated freshman, Alonzo Mourning, he was asked innumerable times how he thought his star freshman would fare.

"There were unrealistic expectations around Patrick when he was a freshman and it's the same with Alonzo," he said. "He should expect that. He can't possibly be what he's expected to be. He will have to make adjustments. My role is to monitor that and be ready for it. We would like to think that what we did with Patrick was the right thing. He graduated, and whether he spoke to somebody or not is not important. Patrick tagged those bases he had to tag and tagged them very well."

"How much a factor do you think it was for Alonzo that Patrick went to Georgetown?" he was asked.

"Patrick going to Georgetown had something to do with

it," he said. "I went into his room and Patrick's picture was all over the place."

His comparison is apt. Mourning is the most heralded freshman to enter college basketball since Ewing began at Georgetown eight years ago. He is 6-10 and expected to emerge as the next dominant player in the sport. One of the last cuts on the Olympic team, he spent the summer playing against pros in regulation games, and he thus might be the most prepared freshman ever to enter college basketball.

Georgetown is a team that's a blend of the old and the new. Along with Mourning, Thompson is also introducing Dikembe Mutombo, a 7-2 freshman from Zaire, John Turner, and Milton Bell. There's also a 6-4 freshman named Ronnie Thompson, described in the Georgetown media guide as "a good all-round player who can shoot, rebound and handle the ball." Interestingly, there is no mention that his father just happens to be the Georgetown coach.

Among the veterans are Dwayne Bryant, Jaren Jackson, and Jonathan Edwards, part of Georgetown's New Orleans connection that started with Steve Martin in the early years of the Big East and also included Perry McDonald. Three years ago Bryant had been hailed as the best schoolboy guard in the South. But his development at Georgetown during his first two years had been slowed by his inability to hit the jumper. Jackson's three years at Georgetown have been marked by inconsistency. Last year he had scored 38 against Seton Hall, sharing an all-time individual Big East scoring record, but there were other nights when he was ineffective, an apparent victim of Thompson's affinity for shuttling players in and out of the lineup. Another veteran guard is junior Mark Tillmon, one in a long succession of D.C. kids who have played for Thompson. He too came to Georgetown with a big reputation but has had trouble hitting the perimeter jumper.

But if Mourning's the showpiece, this is still Charles Smith's team. Four years ago he had been a late recruit by Thompson. He had gone to All Saints in Washington, the school that had once been St. Anthony's, where Thompson had coached. He had been told by Thompson that he would never start, that he was being recruited as a defensive role player. Two years later he came off the bench.

Last year he had emerged as the best player on the Georgetown team, overshadowing the more heralded Bryant and Tillmon. In the summer he had been Thompson's controversial choice to be the point guard on the Olympic team, selected while Douglas and Barros, the Big East's more celebrated guards, were cut. One day, at a practice session at McDonough Gym, Thompson had told the members of the Olympic team to select one player among them to shoot two foul shots. If the player made them, practice would be over. If he missed, they all would run for another fifteen minutes. The players selected Charles Smith.

He made them both.

This team's oddity is freshman Dikembe Mutombo. Thompson first heard of him from a government employee who had worked in Zaire. The man showed Thompson a photograph of Mutombo in which his head all but touched the basket. Thompson showed the man a picture of his Georgetown team and asked if Mutombo was bigger than Ben Gillery, a seven-footer who had played for the Hoyas last year. Bigger, the man said. Send him, said Thompson. Mutombo spent last year at Georgetown learning English. He then spent the summer playing in the Kenner League, one of the best summer leagues in the area, where he was the MVP. Thompson fully expects Mutombo to be an NBA lottery pick three and a half years from now.

"You people will love Dikembe," Thompson says, smiling. "He's not in the Georgetown mold—he loves to talk. He's a newspaper writer's dream."

Could this grinning man really be the secretive John Thompson? Has he been affected by the furor surrounding the Olympics? This seeming transformation will become one of the stories of the season. That his Hoyas will be a dominant force in the Big East once again is almost to be expected. But the surprise will be that the close-mouthed coach will become a voice that rings throughout the land.

SYRACUSE

November 18

There is the Dome Ranger, dressed up in an orange suit, orange hat, and blue mask, all set to run around and shoot a cap pistol at the other team. There is Dome Eddie, dressed in an orange suit and orange wig. There is someone dressed up like an orange. There is the older guy in the first row who continually waves a large orange towel, and sits next to a lady in an orange fright wig who knits constantly. There is the Beast of the East, a guy who runs around in a gorilla suit and then—still in costume—doubles as a radio reporter after the game, interviewing coaches. There are students in orange shirts, men in orange hats, a sea of orange everywhere.

It is just another night in the Carrier Dome, the country's largest basketball arena, in which crowds of over 30,000 have become as routine as binoculars in the upper grandstand. This is the place where one night Cornell was greeted by over 20,000 people turning their thumbs down. Here the students have been known to throw oranges onto the floor during games with their arch rival Georgetown, and one year, after a Syracuse victory, the students stormed the court, overrunning the press table and knocking the Georgetown radio station off the air.

"They used to throw the Christians to the lions," says Tom McElroy of the Big East. "Now we have the Carrier Dome."

It wasn't always this way. Once upon a time Syracuse was a football school, back when Ben Schwartzwalder coached players like Jim Brown, Ernie Davis, Floyd Little, and Larry Csonka, players whose legacies still hover over the basketball program. Basketball was the stepchild, played downtown in the old War Memorial Auditorium. In the midsixties it moved onto the campus to Manley Field House and began building its own tradition.

By the seventies the teams had gotten better, and Manley was affectionately called the "Zoo." It seated almost 10,000 people, and for the students, the games had become a chance to yell and scream and paint their faces orange. Manley also became one of the biggest home-court advantages in the country, and in the late seventies Syracuse never seemed to lose there. The streak was ended by Georgetown in the last game ever played in Manley, after which John Thompson declared, "Manley is officially closed." That was the first year of the Big East, and that game was among the first to be televised during prime time to a national audience.

Then in 1980 the Dome opened on the edge of the campus, a beacon looking out over the city from the hill on which the university sits, a symbolic presence as well as a geographic one. It is a $28 million inflatable dome built with $15 million from the state of New York and a list of area fat cats who lease luxury boxes for 10 years, at prices ranging from $50,000 to $100,000. The Carrier Corporation, which during the Depression had been given $200,000 from the Syracuse chamber of commerce to move their plants in Pennsylvania and New Jersey here, gave a gift of $2.75 million.

The first night the team played in the Dome, the game drew 15,000 people, nearly 6,000 more than the Manley record. Two months later 26,000 showed up for a game against Connecticut, an NCAA record. Soon it was over 30,000 for the big games, and every night in the Dome became as big as college basketball gets. Not only has Syracuse led the country in attendance the past four years, the Carrier Dome has hosted eight of the top ten all-time largest crowds in college basketball history. Last year Syracuse averaged close to 29,000 people a game and sold 24,000 season tickets.

Now the school has, perhaps, the country's most potent football-basketball package. According to an article in *Sports, Inc.* in March of 1988, the two sports generated at least $15 million in 1987. Tickets are up. Alumni gifts are up. A $59 million science and computer center is under construction. The school's $100 million fundraising project is within reach. Since 1985 the school has put about $4 million—mostly derived from basketball revenues—into ultramodern football weight and training rooms, administrative offices, and practice fields.

"In our wildest imagination we couldn't have envisioned this," says coach Jim Boeheim.

Boeheim also couldn't imagine the effect the Dome would have on recruiting. It instantly transformed Syracuse from a Northeastern to a national school. Forget the cold and the long winters. Recruits only saw the Dome. The first glamour player had been Tony Bruin a decade before. He was Tony "Red" Bruin then, from Mater Christi High School in Astoria, Queens, and he was the high-school legend with the 42-inch vertical leap. In the words of Howard Garfinkel, the New York superscout whose flowery prose often makes or breaks a young player's reputation, Bruin was "the greatest swingman since Benny Goodman." He was so heavily recruited that he had to keep changing his phone number, and by the time he arrived at Syracuse there was no way he could have lived up to his legend. He would not be the last Orangeman to suffer such a fate.

The Pearl was next. Officially, his name is Dwayne Washington, but by the time he was a senior at Boys and Girls High in Brooklyn he was simply the "Pearl." No last name was needed. If his career in the NBA has seemed a study in unfulfilled potential, perhaps no one was more suited to the Dome than the Pearl. He was already a mythical figure long before the Carrier Dome. Did he really once score eight straight times in a high-school game, then run by the opposing bench and yell, "Yo, Coach, you better call a timeout"? Did one of his games stop because the opposing team all gave him high fives after one of his moves? With the Pearl was college basketball's version of showbiz.

Pearl's selection of Syracuse not only focused more attention on it, but also gave credibility to Syracuse's emergence as one of the national basketball powers that always has a shot with the best high-school players, no matter where they come from. Was it just coincidence that in November of 1985, the year Pearl was a sophomore, Syracuse signed Stevie Thompson and Earl Duncan, the two best high-school players in California? That's right. Not the two best in New York. The two best in California.

Now a Syracuse basketball game dominates this city in

central New York hard by Lake Onandaga, where the winters
are long and basketball is taken as seriously as the Carrier
Corporation, the air-conditioning company that employs 6,000
people. The directions to the Dome start on the interstates
coming into the city. There are shuttle buses to the Dome
from downtown. The players are celebrities. Many students
sleep in the Dome the night before season tickets go on
sale, so they can sit behind the basket and wave their hands
frenetically whenever an opponent takes a foul shot. Now
Syracuse basketball has become ingrained into this city's
consciousness.

And tonight, it all starts again, another season in which
expectation fills the Dome. It's also the debut of forward
Billy Owens, the most celebrated Syracuse recruit since the
Pearl. People in Syracuse expect Owens to walk across Lake
Onandaga. He has already been on the cover of *Sports
Illustrated*'s college basketball issue, which heralded the arrival
of this new class of superstars.

Boeheim first saw him play one night in a summer-league
game before Owens's senior year. At the time Owens had
narrowed his list of schools to three—Syracuse, North
Carolina, and Villanova. Syracuse supposedly had the inside
track because Owens's brother, Michael, is a running back
on the Syracuse football team. So Boeheim had driven to
Mechanicsburg, a small Pennsylvania town, to watch Owens
play for the first time. He got 63 points that night, scoring
from everywhere.

"It was just a pleasure to watch," Boeheim says. "I don't
want to sound corny, but to watch him play was like seeing
a work of art."

Owens was coached at Carlisle High School by Dave
Lebo, the father of North Carolina star guard Jeff Lebo. As
a freshman Owens had been skinny and didn't like going
inside. The result was that he learned to pass and handle the
ball. Later, he patterned his game after Magic Johnson, so
much so that last year Lebo had to tell him to shoot more.
In the state finals he had 53 points. His Carlisle team won
the state championship four years in a row, the first time in
Pennsylvania history. Garfinkel noted, "Going into college,

Billy Owens is the best all-around player of the 1980s."
Boeheim has called him the best player he's ever recruited.

At the small forward spot is Stephen Thompson, the 6-4
junior who essentially was recruited by television. Thompson
used to come home from school and watch the Orangemen
play on ESPN, awed by the Dome and the spectacle that is
Syracuse basketball. Not only had Thompson been a high-
school All-American at Crenshaw High School in Los Angeles, long one of the top basketball high schools in the city,
he had also graduated fourth in his class. As a freshman at
Syracuse he played sparingly. He became a starter last year,
averaging 14 points and proving he was one of the best
athletes in the Big East, with great leaping ability and slithery
moves to the hoop. He is also an anomaly in the world of
big-time college basketball, someone who is able to play
inside at only 6-4. He has spent a lot of time working on his
perimeter shooting, but that is still the flaw in his game.

At power forward is the controversial Derrick Coleman.
From Detroit, he grew up fatherless, had two close friends
who were shot, and retains a streetwise swagger. Kevin
McNamara, a former sportswriter for the student paper, the
Daily Orange, says Coleman is the worst interview he's ever
had. "If you're on the student paper he tries to intimidate
you," says McNamara. "People are afraid of him. No one
else is even close to being like him. He is the worst."

Coleman got to Syracuse partially because of Boeheim's
association with Dave Bing, the former NBA star and
Syracuse great who was Boeheim's roommate at Syracuse.
Bing, who lives in Detroit, took an interest in Coleman,
even arranging for him to go to Boeheim's summer basketball
camp when Coleman was in high school. When he was a
senior in high school, he and Terry Mills were the two best
players in the Detroit area, both 6-9, both dominating inside
players. The University of Michigan took Mills; Coleman
came to Syracuse.

He quickly established himself as one of the best inside
players in the Big East. As a freshman he was a starter on
the team that lost to Indiana in the national finals in 1987.
He had spent much of last year complaining that he was

being played out of position because he didn't have a power forward's body. All the same, at the end of the year, there was a growing feeling he had yet to show any offensive game outside of a dunk.

The off guard position belongs to the lone white player on the team, senior Matt Roe. From suburban Syracuse, Roe was recruited for his ability to shoot the ball from the perimeter, a three-point specialist.

When Boeheim recruited him three years ago, there had been many who felt it was a wasted scholarship, that Roe would never be able to play in the Big East. He heard himself being called nothing more than scrimmage fodder. But Boeheim believes there's little substitute for shooting ability and he gave Roe a chance. Roe responded by working on his deficiencies. After his freshman year, in which he played sparingly, he worked out with former Syracuse star Leo Rautins. He also put on 20 pounds and dedicated himself to improving as a player. Now he is Syracuse's best outside shooter, a vital part of their offense, especially against zone defenses.

The leader of the team? None other than the spectacular Sherman Douglas.

Douglas is one of the great stories in college basketball. Raised in Washington, D.C., it was his dream to one day play for Georgetown, as it is for most black kids in the District. But after leading Spingarn High School to the metropolitan championship as a senior and being named the player of the year in the District, he was not recruited by John Thompson. One theory is that Thompson considered Douglas to be undisciplined. Another is that Thompson had feuded with Douglas's high-school coach, John Woods, over the recruiting of another Spingarn player, Michael Graham, a few years before, and decided not to get involved with another Spingarn kid.

Whatever the reason, Thompson recruited Charles Smith and Bobby Winston from All Saints in the District and ignored Douglas, as did everyone else in the Big East with the exception of Seton Hall, who gave him a tease. Earlier in the year Boeheim had recruited Boo Harvey to be his point guard of the future. But Harvey had failed to be admitted into the school, and so Boeheim was scrambling for a replacement, someone to back up Pearl Washington for two years.

Enter Douglas.

As a freshman he did what was expected: he backed up the Pearl. Then he got lucky. The Pearl went hardship, and Douglas got his chance to start as a sophomore. He became an instant star. Using his extreme quickness and his ability to penetrate, with the skill of turning the alley-oop pass into an art form, he quickly became one of the elite players in the conference. He became the first sophomore in Syracuse history to score over 600 points in a season and led the Big East in assists. He also guided the Orangemen to the Final Four, something Washington had never been able to do.

Last year had been more of the same. He was named a second-team All-American, and the *Sporting News* called him the best point guard in the country. Many thought he should have been the point guard on the Olympic team. But Thompson had cut him early in the trials, a controversial decision, especially due to the fact that the Olympic point guard became Thompson's own Charles Smith.

Now Douglas is everyone's preseason first-team All American selection and the preseason player of the year in the Big East. He is also on target to finish his career as Syracuse's all-time leader in both scoring and assists.

An hour before Syracuse is to play LaSalle in the opening round of the Big Apple NIT, the Dome is already a scene. Behind the large blue partition that separates the basketball arena from the rest of the Dome is the largest tailgate party in basketball history. A couple of thousand people sit at tables placed on the Astroturf football field. Stretching the entire end zone are concession stands selling everything from Dome dogs to nachos to chili to beer that's unofficially called—what else?—"Dome foam." A large souvenir stand sells enough Syracuse memorabilia to fill a warehouse. A giant TV screen is all set to show the game to the people who would rather stay back here and party than go around the blue partition and watch.

All too soon, however, most of them are streaming to their seats. Minutes later, the crowd stands and waits for the first basket, a tradition here in the Dome. LaSalle is a Philly school with only one great player, Lionel Simmons. Once upon a time Simmons would have justifiably been recognized as one of the best players in the country. But LaSalle is not on television. It is just another one of many schools in the East that have been buried under the Big East avalanche. Now Simmons is a great player in the wrong league.

Douglas and Coleman are great players in the right league. Douglas has a big shooting night, and he breaks the Pearl's all-time assist mark. Coleman is dominant underneath. Once again the 6-9 junior proves he's one of the most effective inside players in the country. Stevie Thompson, the 6-4 slithery forward from Los Angeles, swoops around all night for 24. Syracuse is up 10 at the half, and wins by 16, 92–76.

Afterward, inside the Syracuse locker room, Coleman is getting dressed in front of his locker. He recently said that the two things he doesn't like about college are getting up in the morning and having to go to class, adding fuel to the rumors that this is his farewell season in Syracuse. Later in the season he will say that his goal is to one day "wake up in the morning, have my breakfast, and decide *which* car to use."

Now he is answering some questions as he hangs a large gold chain around his neck. He is wiry and strong, with a shaved head. "If the guys give me the ball I'm going to score," he says. "I don't care who it is. Their job is to get me the ball."

Someone mentions that the supposed weakness in his game is his inability to shoot the ball from anywhere except close range.

Coleman snorts. "I'll show everyone who says I can't shoot the ball. I don't pay any attention to that kind of shit."

The following week Syracuse will go to Madison Square Garden and win the Big Apple NIT, bombarding Indiana in the semifinals and squeaking by Missouri in the finals. The game against Indiana is a Syracuse highlight film: the

Orangemen run and dunk like some Boeheim fantasy come to life. For some schools this in itself might be almost enough to ensure a successful season. But not at Syracuse. Here, nothing less than the national championship is enough.

VILLANOVA

The name of Philadelphia's Main Line is taken from the old train route from downtown to the northern suburbs. Most identified with Philadelphia's old money, the Main Line includes towns like Radnor and Bryn Mawr: this is John O'Hara country. A half hour from downtown is Villanova, and across the street from the train station is Villanova University. With its stone buildings and green lawns, it's reminiscent of Georgetown, only in the suburbs.

The Connelly Center, a modern building in the middle of the campus, is the student union. A small conference room in the basement is the setting for the basketball team's pregame meal. This is one of the customs at Villanova that is special.

There is always loose banter between the coaches and players. Sometimes the freshmen have to sing in a talent show. Sometimes one of the players will do a Massimino impression. But always a Villanova team meal is a testimony to the closeness that exists between Coach Rollie Massimino, his staff, and his players.

Critics sometimes contend that all the talk of "family" at Villanova is overblown media hype, just part of the "Daddy Mass" mystique. That's not true. The closeness here is unusual and lasts long after the players are graduated. Whenever Villanova wins a big game, telegrams will arrive the next morning from the Ed Pinckneys and Stewart Grangers, all the old kids checking in with Daddy Mass.

There's also a great deal of pride here. Not only is Massimino a proud man, the son of immigrants who has made the American Dream come true, but when he talks about his program he displays the pride of a patriarch who looks out over a successful family. There is a page in the media guide, entitled "Life after Basketball," in which Villanova's 100 percent graduation rate for players in the Massimino era is stated. All the players are listed, along with what they are doing now. Even Gary McLain, the point guard on the 1985 team who almost broke Massimino's heart by going public with his cocaine use in college, is listed as a salesman for Kodak.

There are three tables in the room, all with tablecloths. There is a buffet featuring a lot of pasta set up along one wall. In one basket are Italian cookies. "You can't have any," says Massimino to Rodney Taylor, as the other players laugh. Taylor is a 6-6, 235-pound junior forward whom Massimino has been riding for his weight.

The players and coaches eat. Rollie paces. He is usually too keyed up to eat. Either that or he's on one of his many diets. His weight can fluctuate 30 to 40 pounds, and he's forever conscious of it. He is short and dumpy and balding, your neighborhood butcher as basketball coach, complete with the identifiable name: Rollie. During a game his shirt is always out, his suit rumpled, and he always looks like he's on his way to his next crisis. He doesn't just coach a game, he nurses it, bleeds it, infuses it with his emotion. He's the kind of guy who wasn't supposed to win the top prize, coaching at the school that wasn't supposed to win it either. But win it all he did, by beating Georgetown, no less.

Then, just when it appeared he was all set to jump to the New Jersey Nets for the big bucks and the lifetime security, he changed his mind at the last minute. Said he couldn't leave "his kids." Said it would be like leaving his heart behind. What could be any better than that?

All the same, the feeling around the league is that winning the national championship in 1985 made Massimino arrogant. It might be the one attack that bothers him the most. Later the next season, when asked if he thought winning the national title had changed him, Massimino said no. "I'm the same guy. If I'm a prick now, I was a prick then. Jimmy Valvano told me two things would happen after I won. Guys would come out of the woodwork saying they taught me everything I know, and everyone would say I changed."

But if he says he hasn't changed, his life certainly has. He now does Rolaids commercials on national television, where he recreates his sideline antics. He also has two agents screening his business opportunities. He has said he could do seven or eight golf outings every day if he had the time.

But he doesn't. He gives it to his kids. Ask senior Doug West, their star guard. He is articulate and friendly, with a smile that frequently sprints across his face. As a freshman he became a *cause célèbre*, in the center of a recruiting battle that became the genesis for the ill feeling that exists between Villanova and Pittsburgh. Raised in Altoona, a western Pennsylvania town an hour from Pittsburgh, West had been heavily recruited by Pitt. He was talented and he was local, and for a school like Pittsburgh, which had gotten Charles Smith and Demetrius Gore the year before, sending a message to the rest of the Big East that Pitt was getting extremely serious about recruiting, West was a top priority. He was all set to go to Pittsburgh until he visited Villanova and came under Massimino's spell. He later told a Kentucky newspaper during his freshman year that a Pitt alumnus had offered him $10,000. That had been when Roy Chipman was the coach at Pitt, but it became nevertheless the impetus for the Massimino-Paul Evans feud that went public last year, when they both refused to shake hands with each other after games and ended up screaming at each other at halfcourt one night. West has received death threats from people in Pittsburgh and been booed all three years there.

"Coach Mass is . . ." He hesitates, searching for the right phrase. "Coach Mass is just Coach Mass. He's definitely a father figure to us off the court. He lets us talk to the media. He wants us to grow as people. It's not just all about winning here.

"When I visited here, my biggest questions were about Coach Mass. I knew he yelled and screamed a lot, and I was afraid if he did it to me I'd have a complex. But Veltra Dawson and Connolly Brown showed me around and told me not to worry about it. The bottom line was that Coach

Mass cares, and that he'll never degrade you publicly. Which is true. We are a really close team. We also do a lot of the recruiting. We take the recruits to class. We introduce them to teachers and deans. If we don't like a kid, or don't think a kid will fit in here, we tell the coaching staff. Our word is usually the last word.

"I did watch Coach Mass change my sophomore year, though. There were days when he looked like he hadn't slept in a week. He was down. I remember one day after a loss he was still upset the next day and that was very unusual. Then the Gary McLain story broke. I was totally amazed. Everyone on the team was."

It was the worst year of Massimino's coaching life. The Cats lost 13 out of their last 18 games. The freshman class of Tom Greis, Barry Bekkedam, and Rodney Taylor was called overrated, even though Taylor was hurt most of the year. In February, Bobby Martin, who had earlier given a verbal commitment, changed his mind and said he was going to Pitt. Delino DeShields, a guard from Delaware, decided to try professional baseball instead of coming to Villanova. Then McLain went public in *Sports Illustrated* about his cocaine use at Villanova, casting a tarnish on the closeness of Massimino's program, the one thing in coaching the man is most proud of. Even then Massimino stood by McLain, eventually helping him get a job in a pro league in Holland.

"I knew deep down in my heart that I was right," he told the *Philadelphia Inquirer* a year ago. "Gary was a victim of society, not a victim of our program. He's remembered as one of our players, and we love all our players. Before the article came out, Gary told me he was doing the story for the good of society. He said, 'Coach, don't worry, nothing's going to happen. The program will never suffer because of who you are and what you represent.' But obviously there was a tarnish."

Last year, however, Villanova again overachieved. Picked for seventh in the conference, they finished in the final eight of the NCAA Tournament, reinforcing the theory that Massimino's best teams need a few years to learn his complicated system—a match-up zone on defense, a patterned halfcourt offense.

Now four starters are back, including West, Taylor, senior guard Kenny Wilson, and 7-3 sophomore center Tom Greis. Also back is sixth man Gary Massey, last year's Big East defensive player of the year. It is a veteran team, one that Massimino has been touting as potentially as good as the '85 national title team.

The core is the veteran backcourt of West and Wilson. They have started together since their sophomore year and have been called one of the best backcourts in the country. If West is the classic number-two guard, tall and rangy, Wilson is 5-9. Growing up in Jersey City, he played for Bob Hurley at St. Anthony's, the school that this year is supposed to be the best high-school team in the country. While at St. Anthony's, he was a teammate of former Notre Dame star David Rivers, and when he left *Basketball Times* called him a third-team All-American. As a freshman he started a third of the games, then became a fulltime starter the following year. Extremely quick, his individual game has probably been hampered by Massimino's controlled style, but he's experienced and a proven Big East quality guard.

The center is Greis. As a freshman he was a disaster, seemingly physically overmatched in a league as athletic as the Big East. Massimino tells the story of how his team runs a drill in which a player gets a rebound, runs down the court, and gets another rebound. One day Greis did this three times, then fell down, turned his ankle, and was out for three weeks. At the end of the year Massimino told him to either lose 25 pounds or forget basketball. Last year Greis was much better physically and became a third-team Big East selection.

At one forward position is Taylor. He is from Columbia, South Carolina, one of the few Southerners in the Big East. After missing most of his freshman year with a broken foot, he became a starter last year. The other forward spot is up for grabs. Last year it belonged to Mark Plansky, the Cats' best outside shooter and spiritual leader. Two of the leading contenders this year are freshmen Greg Woodard and Marc

Dowdell. From Rochester, Woodard is a left-handed shooter with great range. Throughout the preseason Massimino has told people Woodard's ability to drill jump shots reminds him of a young Chris Mullin. Dowdell is bigger, 6-9, more of an inside player, the player of the year in New Jersey high-school basketball last season.

Massey is again penciled in as the sixth man. A great high-school player in the Bronx, Massey is a perfect example of a "tweener," someone who is caught between two positions. At 6-5, he is a little too small to survive night in and night out underneath in the Big East, yet he lacks the ballhandling skills to play guard. He has compensated by becoming a great defensive player and a spark off the bench.

It is not a particularly deep team. But it is experienced, and it clearly has Massimino's stamp all over it. It's also a team that expects a great year. This past summer they all stayed on campus, playing every night, getting ready for the season, the Final Four as their goal.

The Wildcats were picked third in the Big East and were in everyone'e preseason top 20, but a funny thing will happen in the young season. They'll lose to Southern Illinois. They'll lose to intracity rivals Penn and LaSalle. They seem to miss the leadership and perimeter shooting of Plansky more than anyone ever expected. Sometimes a basketball team's chemistry is as fragile as a fine-tuned engine's. Yes, there are four starters back, but Plansky is gone, and everything seems a little off-kilter. By the end of December, Villanova will have already dug themselves into a hole.

ST. JOHN'S

If you head east out of Manhattan, you follow the signs that point to Long Island, past Shea Stadium and the National Tennis Center. St. John's is synonymous with Madison Square Garden, but in actuality it's deep in the heart of Queens, a commuter school with a host of unattractive tan buildings and a lot of macadam parking lots.

Alumni Hall is reminiscent of a big old high-school gym

where the lockers are always too small and faded cheers from years past seem to echo from the walls. It all seems like college basketball out of the fifties, back when it was played in old college gyms instead of glitzy new downtown arenas, long before there was the Big East and ESPN, back before the glitter. The gym is big and dark with tan walls, and the past stares down from the walls in the guise of a large red banner. On one side is a list of the Redmen's 22 National Invitational Tournament appearances since 1939. On the other is St. John's many NCAA appearances, with a national title in 1952 and a Final Four appearance in 1985 with the team that featured four future pros: Chris Mullin, Walter Berry, Bill Wennington, and Mark Jackson, maybe the best team in St. John's long and rich basketball history.

Last year they were a lowly 17–12. If that seems like a good record, rest assured that at St. John's 20-win seasons have all but become part of the schedule. In the past two decades there have been only six teams that failed to win at least 20 games, and two of those won 19. One has to go back nearly two decades to find back-to-back teams that won under 20 games.

Now it's expected to happen again.

Lou Carnesecca hadn't figured this was going to be a rebuilding year. He thought he was going to have a mix of veterans and freshmen. But during the summer he learned his starting backcourt of Boo Harvey and Michael Porter had both become academic casualities, and center Marco Baldi was going back to his native Italy to play professionally. Good-bye to any thought of a veteran team.

But if it's a rebuilding year, it's not without hope. St. John's has recruited two potential great ones in Malik Sealy and Robert Werdann. Both are city kids, Sealy from Tolentine in the Bronx, where he played for Pitt assistant John Sarandrea; Werdann from Archbishop Molloy in Queens, where he played for famed high-school coach Jack Curran and with Kenny Anderson, generally regarded as the best high-school player in the country this year. With all the homage being paid to Mourning and Billy Owens, neither

Sealy nor Werdann have received the preseason attention they would have gotten in a normal Big East freshman class.

At 6-8, Sealy was named "Mr. Basketball" in New York State last year and was considered to be one of the top 10 high-school seniors in the country. He also had a storybook high-school career: he not only led Tolentine to the state championship, he was also the president of his high school class. Originally, he had said he wanted to come to Providence and play for Rick Pitino, but after Pitino went to the Knicks in the summer of 1987, Sealy cooled on Providence and decided to stay home. Before the season he was picked for the Big East's preseason all-rookie team.

Werdann was also one of the most highly recruited players in the country last year, turning down Duke, Georgia Tech, and Notre Dame to sign with the Redmen during the early signing period in November. He is 6-11, 240 pounds, with a polished offensive game. Already he reminds some people around the league of a young Kevin McHale. His only deficiency seems to be a lack of strength, which should come as he develops physically.

They join junior forward Jayson Williams and veteran guard Matt Brust in the starting lineup. Six-ten Williams was Prop 48* as a freshman. Last year as a sophomore he became a starter midway through the season and quickly showed flashes that he could develop into a quality Big East forward. Unfortunately, he got more notoriety for an incident in the Providence Civic Center, where he threw a chair into a crowd of people behind the St. John's bench after a fight had broken out between the St. John's players and some fans.

Brust is the Big East's version of Rambo: blond, burly, with a body that seems sculpted by the weight room. He is 6-5, 220, from nearby Babylon, Long Island, where he was a leading scorer and a football All-American good enough to be recruited by both Penn State and Miami. He started out his career at North Carolina, then transferred to St. John's,

---

*This is the NCAA requirement that a student must have a combined SAT score of 700 as a prerequisite for participating in athletics.

the continuation of a time-honored tradition of metropolitan kids who discover that you can go home again. Forget Thomas Wolfe. He never could hit the jumper anyway.

This is Brust's third year as a starter, and he is the link between the past and the future. He is also famous for giving impassioned pregame speeches to his teammates and is the acknowledged spiritual leader of this young St. John's team.

And it is young.

In addition to Werdann and Sealy, there are two other freshmen: Jason Buchanan, a skinny six-footer from Syracuse, and Terrence Mullin, younger brother of Chris. Buchanan was a late recruit, given a scholarship in the summer after Carnesecca knew Harvey and Porter would be ineligible. Buchanan was impressive in the Empire State Games, a summer all-star tournament in New York State. No other Big East school wanted either one of them.

So not only is it a young team, it's also one that has to play in the Big East with a pair of freshman guards who were never supposed to have to be playing as freshmen. But even if this is a team expected to have a long winter, they are still the home team in the media capital of the world. St. John's always has a tradition to uphold.

2

ARE THEY REALLY THE ALSO-RANS?

CONNECTICUT

November 26

The University of Connecticut is located in Storrs, about 25 miles away, but Hartford is the spiritual center of Connecticut basketball, and the Hartford Civic Center is the shrine for its dedicated fans. It's a 16,000-seat downtown arena that's inside a shopping mall, and an hour before the game against intrastate rival Hartford, people mill around in the rotunda off the mall and browse in the trendy shops. This is basketball for the upwardly mobile. The nearby restaurants are full, and hordes of people gather on the streets outside. Everywhere is talk that this is the year Connecticut rises to the top.

"Basketball is special here," says Coach Jim Calhoun. "There were so many cameras when I walked into my first press conference, I kept looking behind me to see if Ronald Reagan had walked in. It hasn't stopped since."

In the fall there was a Meet the Huskies night, and kids stood in long lines to shake hands with the players. Four

thousand people showed up at the midnight practice kicking
off the season. Every time the Huskies traveled around the
state during the preseason to practice, the sessions were
mobbed. Calhoun gets a free country-club membership,
clothes, a leased BMW. He gets free haircuts in Storrs. Not
only has he done 160 speaking engagements around the
state in his two years there, but he also has a one-hour
preseason TV show.

Before Calhoun arrived, he had been at Northeastern, a
Division I school in Boston that plays in something called
the ECAC North. In 14 years there he won 250 games and
went to five NCAA tournaments. He was never booed,
never criticized, just ignored. No matter what he did, Northeastern was never a lead story in the Boston newspapers,
not even his last year, when Celtic Star Reggie Lewis led
them into the NCAA Tournament.

That changed the moment he was named the new coach
at Connecticut.

If Calhoun is one of college basketball's success stories, the
former high-school coach who's now making the big bucks,
Dom Perno, the former coach, is the flip side. He had been
a former Connecticut schoolboy star who went on to star for
the Huskies. He had been an assistant coach with Dee
Rowe, had seen Rowe get booed. Perno had also been the
first Connecticut coach to win 20 games three years in a
row.

But in 1982 his best team lost seven out of its last eight
games, finishing 17–8, and he never recovered. Four straight
losing seasons followed. He was booed. He was not announced at home games. A "Dom Perno Coloring Book"
was published underground. There were "Dump Don" post-
ers. He was slandered to the point his wife would often cry
in the stands.

Most observers agree that the three toughest places to
coach in the Big East are Connecticut, Syracuse, and Providence. These are the three places where the Big East team
is the only show in town, where the college basketball team
is treated like a pro franchise. Connecticut just might be the
toughest, if for no other reason than the Huskies are cov-

ered by as many as 14 daily papers, the most of any school in the country. Last year they averaged 13,000 a game, though only winning four Big East games.

Adding to the frustration is that the state of Connecticut has a rich history of producing great schoolboy basketball players. In the fifties it was Johnny Egan from Weaver High in Hartford, who later played and coached in the NBA. In the early sixties it was Dave Hicks and Eddie Griffin; in the late sixties played Calvin Murphy and John Williamson, who both went on to the NBA. The early seventies starred Walter Luckett from Bridgeport, who, before he ever played a college game, was on the cover of *Sports Illustrated*. Later it was Sly Williams from New Haven and Rod Foster of New Britain, both of whom went on to the NBA. Presently the NBA has six Connecticut natives: Wes Mathews and John Bagley from Bridgeport, Michael Adams from Hartford, Harold Pressley from Mystic, Mike Gminski, and Rick Mahorn.

It's an impressive roster, one any state the size of Connecticut could be proud of, yet all these players are linked by a common thread in this tapestry that covers 30 years in the state's history. Not one of them stayed home and played for the state university. Some, of course, couldn't qualify academically. The others merely said, no thanks.

Not that there haven't been exceptions. The biggest in-state plum was Corny Thompson, a high-school All-American from Middletown. He was the leader of the best team Connecticut ever had in the Big East, back a decade ago when the league was forming. But for the most part, the story of Connecticut basketball is that of home-grown kids who have gotten away, only to come back and haunt the Huskies. Villanova came into Connecticut in the early years of the Big East and recruited John Pinone and Harold Pressley. Boston College went to the NCAA tournament with Bagley, Adams, Jay Murphy, and John Garris, all Connecticut natives.

How can Calhoun change this tradition?

He knows he must change the perception that Connecticut is a regional school, caught between its Yankee Conference status in football and the Big East in basketball. In an

18-year stretch ending in 1965, UConn won the old Yankee
Conference in basketball 15 times, but Connecticut's basketball program has never transcended New England. Unlike
every other Big East school, it has never played a national
schedule and never known any national success.

The other drawback is the location of the campus. The
state of Connecticut has many cities, but the university is
located in the rural eastern part of the state. It is the most
rural of the Big East schools. Because it is a state school and
a land-grant institution, complete with dairy barns and an
agricultural school, it does not exactly entice black players
to apply. Dee Rowe remembers a time in the early seventies
when he was recruiting an inner-city black kid, driving him
around the campus. Eventually, the kid turned to Rowe and
said, yeah, this is nice and all, Coach, but you got to get rid
of those chicken coops.

On top of all this was the lack of support systems necessary to compete in the Big East. The budget, the academic
counseling, the practice facilities, all of it was second rate.

So in 1986 a revamping of the athletic department was
one of new president John Casteen's first priorities. One of
his first acts was to establish a task force on athletics. This
could have been dismissed as just another in-house study, if
not for the fact that Casteen had been instrumental in successfully revamping the way the University of Virginia deals
with athletes.

Now UConn has a new athletic director in Todd Turner,
also from the University of Virginia, a new 8,000-seat domed
stadium under construction on the campus back in Storrs,
and a highly successful coach in Calhoun. Not that Calhoun
wasn't aware of what he was stepping into at Connecticut.
His last year at Northeastern he beat Connecticut by 17, and
the first question in the postgame interview was: "What do
you think is wrong with Connecticut?" Midway through his
first year his two best players, sophomores Cliff Robinson
and Phil Gamble, were declared academically ineligible.
That week Calhoun went on TV and talked for half an hour
about it.

"Jim went out and said that everything was going to be all

right," remembers Tim Tolikan, the school's sports-information director, "and people said, 'Yeah, maybe it will.' "

The next year, though, he made good on his promise. The Huskies finished 15–14, the first winning season in six years, though they won only four Big East games. But they won the NIT, their first postseason title ever, and when the team came back to campus they were met by thousands. There is even a sign on certain highways telling motorists that the University of Connecticut is the 1988 NIT champs.

On the recruiting front, he already has a prize freshman in Chris Smith, a 6-2 guard from Bridgeport. Calhoun thinks Smith could turn out to be the best player he ever recruited, no small statement considering he coached Reggie Lewis. He has also signed Scott Burrell from Hamden, considered the best player in the state.

On this night in the Civic Center, there are a couple of pregame cocktail parties going on. In one Casteen, the university president, is hosting a party for key legislators around the state. In another Turner, the AD, is hosting several of the university's biggest athletic boosters.

"It's like the game itself is secondary," says Dee Rowe.

He is standing outside the press room an hour before the game, a stylish man in his late fifties. Rowe's title now is associate athletic director in charge of fund-raising. But for eight years, between 1969 and 1977, he was the coach. He knows first-hand what it's like to be inside the pressure cooker that is Connecticut basketball.

"We are the professional franchise in this state," he says. "But until last year we never were able to give the people what they wanted. The natives were always restless. This is a very difficult place to coach."

Rowe won 17 or more games in his last four years, going to two NITs and one NCAA tournament, but still he was serenaded by chants of "Rowe Must Go." After a while he was eating only one meal a week at home, utterly consumed with being the Connecticut coach. He was also blacking out on the bench, using smelling salts, ice packs, nitroglycerin pills. When he left, he was replaced by Perno, the former local hero. Perno had seen Rowe get booed, but he thought it would never happen to him.

It did.

Now Calhoun doesn't think it can happen to him.

Perhaps he's being optimistic. Sure, Connecticut is led by senior center Cliff Robinson, who's already being projected as a first-round NBA draft choice. On the other hand, their preseason has been in disarray. Senior guard Phil Gamble has missed most of it with a broken wrist. The other guard, Tate George, missed almost a month with a scratched retina. Sophomore Murray Williams missed the entire preseason with a stress fracture. Each in itself is not a big deal, but the cumulative effect is that Connecticut hasn't been able to practice as much together at full strength as Calhoun had hoped. There's the feeling this is a team searching for itself, a team that can go either way once the season starts.

And it does.

Tonight they beat Hartford 67–55, and later breeze through their first few games. But then they play Purdue on the road. It is an ESPN-televised game, a chance to live up to the preseason hype and also prove the Huskies are poised to walk onto the national stage. Instead they get drilled, 88–73. Two days later, though, they beat Virginia at Virginia. It is a great win for them, a little redemption for the Purdue blowout.

So just who are the Huskies?

After the first month of the season no one knows.

PROVIDENCE

Two years ago Providence went to the Final Four under Rick Pitino, one of the great Cinderella stories in recent college basketball history. Then Pitino went on to the New York Knicks and it was pumpkin time. His assistant, Gordie Chiesa, placed in the unenviable situation of trying to follow in Pitino's footsteps, was booed after the third game of the season after his Friars were upset at home by Holy Cross. After that it only got worse. By January, Marty Conlon, the most promising sophomore, had left the team, saying he was tired of Chiesa's "constant abuse," and there were rumors of more defections. By February, Chiesa had become a basketball version of Captain Queeg, clinging to the illusion that all was well while his coaching dream began slipping more and more into the past tense. Here was someone who had paid his dues for years—driving the vans in Division III, sweeping the gym, going to all the clinics, working the camps—doing all the hundred and one things that go into trying to become a big-time college coach. And then when he finally became one, he was all but doomed from the very start.

It was another example of the new axiom that no longer do new coaches have a grace period. Now you win right away or get fired. There is no time for on-the-job training, no time for anything but success right away. There is too much pressure to win, too many dollars at stake, not just in the Big East but everywhere.

Now it is Rick Barnes's turn.

His hiring the past spring is an example of basketball networking. Pitino, who was helping find candidates for the vacancy at the University of Massachusetts, called Barnes to see if he'd be interested in applying for the job at Pitino's alma mater. Barnes had been head coach at George Mason for only a year, but Pitino knew of his reputation as one of the top young recruiters in the country as an assistant coach. Barnes said he wasn't interested, then added he was a big fan of Pitino's and in fact used many of Pitino's coaching techniques at George Mason. They talked for a while, and when the conversation ended, Pitino was convinced Providence athletic director John Marinatto had to talk to Barnes before he decided on a new coach.

"I don't know," Marinatto said. "He's only been a head coach for one year."

"You've got to talk to him," said Pitino.

"I think we need someone with a bigger name," countered Marinatto.

"At least talk to him," said Pitino. "You've got to talk to him."

"Okay," said Marinatto. "I'll talk to him."

Marinatto immediately saw Barnes as a young Pitino.

Barnes is inheriting a program that has become the ba-
nana republic of the Big East: four coaches in five years.
Once the Friars were one of the top basketball schools in
the East, a legacy stretching back over 30 years and including the fabled team featuring Ernie DiGregorio, Marvin
Barnes, and Kevin Stacom that went to the Final Four in
1973 under Dave Gavitt. At the time it was one of the few
Eastern teams to get to the Final Four, but when the Big
East formed five years later, Providence was in a down
cycle, victims of poor recruiting and the growing feeling the
school no longer was capable of enticing enough great players
to ever be a force in the conference. The negatives were
well known: a small school, a lack of impressive dorms to
show recruits, situated in a small state that was lucky to
produce even one future Division I player a year, never
mind someone good enough to play in the Big East. By the
time Pitino arrived, the Friars were 11–65 in the conference
over six years.

Last year they finished eighth and failed to win a game on
the road all season. Pitino had gone, and his era now seemed
like some two-year fantasy in the middle of a black hole.
Chiesa had been the third Providence coach of the past four
to be booed in the Providence Civic Center. Since the
inception of the Big East, only Pitino had been spared the
frustrations of the Providence fans.

And now the Friars were picked to finish last.

The latter was something Barnes hoped to use as a moti-
vational tool for his team. The day after Big East media day
he held a team meeting.

"I was hurt when I found out they picked us last," he told
them. "Hurt that everyone has so little respect for us. They
asked me if I had the experience to coach in the Big East.
They asked Eric Murdock if his good season last year as a
freshman was nothing but a fluke. Every question they
asked showed that they thought we weren't going to be very
good at all. They have no respect for us."

He then went around the room.

"Marty, do you know what the writers asked about you?"
he asked Marty Conlon, the junior forward who had left

Chiesa's team the year before. "They asked if you were going to quit again.

"Carlton, do you know what they asked about you?" he asked Carlton Screen, the junior guard who had spent much of the past season pouting on the bench amid rumors he was going to transfer. "They asked if you were going to pout again.

"Matt," he said to Matt Palazzi, who had quit the team in both the past two years, "they wanted to know if you were going to quit again."

The three players were silent. Barnes continued, his voice low.

"Darryl, do you know what they asked about you?" he asked senior Darryl Wright, unproductive the year before after being a key weapon off the bench in the Friars' march through the NCAA tournament in 1987.

Without waiting for an answer, he turned to Cal Foster, who had spent the year before lodged deep in Chiesa's doghouse. "Cal, do you know what they asked about you?" He turned to Quinton Burton, a junior forward. Two and a half years ago he had been Pitino's key recruit. But he had lost his freshman year, a victim of Prop 48, and last year he had been an undistinguished starter. "Quinton, do you want to know what they asked about you?"

The three players looked at him, expectant.

Barnes glanced at all three of them, drawing out the moment, building up the suspense.

"Nothing," he said finally. "It was like you three guys didn't even exist."

Now he's about to play South Alabama in the Providence Civic Center in the finals of Providence's Fleet Classic, so named for a local bank that sponsors the tournament. The night before the Friars had beaten Niagara in Barnes's first game. Barnes had been nervous all week. South Alabama is the kind of team coaches hate to play: a good team that has little national identity. If you beat them, you get little credit. And you might not beat them. All coaches grow to hate the end of November, the time before the games start. Practice has been going on since October 15. The players are sick of playing against the same faces in practice day after day. The coaches wonder just how good their teams are. Barnes also wondered if he was being hard enough on his players. He had heard all the horror stories from the year before about Chiesa working the players hard and the players rebelling, and he knew that these players he was inheriting were fragile, that they had been beaten down the year before. So he had lessened some of the arduous preseason conditioning he had done the year before at George Mason.

On the other hand, he needs his team to be ready, for he knows he has to get off to a good start. His players need to believe that the skeletons of the year before have been buried and they are starting a new era. The Providence fans also need to know that things are going to be different. So he was all over his players in practice two days before the Fleet Classic began. Afterward, he put his ear on the locker-room door and listened to the sound of happy voices within.

"We're all right," he said, a smile on his face. "If they're happy in the locker room afterward, that means you didn't work them too hard. I learned that from Wimp Sanderson at Alabama. Wimp always would listen at the locker-room door after a tough practice. He said he got it from Bear Bryant."

Barnes again put his ear to the door and smiled.

The night before, Matt Palazzi scored 16 first-half points in leading the Friars past Niagara, the first points he had scored since the 1986 season. His first shot was blocked. His second missed. Then he drilled a jumper from the right corner. Afterward, he was asked what he felt when he saw the ball go in.

"Relief," he said. "I felt relief."

Four years earlier Palazzi had been a highly regarded freshman seemingly ticketed for a storybook career at Providence. He was the kid from nearby Worcester, Massachusetts, who had been an unbelievable high-school star. He was also the son of Togo Palazzi. Togo had been an All-American at Holy Cross, back in the days of Tommy

Heinsohn, and he later played for the Boston Celtics. Togo Palazzi is also, in the words of a former coach, "someone for whom the ball never stopped bouncing." So maybe it was inevitable that Matt began being compared to his father at a young age. There was pressure from his father to continue the Palazzi name at Holy Cross. Two older brothers had played basketball, but not good enough to be recruited by Holy Cross. Matt was good enough. When he announced he was going to Providence, his father didn't speak to him for a month.

Palazzi struggled his first year, a common experience for a freshman in a league as competitive as the Big East. The next year, with Pitino as coach, he was hurt early and always felt he lagged behind everyone else. He felt frustrated, the first time in his life basketball had let him down. Then Delray Brooks, who played the same position he did, transferred to Providence from Indiana, and he became more depressed. When he came back the following fall, his frustrations intensified. He had trouble sleeping. Basketball was no longer fun.

"I got down on myself," he says. "I was really nervous and I put a lot of pressure on myself. It bothered me all the time. Everyone was doing well, but not me."

In October of that year he left school. He just got up one day and, without telling anyone, packed his bags and went home. He thought of transferring. He waited to feel better. For the first time in his life a winter passed without basketball. A month later he came back to Providence. He began working out with the team but didn't dress for the games. It was 1987, the year the Friars jumped into the national spotlight of the Final Four. Palazzi was in the shadows.

He returned last year with new hope, but by November it was the same old story. He couldn't sleep, couldn't do anything.

"I just knew I had to get away from everything," he says. "Basketball, school, everything. I had to get away so I could think if I wanted to continue playing or not."

This time he went to Italy, where his father was coaching.

"I came around the corner and there was Matthew sitting on a car with his Providence College warmups on," remembers Togo Palazzi. "We just started hugging each other and crying."

Palazzi came back to school but didn't play. He figured his career was over and was starting to reconcile himself to it. Then Barnes got the job. One day Palazzi asked him for another chance. Barnes said he had no problem with that, but he wanted Palazzi to take two weeks and think about it. Now Palazzi says it's different for him. No longer does his family care if he plays basketball or not. They just want him to be happy.

"I think what happened to me the past couple of years woke me up," he says. "They saw how miserable I was. Now they don't care whether I play or not. There's no pressure on me."

On this night Palazzi scores 21 points in the second half as the Friars win. Moments later he's named the tournament's most valuable player.

PITTSBURGH

November 28

Pittsburgh has long been the Big East's mystery program, the neighbor no one seems to understand. It was the last school admitted into the conference. It is also, in many ways, different from the other Big East schools. It is a football school in a league where only three of the other schools play football, and one of them—Connecticut—is in I-AA. All the other schools, with the exception of Syracuse, hug the East Coast. Pitt is the farthest west, considered to be in the Midwest by most people in the Big East, who view anything west of Philadelphia as the hinterlands. It is not a Catholic school in a league that has six of them. With the exception of Syracuse, it has never had any basketball ties with anyone else in the league.

With football comes cheating. There has long been the

suspicion within the league that Pitt bends some of the rules
to attract recruits. The rumors were widespread a few years
back that the Golden Panthers, the Pitt booster club, were
all but running the program. They were very visible in the
locker room after games and were rumored to have funneled money to some recruits. So when Villanova player
Doug West said a Pitt booster had offered him $10,000, the
incident at the core of Massimino's anger at Pitt, it only
reinforced the rumors. One of the great stories about Pitt
football is that when Foge Fazio took over from Jackie
Sherrill, he called several players into his office, took out a
sheet of paper that allegedly had details of what payoffs
these particular players were supposed to get, and ripped it
up in front of them.

Is the story true?

Who knows? The point is, many people in the conference
think it's true. Some of this, of course, might be paranoia.
From the beginning there was a certain fear of Pitt among
some of the other coaches in the league, the feeling that any
school with such a big-time football program certainly knows
how to get players, one way or the other.

Two years ago, Paul Evans took over from Chipman, who
said he was tired of his children being physically abused
because the Pitt basketball team wasn't living up to community expectations. Evans came in promising to bring some
discipline to a team that didn't seem to have any. He inherited a veteran team led by such talents as Charles Smith,
Jerome Lane, and Demetrius Gore, players with the reputation of dancing to the beat of their own drums.

He also arrived under the scrutiny of the other league
coaches, a burden that comes with being the coach of Pitt.
His clashes with his veteran players were well documented.
His clashes with some of the boosters were less documented.
One of the first things he did was meet with some of the
Golden Panthers. He told them that he too had heard the
rumors about Pitt and he wanted the rumors stopped. Later
in the season, he will say that if he had it to do all over
again, he would not have retained John Calipari as one of

his assistants, since Calipari was too identified with the Chipman era.

The rumors still persist, however, to the point that at the coaches' meetings in Florida last spring, several coaches had gone after Evans on the cheating issue. Evans, in turn, had defended his program and said that things are different now.

Certainly, the Pittsburgh team is different. It was no secret he'd had his problems the past two years with Lane, Smith, and Gore. They were a group of players who had their own rap song. From Lane, whose ego often seemed as big as the Big East itself, to Gore, whose nickname is Me, the Panthers were fundamentally unsound, stars in their own movies. One of the first things Evans promised to do when he got the job was to make the three of them more disciplined. He and Lane clashed early and often. When Lane didn't do what Evans wanted him to do, Evans threw him out of practice. When the team didn't do what Evans wanted them to do, he made them run. He was forever telling his team they didn't want to be great enough, that they were victims of their own attitudes. His ace was that, under Chipman, the players had had their own way and underachieved. When they did things Evans's way, they achieved.

In his first two years Evans had accomplished what he set out to do: the Panthers attained their highest national rankings ever in the polls, and they won one Big East title and shared another.

All the same, underlying all the success and all the victories, tension remained between Evans and his players. When Pittsburgh lost to Vanderbilt in the NCAA tournament last spring, the players were quick to blame their coach for unraveling in the closing seconds.

Now Evans has his own players. They include Darelle Porter from the city of Pittsburgh, Jason Matthews from Los Angeles, Bobby Martin from Atlantic City, Brian Shorter from Philadelphia, and Sean Miller, from Beaver Falls, Pennsylvania, the town made famous by Joe Namath. (He carries on the showman tradition. As a youngster he traveled all over the country giving ballhandling exhibitions, even appearing on the "Tonight Show.")

It is a nice blend of players. Martin is physical inside. Porter is athletic. Matthews shows signs of one day being one of the best perimeter shooters in the league. Miller is a heady point guard who can pass. And Shorter is a great inside scorer.

In a class that is supposed to be the best to enter the Big East since the Ewing-Mullin class eight years ago, Shorter is the forgotten man. Mourning and Owens got the headlines. Werdann and Sealy got the subheads. Shorter was the afterthought, the kid who spent last year at Pitt prohibited from playing under Prop 48. Ironically, it was fellow classmate Miller, the Big East's rookie of the year, who got the accolades. Shorter spent his time in the classroom working on his grade-point average.

It was not the first time that Shorter seemed to have his career on hold.

After his junior year at Simon Gratz High School in North Philadelphia, Shorter was on course to break the all-time Philadelphia high-school scoring record set by the great Wilt Chamberlain, a record that had stood for over 30 years. He was also on course to never get out of Philadelphia, one of the scores of talented kids who never escape the playgrounds. Simon Gratz was a ghetto school, where survival was much more important than education, and Shorter was one of its victims. When he took the SAT at the end of his junior year, he saw things on that test he'd never seen before. Suffice it to say, the test was infinitely more difficult than scoring points in Philadelphia high-school games.

He decided to go to Oak Hill, a prep school in rural Virginia, to bone up on his academics. He got extra attention. He studied. He got over his culture shock of being far from the city, far from home. More important, he began learning what school was about—all the things he hadn't learned in North Philadelphia.

So even though he entered the University of Pittsburgh as

a Prop 48 student, he didn't see himself as a victim. Instead, he regarded himself as someone lucky enough to have a chance to go to college. Instead of spending last year sulking around his dorm, feeling lost without basketball, he spent a lot of time in the weight room, transforming his body. He also said he wasn't worried about being labeled with the stigma of Prop 48 because "I know I'm not dumb."

"Brian has done something I haven't seen too many kids do in the sit-out year," Evans says. "He's worked very hard and gotten better in some of his deficiencies. His outside shooting has improved. His range has improved. He does everything inside with strength and power, the way we tried to get Lane and Smith to do the last two years. Basketball means so much more to him that it does to the other so-called superstars. It's what got him out of Philadelphia. A lot of kids say, 'I want to be a pro,' but they don't work very hard at it, they just want the glory. Brian really wants it."

It's a team Evans feels he can mold into what he wants.

The newest addition to the Pitt staff is Assistant Coach John Sarandrea. The former coach of Tolentine in the Bronx, he's been hired to give Pitt a strong recruiting presence in New York City. He's already done that. In November, the Panthers signed Jamaal Faulkner from Christ the King in Rego Park, Queens.

Tonight, the Panthers lose to lowly Siena, 80–79, in Fitzgerald Field House, the old-time gym on campus that seats about 6,000. Is this the same team that trounced Oklahoma State two nights earlier in their first game? The entire month of December will go like this. A win over Jacksonville, a loss to West Virginia; a win over Toledo, then a loss to Duquesne. This last is the sort of news that goes out over the wire services like a neon sign: a Big East team lost to Duquesne? It looks like a long roller-coaster ride for Paul Evans.

BOSTON COLLEGE

December 7

It is the first Big East game of the year. It is a nationally televised ESPN game. Commissioner Dave Gavitt is on hand, and following his instructions to commemorate the conference's tenth year, the two teams line up across the court before the game, then meet in the middle, and exchange gifts, as is the custom in international play.

It is also, ironically, a meeting of Boston College and Providence, the two teams picked to finish dead last.

On the other hand, it is also the Big East debut of Conte Forum, BC's new hockey-basketball complex that's attached to the football stadium. The building seats 8,000 and comes equipped with a state-of-the-art scoreboard, luxury boxes at one end, and a parquet floor to remind everyone that this is basketball in Boston. So who knows?

The special basketball supplement of the Boston College student newspaper announces, "High Hopes Surround the 1988–89 Eagles." Last year the Eagles made a wonderful run through the NIT, going to the semifinals before getting beaten by Connecticut. So there are hopes that the Eagles are going to continue their climb up the Big East standings, and Coach Jim O'Brien has been quoted as saying, "We can't wait to get started. We are coming off an exciting season and the veteran players are confident we can build on last year's success."

The biggest reason for optimism is the return of Dana Barros, the leading scorer in the Big East last season. Barros is one of the top players in the country, a quick guard who's a great deep shooter. Plus there are three other veterans returning: senior Steve Benton, a 6-4 forward from Philadelphia, a proven, dependable role player and double-figures scorer; Corey Beasley, a 6-9 sophomore from Baltimore; and Doug Able, a 6-5 sophomore forward, also from Baltimore. Beasley made the Big East all-freshman team last year, showing flashes that he can one day be a fine Big East player. Able reminds people of a young Roger McCready, a former Eagle who survived very well in the Big East wars, though only 6-5. O'Brien also hopes Beasley and Able can make the jump from prospects to solid contributors this year; he also hopes that he can get some help from some of his other younger players, plus John Stovall, a 6-6 transfer from Penn.

But beneath the surface optimism, there's concern that this program lacks talent, especially big people, and that eventually O'Brien will get beaten down by too much losing and by the school's inability to attract the caliber of recruit that the top Big East schools are getting. This has become the one program people in the Big East office worry about. Which is why the arrival of Conte Forum has been so anticipated. A new showcase gym on campus can do wonders for a program that seems too littered with mediocre talent, the kind that makes for a lot of cold, winter nights in the Big East.

It certainly wasn't always this way. Back in the early years of the Big East, the Eagles were the classic overachievers. Tom Davis was the coach then—Dr. Tom—complete with his doctorate in colonial history. And his system.

The Eagles frantically pressed all over the court like hounds after a scent. On offense they attacked, continually getting the ball inside, even though their inside players were usually smaller than the opposition. Every few minutes Davis sent in more players, creating a revolving door. You didn't need a program to watch Davis's teams, you needed a pocket computer. The Eagles also played with incredible intensity, making the game run at 78 rpm instead of 45. In a sense it was a new way to play, and for a while Boston College was very successful. The names back then were John Bagley and Jay Murphy, John Garris and Martin Clark. Even though three of them went on to make the NBA, at the time BC was perceived as the ultimate overachiever.

Boston College basketball was a wonderful story then. Making it better was the fact that basketball had always been the stepchild of the BC athletic program, the third sport on campus. Football was king, since BC is the only school in New England playing big-time college football.

Hockey was next, a hockey school in a hockey town. So even in the years when basketball was going good, there was the feeling it was being done almost by accident. The Eagles played in tiny Roberts Center, a cramped bandbox that spoke of earlier times. Often they had trouble even filling that, even in the good years. The lack of interest was one of the things that drove Gary Williams to Ohio State.

Williams, a dynamic young coach, took over after Davis jumped for a big contract at Stanford. He essentially played the same style and also was successful, but eventually he too became frustrated, feeling that whatever he accomplished was done in anonymity. He had given them an exciting team, a winning team. What more did they want? The feeling that it was never going to be any different began to wear on him. One of the last straws was the final home game of Michael Adams, the tiny BC star who had been one of the most exciting players in all of college basketball. That night Roberts Center was not full. Williams couldn't believe it.

But if Davis left a legacy of success at BC, he also left a legacy of a program that had been built on the backs of some marginal students. This culminated with the revelation in 1983 that one of the stars, Jay Murphy, was enrolled in the university's night school instead of the regular college. Although not technically an NCAA violation, the story was spread all over the Boston papers, to the acute embarrassment of the school.

The result was that Boston College tightened its admission requirements for basketball players. By the time Jim O'Brien arrived three years ago, the Eagles were already slipping. The combination of Roberts Center and tightening admission standards seemed to be relegating the Eagles into the Big East's second division forever.

At least one problem has been solved: Conte Forum boosts BC into the big time. Will there be students, however, to fill it? "For us to be successful," O'Brien says, "we desperately need student support." In that same college paper supplement, captains Dana Barros and Steve Benton have a half-page plea for their fellow students to show up.

The Eagles have not had a strong preseason, despite their 4–1 record. A succession of nagging injuries have kept O'Brien from ever having his entire team intact, and the Eagles have already been upset by Dartmouth. The only name recruit is Bryan Edwards, a guard who is the all-time Massachusetts high-school scoring leader. He is from Boston, but he played at Cohassett, an expensive suburb south of Boston, where he was bussed every day. He was unstoppable, but in a weak high-school league, and even before conference games have begun, he seems bewildered, so once again this is a team of no-names revolving around Dana Barros.

Barros, who this year will be closing in on the all-time Big East scoring record, is from nearby Mattapan. He went to high school in suburban Westwood, two hours on the train and bus every day, because his mother wanted him to get out of Mattapan, a racially mixed working-class area where the future too often stops at next week. For example, one night when he was walking with his friends, he decided to go home instead of going with them for a night on the town. That night his friends stole a car, and one of them was shot in the neck by a cop.

At Xavarian High School, he was more sought after for his prowess in football. He is only 5-10 and he didn't go to any showcase basketball camps. In fact, the only Big East school that showed any interest at all was BC, and theirs was strictly marginal.

"BC didn't really recruit me, I recruited them," says Barros. "They kept coming to see me play, but it was getting late and they hadn't offered me a scholarship. I didn't know anything about recruiting. I didn't realize that if they didn't want me, I wouldn't go."

Just before he played in the Massachusetts state high-school tournament, BC offered him a scholarship. Then he went out and averaged 57 points a game in the tournament. Last year he led the Big East in scoring, at 21.9 a game. Now he's being looked at by NBA scouts. O'Brien calls him the greatest deep shooter he's ever seen.

Providence coach Rick Barnes's strategy is to put Eric Murdock on Barros, and make him expend a lot of energy on defense. It works. Barros doesn't score his first point until a foul shot with 7:15 in the half. A few minutes later he hits another shot and moves into fourth place on the Big East's all-time scoring list.

Right before the half, Barros and Providence's Darryl Wright get into a skirmish going off the court. Dave Gavitt comes over to his assistants, Mike Tranghese and Tom McElroy, and asks them what happened.

"Dave," Tranghese says wryly. "Dana didn't like the T-shirt he got as a gift."

"I'm serious," says Gavitt.

Gavitt is sensitive to his conference's reputation for fighting. After Georgetown's second game against Pitt last year, the second time in one season those two teams had fought, he instituted a rule saying that any player ejected for fighting would automatically be suspended for the next league game.

Two weeks from now, at the Big East office's Christmas party, a video will be shown, set to the Christmas carol "Twelve Days of Christmas." Instead of the refrain "five golden rings," the words "too many fights" are substituted. In a sense, the only real criticism of the Big East as a conference is that there have been "too many fights."

Providence comes out in the second half and takes control of the game. With six minutes left to play, they are up by 20, and they easily coast home 73–52. It is a great win for Providence. It is a devastating loss for Boston College. Not only have the Eagles lost their Big East opener against the other team universally picked to finish last in all the preseason polls, they have been blown out in their own new building.

Barros ends up with only 16 points, 4 of 12 from the field, plus 10 turnovers. It has been one of the worst games he can remember. Afterward, he says he knew right at the beginning he wasn't reading things right, that he felt out of sync. He also says it's depressing to have played so badly on the first big game of the season, because now the BC students might be reluctant to come to the games.

At the other end of the hall from the Boston College

locker room is the conference room. O'Brien walks in. He is wearing dark slacks and a white shirt. Half a dozen reporters sit in front of him. His wife, Chris, sits alone in the back of the room with tears in her eyes. O'Brien stands at the podium and takes a deep breath. His face looks pasty white, as if he's just seen a fatal accident and is now trying to compose himself.

"There's not a whole lot to say," he says in a low voice. "That was a very, very embarrassing defeat. Providence should get all the credit. They were much more prepared to play than we were. We didn't rebound with them. We didn't defend with them. We had our offense completely broken down. We could go on and on, but we are inexperienced. We don't have guys who have been through this before and it shows. We're going to be better, but right now we're not a very good basketball team."

"Is tonight a night you could have used Will Foley?" someone asks, referring to sophomore Willie Foley, who's missed the entire preseason with an injury.

O'Brien looks at him narrowly. Maybe he is wondering if that questioner really thinks Will Foley is the answer to BC's inside woes, the same Will Foley who was a nonfactor last year. Maybe he's asking himself why he is here after being blown out in his own building, listening to this ridiculous question.

"I mean, another big body," the questioner adds.

"Sure, we could have used him," says O'Brien ruefully. "Got any other names?"

SETON HALL

December 10

The bus is late, and Coach P. J. Carlesimo is concerned.

It is 3:30 in the afternoon at the Mariott Hotel across from LaGuardia Airport. In six hours Seton Hall will play St. John's, and now Carlesimo is looking for the bus that's scheduled to take his Pirates over to Alumni Hall for a walk-through. Once upon a time the coaching gospel was to rest your players the day of a game, keep them off their feet. About fifteen years ago, Bill Sharman, then the coach of the Lakers, began bringing his team to the arena the morning of the game for some light shooting and going over the opponent's offensive sets. Now everyone does it.

The players stand in the mirrored lobby in their sweatsuits. Carlesimo is wearing a trenchcoat over his practice gear. With his beard and a soft brown hat, he looks more like a European existentialist author than the coach of a team that's 6–0 and this week is ranked in the top 20, the first time in the school's history.

"Two years ago we got caught in a snowstorm, and it took us three hours to get to St. John's," mutters Carlesimo. "We get there 35 minutes before the game, and we begged for a few more minutes to get ready. We didn't get it." His voice trails off. "We lost by three."

Last year they lost by one at St. John's, missing a shot at the buzzer. Then they lost again to St. John's at home, their 15th straight loss to the Redmen. Not only have the Redmen become the proverbial monkey on their backs, Carlesimo knows that until he beats St. John's no one in New York will take his team seriously. St. John's has been college basketball in New York for so long now that everyone else—the Fordhams, Manhattans, and Ionas—is in the shadows. St. John's is the only New York school that can still pack Madison Square Garden, a throwback to the old days when college basketball ruled the Garden and the NBA was the gypsy league. Even if Seton Hall plays in the same league and last year went to the NCAA Tournament, St. John's has always lorded it over everyone else in New York. Case in point: it's been nearly eight years since St. John's lost to a metropolitan New York team.

So Carlesimo knows that even if he's 6–0, having won the Great Alaska Shootout by beating Utah, Kentucky, and Kansas, and even if the Hall is ranked 20th in the country, a loss to St. John's tonight will nullify everything. Especially since this is a St. John's team that, though 5–0, has lost its starting backcourt over the summer for academic reasons and often plays with three freshmen.

It's also the first Big East game for both the Hall and St. John's. Carlesimo knows he has the veteran team, and if he loses, there will be no excuses. In years past Seton Hall was supposed to lose to St. John's, but no longer.

And now the bus is late.

Carlesimo walks out into the street, looking in vain for the bus. It is a cold gray afternoon with the promise of winter.

"Okay, we'll get into four cabs," he says. "Four guys a cab."

He turns to senior Daryll Walker. "Daryll, you guys go in the first cab. Tell the guy he'll have to wait until I get there until he gets paid. If he gives you any shit, give him a dance."

Walker laughs.

Suddenly the bus arrives. The players get on and fill the air with music. Carlesimo slumps in the front seat, the brown hat pulled low over his eyes.

Soon, the Seton Hall players are casually shooting in Alumni Hall, and the bouncing balls echo through the nearly empty gym. "Take game shots," hollers Carlesimo. "Don't dick around."

He walks back and forth, full of nervous energy. He's been playing in this gym since the late sixties, when he was a freshman at Fordham and came here to play St. John's.

A few minutes later the second team starts walking through the St. John's offensive sets. Carlesimo kneels under the basket, coaching his defense. Assistant Coach John Carroll tells the offensive players where to go to simulate the St. John's patterns. It's all very detailed and is gone over time and time again.

"Run it again," says Carlesimo as one of his players looks confused. "How can you guys defend if you don't know what they're doing?"

You can hear the tension in his voice. Game time is getting closer, the anxiety is rising. The second team runs the same play again and again until Carlesimo is satisfied.

"Okay," he says. "Take a few shots, and we're out of here in five minutes."

John Morton, a sinewy guard, starts shooting three-pointers from the right sideline. When he came to the Hall three years ago, Morton was the personification of a New York City playground player, all flash and dash, without any kind of a jump shot. As a senior at Walton High School in the Bronx, he had led the city in scoring, but in his first two years of college ball he drove Carlesimo crazy. One minute he looked like a reincarnation of Earl Monroe, and the next like he had no clue what was going on. The bottom line was that he was a kid who could keep both teams in the game at the same time. In a sense he seemed to symbolize Seton Hall—all unfocused potential. When last year he was a little more consistent, he became a key weapon as the Hall went to their first NCAA tournament.

Now, he continues to clang jumpers off the rim.

"Hey, John," says Carlesimo, sneaking up behind him. "How about you make one?"

Half an hour later, the Pirates are in an Italian restaurant in Corona, Queens, for a pregame meal. Once upon a time all pregame meals were steak. Now they are pasta. A sign of the times.

"How is Connecticut doing?" Carlesimo asks, referring to UConnecticut's game at Virginia.

"They were down two at the half."

Carlesimo grimaces and gets up to check with the restaurant.

"P. J. really roots for the other conference schools," says Rod Baker, an assistant coach. "He gets upset when they lose. The other night when Villanova got beat by Penn, I loved it. He was upset."

It is one more example of Carlesimo's reputation of truly being one of the good guys of coaching. He is the son of Peter Carlesimo, a former athletic director at Fordham, now the executive director of the NIT. He is 39, has never been married, and he lives near the Seton Hall campus in a condo that is always in a state of perpetual disarray, as if he were a transient in his own life. He came to Seton Hall from Wagner largely on the basis of one great year there. The fact that he is Peter Carlesimo's son didn't hurt him any, either.

In the beginning of his career at Seton Hall, it was thought that one of the reasons Carlesimo was so well liked was because everyone always beat him twice a year. Now it's because Carlesimo is truly a likable guy. In this day and age when so many of the big-name coaches have become bigger than life and don't return phone calls from reporters, Carlesimo is no different than he was when he was in the Big East cellar. He is also the most gracious loser in the league. Many of the coaches are gracious winners. Losing with grace is infinitely more difficult.

"How's he been today?" Carroll asks Baker, pointing at the head coach.

"Surprisingly good," Baker says. "I thought he was going to go off when the bus was late, but he didn't."

"I remember last year," Carroll laughs. "The last thing he told the kids in the locker room was 'Go out and have some fun.' Then in the first timeout he's screaming, 'You mother-fuckers. What are you doing out there?' So much for having fun."

The waitress wants to know if anyone wants any Italian pastries. Andrew Gaze looks perplexed. It's little wonder he's in culture shock. He is from Melbourne, where his father, Lindsay, runs the Melbourne Tigers. Lindsay Gaze is considered the father of basketball in Australia.

He first brought a team to the United States in the early seventies. One of the teams he played on the tour was Providence, then coached by Gavitt, and the two of them became friendly. Two years ago, when Lindsay Gaze wanted to bring his team on another tour of the States, they took on some of the Big East teams. Gavitt offered to pay their plane fare around the league. "Just give us two vans, some lagers, and we'll play some ball," Gaze said. Do you know how far it is between some of our schools? asked Gavitt. Do you know how far it is between Melbourne and Perth? countered Gaze.

It was on that tour that Carlesimo first saw Gaze's son,

Andrew. In fact, he torched the Hall that night for 46 points. At the time Carlesimo mentioned the possibility of Gaze coming to the States to play for a year. Gaze was flattered but said, no thanks. That summer Carlesimo took a team of Big East all-stars to Australia, where they toured the country playing against the Australian national team, of which Gaze was a member. Again Carlesimo offered Gaze a chance to come to the United States, but the Olympics were coming up and Gaze wanted to play for Australia. Seton Hall kept after him, however, particularly John Carroll, who called Gaze constantly in Australia.

"I used to call at 11:30 P.M. because it was 9:30 A.M. over there," says Carroll. "I think."

After the Olympics, Gaze showed up at Seton Hall, the Big East's version of Crocodile Dundee, complete with a deep jump shot. Carlesimo had some concern that his players, a group of inner-city black kids, would resent the high-scoring Aussie with a funny accent. That hadn't happened. Gaze's passing ability helped on the court. His personality helped off it.

"Hey, Jack, you ever hear of canolis?" asks Carlesimo. Gaze is called Jack because in the beginning of the year he used to show up in the weight room wearing a T-shirt from Hungry Jack, one of the largest burger chains in Australia.

"I'm not from here, you know," Gaze laughs, "Australia" all over his speech.

"No shit, Jack," says Carlesimo. "I recruited you, didn't I?"

On the ride back to the hotel, through the darkened streets of Queens, music and laughter resound through the bus.

"Do you believe that we have a major game coming up in a couple of hours?" asks Baker.

"Is the team always this loose?" he is asked.

"Always," he says. "P. J. lets the players make a lot of the decisions. They decide their curfews on the road. They decide what we eat, what time we eat. They have a lot of input. Like last night. We got to the hotel about ten and P. J. asked Daryll Walker—he's the spokesman—what time curfew should be. He said one o'clock. P. J. said no, that was too late, so Daryll says we don't play until nine-thirty the next night, so P. J. says all right.''

One of the reasons he allows this is because he has a veteran team. At its core are four seniors—Morton, Walker, Gerald Greene, and Ramon Ramos. Ramos, 6-8 and built like the side of a building, is from Puerto Rico, where Carlesimo used to coach summer basketball. The other three are from New York City, the products of Carlesimo's first recruiting class that was supposed to start things turning around at the Hall. All had been all-city, and Walker had been the New York State player of the year. In a sense this class was Carlesimo's statement to the rest of the league that things were going to be different. But if Morton has struggled in his first two years, so did Greene and Walker. They, too, seemed over their heads in the Big East. In their first two years, the Hall was once again one of the league's doormats.

This year, however, Carlesimo and his staff thought they had something special right from the beginning of practice. They had the four seniors. They had Gaze. They had great frontcourt depth in Franz Volcy, Michael Cooper, and Anthony Avent, a Prop-48 sophomore. They had a veteran backup to Greene in diminutive Pooky Wigington. They were a team that had learned how to win the year before. More important, from the first day they were the team that worked hard every practice. The team also had something to prove. They had been picked seventh in the Big East's preseason coaches' poll, the thinking being that now, with Mark Bryant off to the pros, the Hall would slide back to where they have always been: the Big East's second division.

Now they are undefeated.

Tonight is also a big night for St. John's in the sense that regardless of their 5–0 record, they really have no idea how good they are. After Coach Louie Carnesecca had learned that both Boo Harvey and Michael Porter, his two starting guards of the year before, were academically ineligible, he said his team should be tenth in a nine-team league. Now he's not sure.

St. John's goes up two at the half. Stellar freshman Robert Werdann is forced to the bench after his fourth foul midway through the second half, though, and the Hall begins to take control. They play intense defense. They never lose their composure. In short, they play like the veteran team they are. Unlike Seton Hall teams of the past, they don't beat themselves. Michael Cooper, who looks like a black Charles Atlas with his sculptured muscles, comes in off the bench and gives them a big lift. They eventually prevail, 74–63.

Afterward, Carlesimo is seated in the small ampitheatre in the basement of Alumni Hall that is used for postgame press conferences. He looks relieved. The tension that was in his face earlier is gone. Not only is his team still undefeated, it has passed its first real test. They are still undefeated. They have won their first game of the Big East season. They have gained their first win in Alumni Hall since before World War I.

3

LET THE BATTLES BEGIN!

DECEMBER 23

The first month of the season is over, and already some things are becoming clear.

As expected, Syracuse and Georgetown are the early front-runners, though they both have yet to play a league game. Syracuse is 11–0 and has won the Big Apple NIT. The Hoyas are 7–0, although the record is irrelevant. The only Division I schools they've played are Oral Roberts, DePaul, and Virginia Tech. Once again John Thompson has cruised through a creampuff December schedule, playing his first four games against non-Division I opponents. The Hoyas started the season in Hawaii, beating Hawaii-Loa by 36 and Hawaii-Pacific by 40. Then they played St. Leo's, winning by 33, before pounding Shenandoah by 74 points, 114–40. Afterward, the question was not how come he beat Shenandoah by so many, but who was Shenandoah?

The DePaul game was on national television. Georgetown never trailed and won by 10, 74–64. Charles Smith scored the Hoyas' last 16 points of the game and finished with a career-high 37, while Alonzo Mourning had 19 points. Mourning had already broken Ewing's record for most blocked shots in one game, getting 11 against St. Leo's.

The two big surprises have been Seton Hall and Providence.

The Hall is 10–0. They won the Great Alaska Shootout, getting by Utah, Kentucky, and Kansas. They beat St. John's on the road, the first time since 1913. They have also won the games they were supposed to win. An old coaching adage says there's nothing better than a senior backcourt, and so far Greene and Morton have lived up to the adage. The Hall is starting to believe it can play with anyone.

Providence is 8–0, with four quality wins: South Alabama and Rhode Island at home, Boston College and Holy Cross on the road. More important, the chaos that surrounded the Friars last year is over. This has been Barnes's major challenge, and the 8–0 record is gravy.

At 6-1, St. John's has also been better than expected. Sealy and Werdann have already proved they can make an impact in the league as freshmen. In addition, Carnesecca has gotten decent guard play out of Jason Buchanan. What's more, in a few days St. John's is expected to get Boo Harvey back.

Connecticut, which began the season with such high expectations, is closing out the first month still as the league's mystery team. Are they the team that came in last in the conference last year? Are they the team that won the NIT, the one picked in the preseason top 20? They are 5–1, but that's deceiving, for theirs was a December schedule laced with the usual post-Thanksgiving turkeys. Their first big game was at Purdue. In a sense it was their showcase game, complete with a national TV audience. They were blown out, embarrassed. Cliff Robinson was particularly ineffective, but the entire team looked intimidated and overwhelmed. Not what a Big East team is supposed to look like, regardless of who they're playing. It was one of the few times in Calhoun's two years at Connecticut that this has happened, and afterward there had been a sense of shock.

But Connecticut had come back to win at Virginia, in one of those early must games, and Robinson went for 31. A loss on the road to Purdue they could live with. A double dip, and there's no question they would have again heard boos when they came back to the Hartford Civic Center.

The early season disappointments?

Villanova, Pittsburgh, and Boston College.

Villanova is 6–4, with losses to Southern Illinois, Penn, California, and LaSalle. They have been hampered by the inability of anyone besides Doug West to hit an outside shot. Throughout the fall Massimino had been saying freshman Greg Woodard from Rochester was going to have an immediate impact as a shooter, even going so far as to say he reminded him of Chris Mullin. So far Woodard hasn't shot well in games. Neither has anyone else.

Pittsburgh is 5–3, with losses to Siena, West Virginia, and inter-city rival Duquesne. They have one quality win on the road at Florida. Yes, Evans did get rid of the titanic egos he inherited two years before, but they have been replaced by young players who have played just as erratically as anyone might expect. Rod Brookin, who had been an academic casualty midway through the season, had showed up for practice in October 30 pounds overweight. Sean Miller, who last year started as a freshman at point guard, was now expected to have a bigger presence with the loss of Smith, Lane, and Gore. So far he hasn't. The Panthers have lacked outside shooting, experience, and depth.

The one bright spot has been Brian Shorter. Already he's emerged as one of the conference's young stars. Even last year, which he sat out, the Pittsburgh coaching staff was convinced he was going to be a great one. Last February, when there were strong rumors Jerome Lane was going to go hardship and forego his senior year, Pitt assistant John Calipari said, "We really don't care, because Shorter already is as good."

Boston College is 6–3. Not only were they awful in their first Big East game against Providence, they were beaten by Holy Cross and Dartmouth. The loss to Dartmouth was especially troubling, since Big East teams are not supposed to lose to Ivy League teams. Ever. Because the Eagles have gotten little inside scoring, their offense has been limited to the three-point bombing of Dana Barros. It's been a disappointing first month, one that does not bode well for the future.

JANUARY 3

Its official name is the Brendan Byrne Arena, a large white structure that sits across a parking lot from Giants Stadium, but everyone knows it as the Meadowlands. Located in East Rutherford, New Jersey, a jump shot away from the Vince Lombardi rest area on the Jersey Turnpike, it is perhaps an odd setting for New York's two professional football teams, but it suits the rise of a certain local basketball team very well.

Tonight the Brendan Byrne Arena is sold out. Over 19,000 people, the largest crowd ever to watch a college basketball game in New Jersey, have come to see 10th-ranked Seton Hall play fifth-ranked Georgetown.

A great many people have come to see Alonzo Mourning, the most celebrated freshman in college basketball. A year ago Mourning was billed as the next great player in college basketball, the latest in a conga line of prodigies that seem to be as much a part of the game as recruiting and cheerleader pyramids: Lew Alcindor, Tom McMillen, Bill Walton, Moses Malone, Darryl Dawkins, Sam Bowie, Ralph Sampson, Patrick Ewing, and now Alonzo Mourning. While in the eighth grade he was already going to Five Star, the showcase summer camp run by Howard Garfinkel. It was there, legend has it, that he blocked a few shots of J. R. Reid, who at the time was the most celebrated high-school player in the country.

His adjustment to the college game seemed to take about as long as it took him to lace up his sneakers. In his first home game he broke Ewing's Georgetown record for blocked shots. Already he's the main man for a Hoya team that's the most feared in the Big East, a team everyone thinks will be on center stage when the NCAA dance gets underway in March.

Now, on this night of his first Big East game, there's the feeling the future has arrived.

Throughout the past month the word was that if he were available for the NBA draft in June he would be a guaranteed lottery pick. Recently that opinion has been upgraded. There's growing sentiment that if he were available, he would be the first pick in the entire draft, before Danny Ferry of Duke, before Stacey King of Oklahoma, before Sean Elliott of Arizona.

All the same, the majority of spectators have come to see the local upstarts.

The week before, Seton Hall won the Sugar Bowl Tournament in New Orleans, beating Virginia and DePaul. The Pirates are now 12–0, and tonight they play before a sold-out Meadowlands crowd. The contrast to last year couldn't be more stark. Then the Meadowlands seemed like a tomb, a monument to frustration and defeat, and Carlesimo was lustily booed.

Forget all the obvious negatives that surrounded the Hall: a small, old campus gym; a school that had never gone to the NCAA Tournament; a school dwarfed in the metropolitan area by the tradition of St. John's. It was all Carlesimo's fault, or so the thinking went. He was booed at games. The student senate called for his resignation. The word throughout the basketball world was that P. J. was done for.

Now Seton Hall was off to the best start in their history.

"There isn't an S.O.B. in the country that thought this was going to be a game between the number five and the number ten team in the country," says Seton Hall assistant Rod Baker.

He stands in the runway of the Meadowlands watching the preliminary game, St. Peter's against Jacksonville. The big building is still mostly empty.

"What's the difference?" he's asked.

"Experience," he says. "Our guys just don't bend. Forget breaking. They don't even bend. They know now that if they do what they're supposed to do, they'll win. We have nine guys who can play, so each individual doesn't have to worry about being good. All they have to do is play. Some days some guys shoot it, some days other guys score inside. No one has to worry about carrying us. Ramon Ramos has a bad half against DePaul. Anthony Avent comes in and carries us. Andrew has a bad shooting game, John Morton scores.

"You can't overemphasize experience. There wasn't a whole lot of teaching going on before the season. It was more like a carryover from last year. It was all there, and we just refined it. And the younger guys just sort of blended in."

"What's the biggest thing that's surprised you?"

Baker thinks for a moment.

"How oblivious the kids are to P. J.'s rantings and ravings. He's brutally honest with them, but they don't take it personally. They seem to sift out what they have to know. Again, that's experience. You have to mature to that level.

"They also are unselfish. P. J. won't stand for anything else. He'll say right to them, 'You selfish motherfucker.' He's probably said it to the veterans a hundred times since they've been here. And they've survived that. So we don't have to worry about ego. Anthony Avent is a young player, but he can't get upset when he gets yelled at because Ramos, who's a senior, gets the same thing.

"Take the other day in practice. After John Morton throws a couple of terrible passes, P. J. stops practice and says, 'You know, John, I used to get upset when you threw passes like that, because it used to kill us. But now I like it. You know why? Because every time you throw a stupid pass, it's taking money out of your pocket. Because no pro team is going to take anyone who throws stupid passes like that. So keep throwing them. Because now they make me happy.' Morton got the message. These guys are survivors. From P. J. on down. And now they're all reaping the benefits from all the bullshit they took."

Thompson gets the biggest crowd response in the pregame introductions: a cacaphony of boos rolls down from the stands across the court. Thompson appears oblivious. Certainly he's heard boos before. There are some in the league

Bill Reynolds

who believe he likes it, just as he seems to revel in controversy.

On the bench is Mary Fenlon, a former nun with short strawberry hair who came to Georgetown with Thompson 16 years ago. At the time he told her that he wanted to be a basketball coach and it was going to be her job to make sure he was going to be able to do that. He knew her from St. Anthony's where she had been a sort of volunteer academic support service for the team.

"I was impressed with her ability to motivate without relying on any pretense," Thompson has said. "She was a teacher, not a temporary mother or guardian, and she got the students to do what they were supposed to do in school without the pretense of being overly affectionate with them."

At Georgetown she began by being in charge of the players' academic life. Her job soon evolved. In the beginning there was no basketball secretary, so she answered the phones, did the typing, handled the budget, the behind-the-scenes administrator. She had input into all parts of the program, the scheduling, practice schedule, all of it except the x's and o's. She also became the buffer around Thompson, screening him from the people making demands on his time, to the point that Mary Fenlon became for many a symbol for the paranoia that surrounds the entire program. She has been the one standing by the locker room door telling reporters that the room will only be open for two more minutes. She has been the one seen scurrying the players out of the locker room, as if one more minute with a reporter might cause the walls to come crumbling down. In many ways she's been cast as the heavy in the entire Hoya scenario.

There is even an apologia of sorts in this year's media guide, in the brief bio of her. After recounting that part of her duties include handling Thompson's schedule, it says, "Since this may mean disappointing people who desire Coach Thompson's time, it's not the easiest or most popular position in the basketball office."

Amen.

It is a great game, a sneak preview of the intensity of an

NCAA tournament game. Mourning blocks shots. He runs the floor. He rebounds. He goal tends. He posts up inside. His passion for the game shows in his every move. When he fouls out near the end of the game, he has 18 points, 8 rebounds, 8 blocked shots.

The Hall is down by 8 with 12 minutes to play, in danger of letting the game get away from them. Then Carlesimo adjusts and puts his players in a zone. It's the first time the Pirates have played zone all year, but the strategy works. Georgetown's offense starts to sputter. Mourning doesn't get the ball as much and becomes less of a dominating presence in the game. The Hall eventually wins by 8, 94–86, but the victory is not as important as the fact they have played Georgetown in front of a capacity crowd and fought back when they were down.

Afterward, a reflective Carlesimo stands in the hallway in front of a small podium, trying to put the night in perspective.

"I believe we're a good basketball team," he says. "A very good basketball team. The difference is that now we think we can win anytime we go out. We didn't used to think that. But I just want to get to be a good enough team so we don't have to keep on proving it. So even if we lose, people can come out and see a good Big East basketball game without being disappointed."

Carlesimo goes on to laud Georgetown. Part of this is due to his deep respect for Thompson. Not only was Thompson one of the coaches who supported Carlesimo in his time of need, last year Thompson had taken the microphone in the Meadowlands, moments after Georgetown had beaten Seton Hall, and said, "This is the only building in the Big East where we don't sell out. And we've had some great teams." It had been a further defense for a young coach under siege.

But Carlesimo also knows how good Georgetown is. They came in after playing a weak December schedule, and with their young frontcourt they showed that they will indeed be a force in the Big East. But all that's for the future. Tonight is for celebrating.

"It was a very special night with the crowd and all," he

says. "That is the product of not just this team, but a lot of other teams that worked awfully hard in the past."

JANUARY 4

Mike Gorman is sitting in the press room of the Hartford Civic Center. In a few hours Connecticut will play Villanova, but now Gorman is having his pregame meal and talking about the long, winding road that's taken him from a small radio station in New Bedford, Massachusetts, to becoming the most recognizable voice in the Big East Conference. He now does as many as 40 Big East games a year, from the national Monday-night games on ESPN to specific games in cities throughout the league.

Gorman grew up in Dorchester, a working-class section of Boston, where he played all sports, then went to Boston State with the vague notion of being a teacher. But the Vietnam War got in the way, and he ended up in the navy, spending five years as a flier. By the time he got out he realized that he disliked the navy so much that he promised himself he would get a job doing something he liked.

Like be around sports.

His first radio job was as an all-night disc jockey. It also was the first chance he got to broadcast sports, when he and Frank Daly, who's also now broadcasting some Big East games, decided to broadcast a local golf tournament for an entire afternoon. So what if their only equipment was a phone in the clubhouse lounge?

"We'd say things like, 'Here we are on the 14th fairway,' " Gorman recalls. "We'd just make it up. But no graduate school with the finest of equipment could have given you that kind of experience."

The following year Gorman went to a larger radio station in Providence, where he was the cohost of a morning radio show. He soon talked the station into doing some University of Rhode Island games, his first foray into play-by-play. A few years later he became a weekend anchor on a Providence TV station, going fulltime there in 1979. He then began doing some Providence College games on television.

The Big East was getting underway at the time, and the new conference was formulating plans to get its games on TV. Gavitt and Tranghese approached Gorman about doing some work for the conference. There was going to be a Monday-night game of the week, for which they wanted a recognizable face—Lenny Berman, then on TV in New York. They wanted Gorman to do a halftime report, with highlights of games from around the league.

"Every Sunday Mike and I would tape this highlight show," recalls Gorman. "We created this little studio that looked like it came out of a box and then every Monday night Mike would take the tape and play it during halftime of the broadcasts. Back then Big East television was like a mom-and-pop store, but Dave and Mike were not afraid to go out and learn someone else's business. Mike Tranghese sat in the TV truck every Monday night that first year trying to learn the business. This was back in the days when he always used to pass out Big East T-shirts to the cheerleaders before the games so they could be photographed on the broadcasts. Dave was doing the color with Berman on the broadcasts, learning what it was like to do a live TV game. TV is not as difficult as TV people want you to think, and Dave and Mike were perceptive enough to see that and not be afraid to do it themselves. I remember early on when I was supposed to do a game at Villanova with Gavitt, but when I got to the Philadelphia airport, there was a blizzard. I had no way to get to the game. So Dave had to do it alone. And he was great. He did the play-by-play, the color, and the interviews, all by himself. After that, I always had the feeling Dave was never going to be intimidated by TV again."

In those first few years Gorman would fill in on Monday nights if Berman had a conflict. He also continued to do both the halftime reports and some TV production work for the conference. Then the Big East also began televising Saturday-afternoon games. Gorman broadcast them, sometimes doing a game in the afternoon, then flying somewhere else afterward to do another Big East game in a different city.

Eight years ago he also began doing Boston Celtics games on SportsChannel, while juggling the Big East games and his local TV-sports anchor work. But he never saw being a TV sportscaster as a lifelong career. He considered it too high gloss, too transparent. He didn't want to be a slave to the way he looked. What he wanted to do was play-by-play. So three years ago he quit the Providence TV station.

It was a changing time in the television industry and the future said *cable*. Cable was going to be the goose that laid a thousand golden eggs, and everyone was jumping in. Syndication companies were springing up overnight, reaching out for talent like the old-time Hollywood producers once reached out for starlets. There were going to be games and more games and everyone was going to get rich, right?

Not exactly.

Now the cable industry is in transition. The glut of games is shrinking, and the air smells of instability. Syndication companies come and go like ships in the night, and broadcasters play their own version of musical chairs.

"Forget about job security," says Gorman. "I've always had a one-year contract with SportsChannel, and now I have the same thing with the Big East Network. There's no dental plan. No one takes your taxes out. There used to be a time when my goal was to get a fulltime network job—and I would still one day love to be the voice you hear when you turn on the Final Four, or the NBA playoffs—but I don't really know anymore if I want to do auto racing from Daytona, too. Seven or eight years ago I would have leapt at that opportunity. Now I just want to do the most good basketball games I can. People say to me that it's a gypsy life, that they see me on TV all the time, and I must never be home. But if that's the case I'm at a lot of good games and I like that."

Now he does halftime features, tournament features, music videos, and other production work for the Big East. He has done a recruiting film for Seton Hall. He and his wife, Teri Schindler, are doing a 10th-year Big East video for the conference to be sold in the spring. But his main work for the Big East has been being their most recognizable voice, not to mention being a witness to the conference's phenomenal growth.

"The biggest surprise to me is that the people haven't really changed all that much. The Dave Gavitt I knew in 1979 is the Dave Gavitt I know now. Mike Tranghese treats people the same way now that he did when he used to be the sports-information director at Providence College. He's aways treated the guy from the *New York Times* no differently than some guy from the smallest daily in Rhode Island. You walk into the Big East office now and, with the exception of Chris Plonsky, there haven't been any new staff members in five years. Now with Dave Gavitt's involvement in international basketball, the Big East Conference is known all over the world, but what are we talking about? Eight or nine people in the entire office, including interns? The CBSs of the world could learn a few lessons."

Gorman is asked how he's seen the coaches change.

"I'm not the kind of guy that goes down to the locker rooms after games or spends a lot of time visiting with the coaches beforehand, so it took me a long time to build relationships with coaches. Looie and John Thompson were probably the first who were the most cooperative, the most open. Then Rollie. Not that Boeheim was uncooperative. That's just his personality not to be all that open. But Looie's Looie. I haven't seen him change. He's always been a very decent man. I think people are beginning to understand John Thompson. I think he becomes more approachable, less intimidating, the longer you are around him.

"One of the things I've done for years is preseason previews where we go to each school with a camera and interview the coach and one or two of the players. That's where I've gotten to know most of the coaches. Obviously, in the beginning I didn't know what to expect from Thompson. I had heard all the horror stories. But he never dodged a question. He always was on time. And he always gave me as much time as we agreed upon. That's the John Thompson I always found. Am I John Thompson's friend? No. I don't think if you asked him if Mike Gorman is his friend he would say yes. But I think people are beginning to see that John Thompson's way works for him. He doesn't necessarily want you to criticize it, but he's really not asking for your approval, either. But I've found that if you show him respect he will show you respect.

"Rollie's players always say he will do anything for you, and that he doesn't have to be asked. Boeheim hasn't changed. Some days he's friendly and will talk to you for hours, some days he won't. But that's just him. The newer coaches in the league all are good, because they all essentially want publicity. Paul Evans is a personality. He basically will be Paul whatever happens.

"The only real change in all of them I've seen is that the quality of their sports jackets has increased dramatically. That, and that they are now much more comfortable in front of the TV camera than they used to be. The first few years you got the feeling you were kind of an imposition on their time. That's no longer true. Their comfort level in front of the camera has risen 200 percent.

"But you know, they are different than most people you see on TV. Most people you see are there because of the way they look. Basketball coaches are on because of how much they win. They are allowed to be themselves. No one's writing a script for them.

"And the players very much mirror the program. The Georgetown kids always are in jackets and ties. They always are prepared and very polite. The Villanova kids are very loose, like you are meeting them over at Rollie's house. The St John's kids are New York kids, no pretense. Syracuse is the biggest cross-section."

Gorman has interviewed scores of Big East players over the years, everything from perfunctory postgame things to more in-depth interviews.

"Maybe the best one was one of the first years of the Big East tournament in the Garden. We were all set to interview the Pearl between games, and we only had a few seconds before we were due to be on. So I said to him, 'We're going to run some highlights of you and you just comment on them, all right?' He shook his head, yes, but we started rolling the clip of the Pearl coming down the court, dribbling through his legs, then making a move to the hoop, and he didn't say anything. There were a few seconds of silence, then all you heard was Pearl's voice, almost reverently saying, 'Hey, there's the Pearl on TV—check it out.' "

As Gorman gets ready to leave, he is asked what surprises him the most after all these years. Is it the money? The number of games on TV? The success of the conference? What?

"I'm amazed time and time again that they're still kids," he says. "Sometimes they're on TV so much it's easy to forget that."

The big news tonight is that Connecticut freshman Chris Smith is hurt, out for a few games with a bad ankle. Calhoun is not happy, especially now with the start of the Big East season, Villanova tonight and Providence four days away. His Huskies, though 8–1, have been erratic, out-of-sync on offense, still looking for the rhythm they had last March when they won the NIT. They were recently down to lowly Pepperdine 15–5 here in the Civic Center before pulling away.

Smith's injury is the kind that affects a team more than the average fan realizes. Not only is he considered a great talent, he's also able to play both guard positions. With him not available and backup Steve Pikell being red-shirted with a shoulder injury, Tate George becomes the only point guard on the club.

"This really hurts us," says Tim Tolikan, who is probably as involved with the program as any sports information director in the conference. He is knowledgeable, informed, and very close personally with Calhoun.

"Now it's all up to Tate for a while, and he hasn't been playing particularly well. He is basically a coaster, someone who has to be pushed. And when he strolls, he's not a good player. Jimmy gets all over Tate. But every time he's been down before he's usually bounced back."

George is a 6-6 junior guard from New Jersey whom

Calhoun always seems at odds with. One of the reasons is that Calhoun thinks he is not as committed to basketball as Calhoun would like him to be. He is a student. He has a social life. His life doesn't seem to be confined inside the borders of the court.

"Tate's a charmer, but when Tate plays well we are a good team," continues Tolikan, "and he played five good games for us last year in the NIT. That's why we won the NIT. Phil Gamble was the MVP and Robinson played well, but the reason we won is that Tate ran everything and got the ball to the right people at the right time."

The name player for Connecticut is Cliff Robinson, a 6-11 senior whose career has been marked by inconsistency. Still, he is being talked about as a possible first-round draft choice. Over the summer he spent a week informally scrimmaging against many of the Celtics and impressed them with his talent. As a freshman he had been in and out of the lineup, all potential with little performance. When Calhoun got the job, he began developing a special relationship with him.

"Don't take this wrong," says Tolikan, "but I think Jimmy does a better job with black kids than white kids. He had a lot of tough, inner-city black kids at Northeastern, and he knows how to deal with them. Basically, he's a tough, blue-collar guy himself. When he got the job he went right at Robinson, who is an inner-city kid from Buffalo. He's really the toughest kid to deal with that we have. Basically, Jimmy told him what he had to do to be a pro. And he has brought him along academically and socially, as well as in basketball. Now how far Cliff goes is up to him. He's not someone who's going to work hard in the weight room. But right now they're talking about him being a first-round draft choice. We're talking about a kid who could be making a million dollars next year."

He's never been a popular player with the Connecticut media. He often plays with a perpetual pout on his face. His game is marked by a propensity to take medium-range jump shots, not bang inside. In his first three years at Connecticut there have been too many times when the whole didn't seem to measure up to the sum of the parts.

The game is a grind, a typical Villanova game. Played at Massimino's pace, each possession becomes important. Both teams are tenacious on defense, deliberate on offense. Maybe it's only fitting. If Calhoun is not personally enamored of Massimino, it's the Villanova program the Huskies are most trying to replicate. Calhoun believes that Connecticut is never going to be able to attract the best talent in the league, and so they are going to have to be smart, well coached. It's essentially the same basic philosophy that Massimino has won with.

Villanova is up two at the half, but Connecticut holds the Wildcats scoreless for nearly eight minutes in the second half and takes a 9-point lead. Once again Villanova's inability to consistently hit perimeter shots hurts them badly. But with six seconds left the game is tied. Villanova has made a comeback, Kenny Wilson has hit a three-pointer with just eight seconds remaining on the clock, and it appears to be another game the Cats are going to pull out in the final seconds. Then Murray Williams, a Connecticut sophomore from nearby Torrington, gets an inbounds pass in front of the Villanova bench. He starts dribbling down the right sideline, crosses midcourt, makes a cut to the basket, and scores a layup as the game ends and pandemonium erupts on the Civic Center court. It is the first time in 15 games that Connecticut has beaten Villanova.

Afterward, Calhoun is in the interview room in the bowels of the Hartford Civic Center, saying what a big win it is for his kids, when Massimino walks into the back of the room. Next to him is Craig Miller, the Villanova sports information director. It becomes quickly apparent he's in no mood to stand in back of the room and wait for Calhoun to finish his interview. Maybe it's because Massimino and Calhoun were once old Massachusetts high school rivals when they both were starting their coaching careers, and the old rivalry has carried over. Maybe it's because while Massimino is considered a gracious winner, always praising the other coach, he's generally considered the worst loser in the league.

"How long is this going on for?" he says to Miller in a loud voice, glancing up at the front of the room at Calhoun.

"Let's go," Massimino says, his voice louder now.

Calhoun looks over, surprised by this rudeness.

"I guess the coach wants to say something," he says, somewhat sheepishly. He starts to walk out of the room. As he and Massimino pass, they don't look at each other. Calhoun leaves the room, followed by several writers. Massimino stands in front of the lectern and begins lighting a large cigar.

Outside in the corridor, Calhoun is surrounded by several writers. He is asked if he had a special play all set for the last six seconds.

"We just wanted to go to the basket and see what happened," he says. "It's the toughest play to defend in basketball: someone coming right at you in the closing seconds. I know it doesn't sound very complicated, but I'm not Billy Tubbs either. We run a lot of things. But what do you do with six seconds left? Explode to the basket."

Next to him is Tim Tolikan, Connecticut's SID.

"What was Rollie doing in there?" he is asked.

"Fuck him," Tolikan says loudly. "Fuck him and all his Daddy Mass bullshit. He comes into our building and pulls that stuff. Like we aren't big enough for him. Fuck him, and all that wheelchair stuff and what a good guy he is. The man's a fraud. And no one writes about it. Our radio guys used to do the Villanova games, and they say that he wouldn't walk from here to there unless there was something in it for him. Fuck him."

JANUARY 8

Sunday morning, Chris Plonsky, the Big East's director of communications, is at work in the Big East office. From Tallmidge, Ohio, on the outskirts of Akron, she is a former player who learned about basketball first by following the boys who lived down the street, later by hanging around a public park called "the courts" that still has a picture of local legend Gus Johnson hanging from a light tower. Coming of age at a time when women were starting to take playing seriously, she played throughout high school. Not recruited, she walked on at Kent State, made the team, and earned a scholarship. She also wrote for the school paper and became the first woman to work in the school's sports information office. After Kent State, she worked in the sports-information office at Iowa State, then at Texas, before coming to the Big East.

She is constantly on the phone, plugging herself into the basketball network of sportswriters and sports-information directors. Sundays, she gets a recap of all the games from the night before, all the stats. She talks to many of the beat writers who cover the Big East teams. She also selects the Big East player of the week and the rookie of the week, names that usually go out over the wire services Sunday afternoon.

The day before was busy.

• Providence beat Connecticut by 2, 80–78, in the Hartford Civic Center, after twice being down by 9 in the second half. Afterward, Calhoun said his Huskies had had a bad game, then grumbled that his players can't practice three times a day because they have to go to class, a blatant swipe at Providence. He also hadn't been pleased with his team's intensity. He said if his team had won, "I wouldn't have cared. It would have been a lousy win. Apparently, Providence College thinks that winning a game in the Big East Conference is a little more important than we do." The Friars are still undefeated. They are also now 2–0 in the Big East, after having crushed St. John's at home early in the week.

• St. John's beats Villanova by 19, 81–62, making 35 of 37 foul shots. It was their first conference win, and it dropped the Cats to 0–2. Villanova's now 8–6 overall, leaving them, even at this early date, at a precarious position for an NCAA bid. Worse, the Redmen had played without freshman center Robert Werdann, going instead with 6-6 Billy Singleton to guard 7-3 Tom Greis. The only bright spot for

Villanova was freshman Greg Woodard, who finally hit some perimeter shots. But once again the Cats overall had trouble scoring.

• Boston College beat Pittsburgh in Pittsburgh by 12, 95–83, getting 43 from Dana Barros. It is a Big East scoring record, breaking the old mark of 38 held jointly by Mark Bryant and Dan Callandrillo of Seton Hall and Jaren Jackson of Georgetown. Barros also took 16 three-point attempts, making nine. This is another Big East record. Plonsky has already decided Barros is the player of the week.

"Some of the other SIDs gave me some other candidates, but when I told them that BC beat Pitt on the road and Dana had 43, that kind of stopped it," she remarks wryly.

• Syracuse had entered the week undefeated and ranked number two in the country behind Duke in the Associated Press poll, but they had been upset in the Dome by Pittsburgh, 81–76. Once again their inability to make free throws was their Achilles heel. But they came back last night to blow out Seton Hall by 24, a game the Hall was never really in and that extended the Pirates' streak of never having won in the Carrier Dome. Syracuse is now 14–1, the Hall 13–1.

• Georgetown blasted Miami, 112–79, in a nonleague game at the Capital Centre in Landover, Maryland. Alonzo Mourning had another monster game and is named the freshman of the week. He had played with an upset stomach, the second time this week. Thompson thinks he's getting these upset stomachs because he continually eats jelly candies called gummi bears before games.

"Do you believe it?" says Plonsky. "Our freshman of the week eats gummi bears!"

It's been a strange week. Pitt beats Syracuse in the Dome, then gets beaten at home by Boston College. St. John's gets annihilated on the road at Providence, then comes home and climbs all over Villanova. Providence wins two to go 3–0 in the conference and take sole possession of first place.

One week into the conference and the world as we know it no longer seems to exist.

In an article under the subhead "Unlikely front-runners Seton Hall and Providence top the talent-rich Big East," Alex Wolff writes: "Upon reaching the ripe old age of 10, any league with two NCAA basketball titles, a full calendar of TV dates, and a ton of money is entitled to raise a glass to itself. But having made the toasts and downed the drinks, does the Big East really have to take 'Bottoms Up' so literally?"

JANUARY 9

Rollie Massimino is watching his team finish their shoot-around. Tonight his Wildcats play Syracuse in what is already a must game for Villanova. A loss tonight, plus another later in the week to undefeated Providence, and this could very well become the season that never was for the Wildcats.

"See that kid?" he says, pointing at freshman Greg Woodard. "I think he's going to be a great one. All fall I felt he was going to be another Chris Mullin. I really did. He's 6-7 and he never misses in practice. Then he gets in the game and doesn't shoot well. I've been all over him. I tell him that I'm going to drive him crazy, but in the end he's going to be great."

He took this same approach with Tom Greis, the 7-3 junior, the year before. As a freshman Greis seemed lost, an overgrown kid who was nowhere near ready to play in a league as physical as the Big East. So began the transformation. Massimino told him to lose 25 pounds or forget playing.

Not that transformations are always successful. A few years back Massimino recruited two large white kids, Wyatt Maker and Chuck Everson. Both were close to seven feet and huge. Both were also slow and unskilled, what's called in the trade "projects." (Rest assured, projects are never 5-11.) Wyatt and Maker never became the players Massimino envisioned, though. "I got 14 feet worth of shit," he recalled.

No one ever said "projects" came with a guarantee.

Woodard is taking soft left-handed jump shots from the

three-point line. Nearly every shot goes in. A year ago he was a senior at McQuaid High School in Rochester, one of the most sought-after recruits in the East. Now Massimino watches him as he keeps knocking down jumpers and shakes his head.

"Look at that," he says. "The kid never misses. And he's not selfish either. Maybe that's his problem. Shooters shouldn't care if they miss. Shooters have to have the confidence that no matter how many they miss, the next one's going in. He doesn't have that yet. He misses in a game and he gets tentative." Woodward sinks another one, and Rollie shakes his head. "He just plain never misses. We've never had a kid like that. Never."

Doug West comes over and jokes that he needs more shots tonight.

"More shots?" says Rollie in feigned annoyance. "More shots? I'll give you a shot in the snoot, that's what I'll give you."

West laughs and dribbles away.

"We got great kids," says Rollie. "I love them. I break their balls, they break mine. It's great. I'm having as much fun as I ever had. The only year I didn't was two years ago with the McLain thing. But now I'm having as much fun as I ever had. They know what I think about them. I tell them, 'The worst thing about coaching is that the people you love the most, you see the least: your family. So you are my family and I am your family, and that's the way it is.'

"I do the same thing I did thirty years ago. I treat the kids the same way. I yell and scream at them, and I demand things. I am a very demanding person. I don't want half their effort. I want their total effort. I talk about them as my family and I mean it. These kids are like my own kids. And winning is only part of it. I want to see them develop as people and see them leave here with degrees. The longer I stay in this job, the more I realize that's what it's all about."

Rollie Massimino is one of the great success stories in college basketball. People can say he changed after he won the national title in 1985. People can say his image has been a media creation. But no one can say he hasn't paid his dues.

He grew up in Hillside, New Jersey, the son of Italian immigrants. His father worked as a shoemaker. He probably would have been a shoemaker himself, but his older brother Carmen, who now owns a shoe store in Hillside, insisted he go to college. So he went to the University of Vermont, intending to be an accountant. He played varsity ball for three years, graduating in 1956.

He began his coaching career as a high-school assistant at Cranford High School in northern Jersey in the late fifties. This area produced several people who went on to become name coaches: Hubie Brown, Mike Fratello, Tates Locke, Lou Campenelli. In the summers they all ran a local swimming club. Their players were the cabana boys by day and then played games at night. Afterward, they would sit around and talk about strategies. It was a basketball education for a young coach.

"It was all one big clique," he says.

He was an assistant at Cranford for four years before becoming the head coach. Then he went to nearby Hillside, and in 1962 his team went to the state finals. He was more than just a coach, though. He also taught typing, shorthand, and consumer economics. The next year he went to coach at Lexington High School, in the Massachusetts suburb best known as one of the birthplaces of the American Revolution. He already had five children.

And still a college coaching job was the siren call always beckoning to him. He turned down several jobs as an assistant coach because they didn't pay enough money. Yes, he wanted to get to college, but he never wanted his family to have to mortgage their lives for his coaching dream. The two college jobs he wanted were Harvard and Dartmouth. Dartmouth, because of his friendship with Doggie Julian, the old Dartmouth coach he knew from a summer camp in New Hampshire. Harvard, because it was close to Lexington, and he wouldn't have had to uproot his family. He almost got the Harvard job in the early seventies.

When he was thirty-four he got a call from Stony Brook, a

division of the New York State system located on Long Island. "Where the hell is Stony Brook?" he thought.

"The guy who hired me said he wanted to make Stony Brook the UCLA of the East." He laughs. "He was a screwball."

He was at Stony Brook two years when Chuck Daly called. Daly was at Penn at the time, and Massimino knew him from his days at Boston College.

"I meet him in Newark Airport at eight in the morning," says Massimino, "and he offers me an assistant's job at Penn for something like $13,000. I'm already making $19,000. I got a wife and five kids and no money. I'm driving a beat-up old Pontiac and I don't know where my next meal is coming from. But my wife said let's go."

The rest is history. In 1973, after two years as Daly's assistant at Penn, he became the coach at Villanova, succeeding Jack Kraft. He boldly announced that his immediate goal was the reemergence of Villanova as a basketball power and quickly developed his "family atmosphere." Two years later the Cats began winning. Now they have a record of unparalleled success at Villanova: 12 postseason tournaments; eight NCAA Tournament appearances in the past nine years, including five trips to the Final Eight; a 15-year average of almost 20 wins a season.

Then in 1985 he won the national championship, upsetting Georgetown in one of the most memorable finals in history. Soon after, he turned down a mega-offer from the New Jersey Nets, changing his mind at the last minute. Villanova came back with a salary commensurate with someone who had won the national title.

Then the world started to change for Roland V. Massimino, the shoemaker's son from Hillside.

Maybe it was inevitable. Maybe there had been too many years at too little pay, too many nights on the road recruiting, too many nights spent away from home at summer camps looking at kids who can't play anyway. For the first time in his life Rollie Massimino had money, and his image started to change. He began wearing more expensive suits, expensive jewelry. And with the changes came the charge that Massimino himself had changed, that something irreplaceable had been lost that night he won the national title.

The Spectrum in Philadelphia is across the street from Veteran's Stadium, a few miles south of downtown. Inside, the seats are red, and red banners honoring Julius Erving, Hal Greer, and other Philadelphia 76'er legends hang from the rafters. Though Villanova is in the northern suburbs and plays most of its home games in its new duPont Center on campus, the marquee games are played here. Tonight it is Syracuse, and the Spectrum is filled nearly to capacity.

Each season every team has various turning-point games that, in retrospect, are the ones that determine how the rest of the season gets played out. By all consensus, this is one for Villanova.

The two Philadelphia newspapers have stories that essentially ask, "What's wrong with the Cats?"

"But Rollie is a crisis coach," says Billy Raftery, here to do the game for ESPN. "He lives for games like these."

The game is played according to Massimino's game plan. He is a product of Eastern basketball back in a time when its coaches were generally considered the most cerebral in the game. His teams play smart on offense, always under control. He wants the game to be played at his tempo, and invariably, when the game is played at a slower pace, making each possession important, Massimino teams have been successful. Case in point: Villanova's upset of Georgetown for the national title in 1985.

Massimino plays a match-up zone defense. It's a zone defense with man-to-man principles, which essentially means that each Villanova player is always paired with an opposing player. The originator was Joe Mullaney, back when he began coaching at Providence in the midfifties. For years he won games he shouldn't have because other teams bumbled against his defense, treating it as though it were a straight zone. Later, Jack Kraft did a variation of it when he was at Villanova, calling it his "ball defense." It's a complicated system, for the players always have to trade players off to someone else and pick up the next player who comes into

their zone, and it requires hour upon hour of teaching. It's
not by accident that Massimino's teams always seem to be
better when his players are upperclassmen, or that the Cats
always have good fortune in the NCAA Tournament, especially against teams that don't see them frequently.

That night Syracuse certainly struggles against it. Once
again their lack of consistent outside shooting and their
inability to play well in a halfcourt offense makes them look
very different than the team that won the Big Apple NIT
just six weeks ago. The Wildcats play like they are defending the Alamo, spurred on by Massimino, who in turn periodically spurs on the crowd. This is the Rollie of legend,
stamping his feet, his hair disheveled, his face contorted,
primed for the upset.

The Cats win in a great game, and afterward Massimino
strolls into the interview room like an old ward healer who
once again has delivered a winning ticket on election night.

"The key to this game was 'TNT,' " he says, holding his
omnipresent postgame cigar. "Tempo negates turnovers."
He takes a puff from the cigar. "I'm very much impressed
with our team," he says. "It's a team with a lot of character.
I've always said that."

The locker room that Villanova is using tonight is full of
reporters and minicams. Standing in front of one of them is
star guard Doug West.

"What does 'TNT' mean?" he's asked.

He is 6-6, lean, sinewy, with an engaging smile.

"Tempo creates turnovers," West says, then realizes what
he's said and covers his face in mock horror. "I don't know
what the 'N' stands for. I just heard the two 'T's.' "

"So you don't hear that one very often?"

West laughs. "I never heard it before yesterday."

Down the hall in the Syracuse locker room, most of the
players have already left. Boeheim sits in one corner talking
quietly with Billy Cunningham. Across the room is Billy
Owens. He's wearing his orange and blue Syracuse warmups. On his head is a dark blue Villanova cap, his gift from
the pregame ceremony. He has scored 9 points but not

taken many shots. His homecoming back to Pennsylvania has been a personal disappointment.

"Are you happy with the way you're playing?" he's asked.

"I think I'm playing all right," he says softly. "Maybe the fans don't think I am. They expect me to come out and score 30 points a game. I've heard people say, 'When are you going to start doing something?' "

He hesitates, then goes on. The words come out haltingly. "They have to understand that I'm playing with veteran players. I'm trying to keep everyone happy. In high school I had the green light. I just got the ball and went. It's different here. Sometimes I know I can drive, but I pass it up. I don't know why, but I do it. You see DC posting up, you give him the ball. I try to keep everyone happy."

He shrugs in resignation.

"Do you talk to anyone about this? Coach Boeheim? The other players?"

"I talk to my brother."

"What does he tell you?"

"To just keep on playing my ball. Don't worry about anybody else. They ain't out there playing."

The room is nearly deserted now.

"In retrospect, do you think it was a good idea being on the cover of *Sports Illustrated*?" he is asked.

He pauses. "I wish it never happened," he says softly. "People are expecting too much."

He picks up his traveling bag and gets ready to leave.

"You talk about keeping everyone happy. Are you happy?"

He pauses again. "Yeah," he says. "I'm happy."

But he doesn't sound it.

Five nights later, before a record crowd in the Providence Civic Center, the Wildcats do it again. The Friars have all sorts of trouble with Greis, who goes for 25 points and 10 rebounds. West chips in with 24, and the Cats win by 9, 76–67. The victory is the 300th of Massimino's career, a significant milestone, and in the final seconds he is hugged by his assistant coaches. It is also Villanova's second Big East victory in a row, evening their conference record at 2–2. The Cats' season has turned around. At least for now.

4

COLLEGE BASKETBALL GAINS A SPOKESMAN

JANUARY 14

There is a white towel draped over an empty chair in the middle of the Georgetown bench. The Hoyas, ranked number three in the country with the loss to Seton Hall the only blemish on their season, are set to play Boston College in the Capital Centre. But their coach has already walked off to the locker room, surrounded by cameramen.

He is protesting Proposition 42, the new NCAA edict that if a high-school student doesn't score at least 700 on the SAT, he is no longer eligible for a scholarship.

Proposition 42 is an extension of the controversial Proposition 48, which was passed by the NCAA in 1986. Prop 48 states that any high-school student who does not have either a 2.0 in the standard high-school core curriculum or a combined total of 700 points (out of a possible 1600) can receive a scholarship but is not eligible to play in games or practice with the team the entire freshman year of college. Now Prop 42 is taking away the scholarship, and Thompson believes it discriminates against inner-city kids.

"The events of the past week at the NCAA Convention in

reference to Proposition 42 are disquieting and disturbing because they affect a group of individuals who are least able to defend themselves. I felt I had to personally take a stand in reference to Proposal No. 42.

"Many of the proponents of Proposal No. 42 may have laudatory academic and athletic goals in mind. However, this proposal fails to take into account the significant detrimental effect that it will have on socio-economically deprived students. They will no longer have the opportunity to show that a poor test score in the SAT or the ACT is not a result of the lack of native intelligence but is a result of the cultural bias of the test and the deprivation that has existed in their lives because of socio-economic and racial issues that are, unfortunately, inherent in our society today.

"In an effort to rekindle discussion in this proposal and to highlight the inequities inherent in it . . . I will not be on the bench in an NCAA-sanctioned Georgetown game until I'm satisfied that something has been done to provide these student-athletes with appropriate opportunity and hope for access to a college education."

His move has met with mostly favorable responses.

Of the 12 Prop 48 players in the Big East since the rule was instituted three years ago, 11 are black. The lone white player is Connecticut's Marc Suhr, a sophomore from West Germany. Connecticut appealed the NCAA's decision on the grounds that Suhr should have been able to take an untimed SAT because of the language barrier. The appeal was denied. Thompson has never taken a Prop 48 kid, nor has Boston College or Villanova.

In fact, Villanova was the only Big East school that voted for Prop 42. Later, Villanova AD Ted Aceto will say, "We respect John Thompson, but contrary to what he is saying, racism had nothing to do with our position."

When informed that night at Providence, Massimino says that what Thompson is doing is right. "Outside of Jesse Jackson, what black is any more visible than John?"

For John Thompson is no longer merely a college basketball coach. He has become a national figure. He has also come a long way from the young kid growing up in Washington in the fifties who once was called "uneducable," kicked out of a Catholic elementary school by teachers who told his mother he was retarded. She didn't believe it.

He grew up the youngest of four children and the only boy. His mother had been a teacher in southern Maryland but had lost her teaching certificate and cleaned houses for four dollars a day. His father couldn't write his name, having gone off to work as a child. The family moved many times throughout Washington. Finally they moved in with Mrs. Thompson's mother on W Street, and young John slept on a couch in the kitchen. Later, Thompson would say he never knew he was poor.

In the fifties the District of Columbia was still segregated, for it is in many ways a Southern city. It's often been reported that one of Thompson's indelible childhood memories is of going to his father's church in Maryland and wondering why he had to sit in the back.

Dave Kindred, the excellent sports columnist for the *Atlanta Journal & Constitution*, has written about the influence Thompson's mother had on him. She taught him to have faith in himself, even when his teachers were saying he never would be able to read. To speak his own mind. To keep family problems in the family. His mother told him not to get caught up in the world's inequities but to keep moving ahead. And most of all, she taught him that "you can do anything you think you can."

It was through basketball that he found his identity. At Archbishop Carroll, a Catholic high school in Washington, he became one of the most imposing high-school players in the country, leading Carroll to 55 straight wins and two city championships in 1959–60. At this time the NBA had something called the territorial draft, which meant that a professional team essentially had access to any college players within a 50-mile radius. Enter Red Auerbach. However closely he is affiliated with the Boston Celtics, Auerbach has always lived in Washington. In his younger days he used to spend time in the summers around various playgrounds in the District, familiarizing himself with the young talent, such as Thompson. By the time he was a senior in high school, Thompson was 6-10. Auerbach, thinking four years down the road, steered him to Providence College, the number-one basketball school in New England at the time, and, more important, just within the Celtics' 50-mile radius.

Providence College was a small Catholic school then of 3,000 students, all male. With only a few exceptions, the only blacks on campus were basketball players. The coach was Joe Mullaney, in the middle of transforming Providence College from a small Rhode Island school no one ever heard of into one of the name basketball schools in the Northeast. The key players in this transformation were Lennie Wilkins, now the coach of the Cleveland Cavaliers, who graduated the year before Thompson arrived; Johnny Egan, who later both played and coached in the NBA, three years ahead of Thompson; Jim Hadnot from Oakland, considered Bill Russell's protege, also at Providence because of the 50-mile radius. He was two years ahead of Thompson, and Ray Flynn, now the mayor of Boston, was a year ahead of him.

Thompson was an economics major at Providence and received the "Outstanding Senior" award right before his graduation in 1964. On the other hand, he never became the player he was supposed to be at Providence. The Friars went to one NCAA tournament and two NITs in Thompson's three years of varsity ball, and when he was a senior he was named the best player in New England, but there was always the feeling he never really lived up to the promise of his high-school career. He was slow, somewhat plodding. His strength was his shooting touch.

"He always was complaining he didn't get the ball enough," remembers one teammate. "Not in an overt way, but it was always an undercurrent. He always said the guards shot too much, that they wouldn't pass him the ball. He thought it was hurting his pro potential. For a while there every time he went home on vacation he'd say beforehand that he wasn't coming back. It was like nothing was ever right. John Thompson the coach would not have liked John Thompson the player.

"But that's not to say he was ever any problem. Just the opposite. He was a model citizen. He had been to a Catholic high school and now he was at a Catholic college and he knew what to do. Some of the blacks had problems adjusting back then, but John didn't. He went to every class. He was never late. He worked hard, both as an athlete and a student. He got along with people. He is someone who did everything the way it was supposed to be done. But I was very surprised years later when he went to Georgetown and became a sort of spokesman for blacks because I never saw any evidence of that side of him. He didn't even hang around much with the other blacks on the team. His friends were white. I'm sure he had encountered some racism growing up in Washington, but in no way, shape, or form did he give any indication back then that he one day would be any kind of spokesman for blacks."

In 1966, after two years with the Boston Celtics as a backup center to Bill Russell, Thompson came home to Washington. He had been left unprotected in the NBA's expansion draft and decided he had had enough of professional basketball. He worked for awhile for the United Planning Agency, then for the National 4-H Council. Soon he got a part-time job as the basketball coach at St. Anthony's, a Catholic school in the northeastern section of the District.

His name, plus his contacts in the police boys' clubs and throughout the District, soon provided him with many black kids other schools didn't know much about. And from the beginning his teams played a tough, physical style, the same style his Georgetown teams employ to this day.

Schoolboy basketball in the District had long been dominated by Morgan Wootten, the highly successful coach at DeMatha, a small Catholic school located in nearby Hyattsville, Maryland, and by Joe Gallagher, who still coaches at St. John's in the District. The two are very close, for Wootten got his coaching start as Gallagher's assistant. The two even run a summer camp together. They are the deans of the local coaches, prime forces in selecting which D.C.-area kids get to play in the prestigious Capital Classic all-star game each spring. Two white men in a city that's overwhelmingly black, they are the leaders of the old-boy network that runs schoolboy basketball in the area.

When Thompson first came to St. Anthony's, he was excluded from the old-boy network. As St. Anthony's got better, the antipathy deepened between Thompson and Wootten. Neither Wootten nor Gallagher would play St.

Anthony's. Once, when DeMatha consented to play St.
Anthony's in a summer-league game, Thompson started two
managers and the worst three players on his team. His team
got drilled. So much for any showdown.

To this day, for all his recruiting success at Georgetown,
Thompson has never gotten one player from DeMatha,
though it's a Catholic school only a few miles away and
routinely produces kids who play at many of the top basketball schools in the country. Old wounds die hard.

In the early seventies, a turbulent time when racial tensions were like kindling waiting for a match, Georgetown
began reexamining its commitment to the community. The
school was virtually all white, a prestige school for Catholic
preppies in a city that was nine-tenths black. Across the
country many schools were trying to make themselves more
accessible to minority students, to the point of starting to
develop different admission requirements for minorities so
that they would not be judged by the same criteria as people
with more advantages.

Into this climate came John Thompson. In 1972, the basketball program at Georgetown had hit the skids, going
3–23 the year before. The Reverend Robert Henle, then the
president, was impressed with Thompson. He, in turn, promised he would not bring in kids who were going to flunk out.
He also wanted someone to monitor his players' academic
development, paving the way for the hiring of Mary Fenlon.

In his third season, after a six-game losing streak, a banner that read "Thompson, the Nigger Flop, Must Go" was
thrown onto the floor. Perhaps this goaded him, for that
year the Hoyas beat West Virginia in the ECAC championship game and qualified for their first NCAA Tournament
in 32 years. His first star black player from Washington
came at the same time, Al Dutch. Another was Merlin
Wilson, who had played for him at St. Anthony's. They
were soon followed by two others, Craig Shelton and John
Duren. They would not be the last. He had become successful at St. Anthony's by using his influence in Washington;
he became successful at Georgetown the same way.

A few years later he used his friendship with Bob Wade,
the highly successful black coach at Dunbar High School in

Baltimore, to land David Wingate and Reggie Williams. Wade was at odds with Maryland's Lefty Driesell then, in much the same way Thompson and Morgan Wootten were, and he would not send any of his players to the state university. Thompson became the beneficiary. A couple of years ago when Driesell left Maryland and the school was looking for a new coach, Thompson pushed for Wade, who got the job.

There is no question that John Thompson is a complicated man.

He is a child of racism, yet he has been accused of being a racist in that he has no white players. He is criticized for being overly protective of his players while also criticized for not doing more for the black community in Washington. He has browbeaten many a reporter through the years, but when he discovered Katha Quinn, the St. John's sports-information director, was battling cancer, he was always sensitive and caring.

For such a public figure, his family life has remained remarkably private. He has always been better after losses than after wins. He can be an arrogant and belligerent bully, but he has also displayed a tender side. In the NCAA finals in 1983, a player of his named Freddie Brown panicked in the last seconds and gave the ball to North Carolina's James Worthy, a play that lost Georgetown the national title. Thompson embraced Brown after the game and went out of his way to protect his player from the press.

Over the years some of his former players have been quoted as saying that Thompson's overriding message is that no one is ever going to give you anything, whether it's on the basketball court or in life. He also strongly believes that economic power is a way of overcoming racism. Thompson told the *Washington Post* last summer that he tells young people, "Put yourself in a position of power where you create a need for yourself that has an economic effect on somebody. The word is not black or white as much as green. And I think our kids have got to understand and learn that."

In a story last August in the *Washington Post* magazine, writer Juan Williams recounted the story of the day Thompson stood in the doorway of McDonough Gym and talked fondly about James (Jabbo) Kenner, who was the coach and counselor for the Metropolitan Police Boys and Girls Clubs in the District for 40 years. Thompson recalled that in the midseventies some bureaucrats began questioning Kenner and eventually cost him his job.

"I saw what happened to Mr. Jabbo," Thompson told Williams, jabbing his finger into the air, "and I said to myself, 'I'm never going to let this happen to me—I'm going to stay in control.'"

Certainly, Thompson's coaching career has been marked by his propensity for keeping control. Practices are always closed. Requests for interviews go through Mary Fenlon. The locker room is open for 15 minutes after games and not a minute more. Everything is done the way John Thompson wants it done, to the point that Georgetown no longer plays other schools in the D.C. area because John Thompson does not want to play them. With the ones whose basketball programs are inferior to his, he figures he has nothing to gain and everything to lose by playing them. With the University of Maryland, the ACC school that's only a long jump shot away and one Georgetown traditionally played, he ended that relationship in the early eighties after a dispute with Driesell, whom he once called a motherfucker in front of several thousand people in the D.C. Armory.

One former player has said that one of Thompson's favorite sayings to them is "I am Georgetown basketball. I built this program. I made it. I am Georgetown basketball."

In the Providence Civic Center four days later, facing his alma mater, he is still missing. He had ended the suspense the day before by walking into the sports-information office at Georgetown and telling one of the people there, "Tell anyone who needs to know that I'm not going to Providence."

He also said that he wasn't sure how many more games he would boycott, only that he had to talk to some "people we feel are of influence," and "I have to feel sincerely we are moving in the right direction." He reiterated it was now a day-by-day decision on when he would be back, and while he had been at practice with the team, he wasn't coming to Providence.

The chair in the middle of the bench remains empty except for the white towel draped over it.

Thompson returns to the bench for Saturday afternoon's game against Connecticut in the Capital Centre, a close game the Hoyas win by four. After traveling to Kansas City to meet with NCAA officials, Thompson says that although there hadn't been a complete solution to the problem, he was satisfied enough that everyone was moving in the right direction to return to the bench.

"I would like to make it clear once again that I am in support of core curriculum, I am in support of cumulative 2.0, but I am opposed to a misuse of standardized testing, which fails to consider individual opportunity or situation. There is nothing more unequal than the equal treatment of unequals. . . . I am grateful to all those who lent their support to change this legislation and I am presently satisfied enough to end my protest and return to the bench."

Thompson told the *Washington Post*, "I was glad to get back because this is what I do. I'm not a protester. I'm a basketball coach."

Charles Smith said later that Thompson's spirit was with the Hoyas at Providence even if he wasn't, and Jaren Jackson said, "I don't think other players on other teams have experienced such things the way we have with Coach Thompson. You never know what's up. You never knew Prop 42 would come up. You never knew Coach Thompson would depart from the court. You never know what's going to happen. But whatever happens, you know it will be in the best interests of all of us. And that's why I'm here."

Jackson was asked if it really made that much difference to have Thompson on the sidelines.

"Everyone knows Coach Thompson's presence." He smiled. "There's always a difference."

5

THE SEASON TAKES SHAPE

JANUARY 15

Tonight it's Syracuse against Connecticut in the Hartford Civic Center, and Jim Boeheim is worried. So far his team is 1–3 in the league, and he knows that playing Connecticut at home is always tough.

Boeheim has been the coach of Syracuse since 1976. You can't go home again? Boeheim wouldn't know. He never left. The son of a mortician, he grew up in Lyons, New York, a small town an hour west of Syracuse. From the time he first started playing ball as a kid, he knew he someday wanted to coach. The role model was his high-school coach, a man named Dick Blackwell.

"He was years ahead of his time," says Boeheim. "We pressed, had zone traps, ran the shuffle offense. He got me to understand the game as well as play it."

He wasn't recruited coming out of high school in 1962. Syracuse was trying to make a name for themselves in basketball, and they knew they weren't going to get there by recruiting 6-3, 150-pound kids from nowhere towns in up-state New York. He thought about going to play at Colgate,

and decided instead to walk on at Syracuse. His friends
thought he was crazy and said he'd never play there. There
were eight scholarship players in his class, but at the end of
the year he had played well enough to earn a scholarship.
For the next two years he roomed with Dave Bing, the
greatest player in Syracuse history and former Detroit Piston great: the white son of a mortician in upstate New York
and a black kid from a District of Columbia ghetto. Boeheim
went on to start for two years with Bing in the backcourt.

Syracuse was a football school then. There was no Dome.
The Big East was still nearly 15 years away. Manley Field
House had just been built, primarily as a football practice
site. Boeheim remembers many times when it would be
raining and the football team would come inside and start
practicing, basketball be damned.

When he graduated in 1966, Boeheim became the grad
assistant at Syracuse, then an assistant coach to Roy Danforth.
He also played weekends in the Eastern League, a semipro
league located mainly in the small cities of Pennsylvania and
New Jersey, featuring small gyms, boisterous, hostile crowds,
and dank locker rooms where the lockers were always too
small and the water never quite hot enough. For his first
two years the Eastern League was the NBA's minor league,
and its rosters were full of guys one step away from the big
time. Then came the birth of the ABA and many of the best
players left. Boeheim remained.

He played for Scranton, so he always started his weekend
odysseys by first driving to the town two and a half hours
away. He played on Saturdays and Sundays throughout the
two-state area, then would drive back to Syracuse. He did
this for five years. His first two years he also taught history
at a junior high in Syracuse. Then he went off to practice,
usually getting home at ten at night.

"I look back on those days now and don't see how I did
it," he says. "But I wanted to play and I wanted to coach."

When Danforth left in 1976 to go to Tulane, Boeheim
wanted to become the head coach. He had been there for
ten years. He had recruited most of the players and he had
their support. He felt he'd paid his dues. Eventually, he was

told that though he was under consideration, the job was
going to be opened up.

"I gave them an ultimatum," he says. "I told them, 'Who
recruited all the players? Who's been here? I did the whole
thing. I'm either getting the job now, or I'm not going to
take it.' "

Then he walked out of the room. Soon afterward he got
the job.

He was 31 years old.

Now he is wearing gray slacks and a light blue sports
jacket along with his customary agitated look. It's been a
tough two weeks for the Orangemen. Upset in the Dome by
Pittsburgh, by Villanova in Philadelphia, then two days ago
in the Garden by St. John's.

Tonight they are meeting a Connecticut team that's starting to feel the effects of not living up to their preseason
hype. Before the game Jim Calhoun and his staff held a
meeting in a room at the Sheraton, the hotel adjoining the
Civic Center. In another room the players were having their
own meeting, trying to come up with something, anything,
to get the team back to winning. That morning *Manchester
Journal-Inquirer* columnist Randy Smith questioned Cliff
Robinson's ability to be a dominant player, calling him
George Gervin hiding in Patrick Ewing's body and casting
other doubts on his leadership. The article left Robinson
fuming. Afterward, he will say he never claimed to be an
intimidating player and he can't understand why Smith would
write something like that.

The Orange are quickly down 13–2 in the game, throwing
the ball away against the Connecticut press and looking very
unlike the team that was ranked number two in the country
only two weeks ago. Boeheim walks up and down the sidelines
in front of the Syracuse bench, complaining about every call
that goes against him. Not that this is anything new.

Boeheim has long had a reputation of whining at the
officials. He views it as nothing serious, just another part of
the game. Certainly the baiting of officials is as common in
college basketball as slam dunks and cheerleader pyramids.
It is partly based on the theory that complaining early in the

game will get you a call later on. Also, if you don't get on
the officials, your opponent will, and you'll be at a disadvantage, the inference being that officials often respond to
the coaches. In a sense, the baiting of officials has become a
skill in itself, and each coach in the Big East has his own
style. Thompson tries to intimidate them, using his size and
his glare. Massimino and Carnesecca get their attention with
emotional antics. Boeheim whines the entire game.

Periodically he glances over at Art Hyland, who is sitting
at the press table some fifteen feet away from the end of the
Syracuse bench, and waves his hand in disgust.

Hyland is the director of the Big East officials. After
playing at Princeton in the early sixties where he was all-Ivy,
he became a lawyer, then went to work for the ECAC, then
headquartered in Manhattan. When the ECAC moved to
Cape Cod several years ago, Hyland moved with them. As
fate would have it, he bought a house near Craigville Beach
in Barnstable, very close to Dave Gavitt's summer house.

"They suck, Artie," Boeheim yells over.

Hyland says nothing. He just keeps watching the game.
The Orangemen continue to have trouble. The times they
get the ball successfully through the Connecticut press, they
have to confront a variety of zone defenses, the kind of
defense Syracuse always seems to struggle against. No team
in the Big East wants to run as much as Syracuse. When they
run, they are as good as anyone in the country. Conversely,
when they don't, they often look confused, a different team.

Their offense against zones sometimes seems to come
down to Sherman Douglas throwing low-percentage alley-
oop passes and Matt Roe shooting three-pointers. Tonight is
no exception. They get little movement against the zone,
Connecticut's interior defense takes away the alley oops,
and the Orangemen struggle. The result is that Stevie Thompson, who's great when the Orangemen can run, is not a
factor. As he had been the week before in the loss to
Villanova in the Spectrum, he seems stymied. So does the
entire team. After eleven minutes they only have 9 points,
and Boeheim is getting more frustrated.

Every time a call goes against Syracuse he glares at Hyland.
"The officials are the only thing in the game the coaches

can't control," says Hyland. "They call the defenses. They set the offenses. They run the practices. They determine who plays. The officials are the only thing they can't control and it drives them crazy."

Near the end of the half the Orangemen are down by a dozen, still inept against the Connecticut zone, and Boeheim is still glaring over at Hyland every time a call goes against him.

"If Jimmy spent more time on his zone offense and less time looking over at me, he'd be a lot better off," mutters Hyland.

After the half, Syracuse makes a run and narrows the Connecticut lead to 2. Boeheim's looks over at Hyland stop.

"The officiating always looks a lot better when you start putting the ball in the basket," says Hyland with a smile.

Syracuse eventually loses by 6, 68–62. They are now 1–4 in the Big East. They are tied for last.

"What would you have said two months ago if someone had said you'd be in last place on January 15th?" Sherman Douglas is asked afterwards.

"I would have said it must be April Fool's Day," he says.

Two days earlier, in the loss to St. John's, he hurt his back in the opening minutes and missed most of the game. His back is taped, but it's been obvious he's hurting. But as he says with a shrug, "We're in last place, I have to play."

"Are you surprised you're in last place?"

"It definitely surprises me," he says. "It's not any one thing. It's a combination of several things. Rebounding. Not scoring enough points. We played outstanding ball early in the season, but we haven't adjusted to the conference. We played a lot of easy games in December and we got into some bad habits. Now we're still playing the same way and it's hurting us. Certain teams are going to walk the ball up the court against us, and there's nothing we can do about it. But it's our fault, no one else's. We have dug ourselves a hole, and now we have to dig ourselves out. It might take a miracle."

Douglas is the only player talking in the Syracuse dressing room. The others have either already left or are uncommunicative. The Orangemen have the reputation of being testy with the media even when they win, never mind when they're last in the Big East. Douglas and Roe are considered the only good interviews on the team, to the point that they are on local television in Syracuse almost every night.

Across the hall in the interview room, a group of writers is waiting for Boeheim. Calhoun has already been in, and has admitted his team has been under siege a bit. He said it has been a tough ten days. Calhoun also said the Huskies were a good basketball team, not a great one.

Then he turned prophetic. "We're probably going to lose again," he said. "It's hard to tell everyone that. But it's true."

Boeheim is simple and direct. After admitting that without a healthy Douglas the Orangemen are going to have to struggle, he's asked about his team's woeful performance in the first half.

"I think the first fifteen minutes were as poorly played as we have played basketball since I've been at Syracuse," he says, "and I really don't have any explanation for that."

The Orangemen are now 1–4 in the Big East, tied for last place. Who would ever have believed it?

JANUARY 17

Pitt comes into Conte Forum on the Boston College campus tonight with a record of 8–6, fresh off an upset win over Oklahoma in Fitzgerald Field House on the Pittsburgh campus, a game that had ended an 11-game Oklahoma winning streak. In that game Brian Shorter scored 37 and Rod Brookins came off the bench for 24, his best performance of the season.

Both Boston College and Pittsburgh are 1–2 in the conference, BC having lost to Providence and Georgetown, while beating Pitt, the night that Barros went for 43. Pitt has beaten Syracuse in the Dome while also losing to Georgetown.

All the trappings are there for a Big East game. The Conte Forum, complete with its parquet floor, is shiny and new. The scoreboards at each end, complete with video screens, are state of the art. Championship banners hang in the rafters. There are about 6,000 people here, a good crowd, but there is little noise, no energy. The crowd seems like a theater audience, there to applaud good plays, not cheer their team to victory.

At the press table is P. J. Carlesimo. He is wearing a light brown jacket, khaki pants, and a pink tie. He is here to scout Pitt, having flown from Newark to Boston after practice. Off to their best start in history, his Seton Hall Pirates are now 16–1, losing only to Syracuse in the Dome. He is asked the reasons why.

"We've learned how to win," he says. "That's one big difference. And we have better players than we used to have. And we've really benefitted from lifting weights. We used to always do Nautilus and didn't see results. Two years ago we started lifting free weights under a program set up by Greg Mackrides, the Knicks' strength coach, and it's really made a difference. We are a very strong team now. You should see the before and after pictures of all the players. You wouldn't believe it. Now we lift twice a week during the season."

Both teams come onto the court to warm up, and the bouncing balls echo through the quiet building.

"I couldn't have a better situation than I have now," Carlesimo continues. "We hardly want for anything. Once we got the contract last year, we had stability, so now the thing is to sustain it and take the program to the next level."

"So do you feel vindicated now?" he is asked. "Have you proved something to all the people who said you couldn't do it?"

Carlesimo grimaces a bit. Gloating doesn't come easily to him. He has spent all year praising his players and his assistant coaches for Seton Hall's success, minimizing his own role.

"I guess I feel vindicated, but how can you say that?" he says finally. "I always thought I could coach. I thought that people in the profession knew I could coach. Now I hope other people do too."

Pittsburgh starts Shorter, Bobby Martin, and Darelle Porter up front, with Jason Matthews and Sean Miller in the backcourt. They all are sophomores, and now they are starting to get together. They immediately go out in front, 15–5, for Boston College has no answers for Pitt's inside game. Adding to BC's woes is that Dana Barros misses his first six shots. Barros has not shot well in Conte Forum, and he complains that the new rims are too tight. Shooters like soft rims, ones that have been worn down by constant use. Because Conte Forum is used most of the time for hockey, becoming a basketball court only on game days, the rims get little use.

All the same, the Eagles narrow the Pitt lead to 5, 36–31, at the half. Does this bring the crowd to life? Hardly. The building seems dead.

Pittsburgh coach Paul Evans isn't dead. He's mad as hell. As the first half is about to end, he gets off the bench to yell at one of his players, and Carlesimo laughs.

"That's the way Paul coaches," he says. "He's very negative. One night I was sitting behind his bench and he says to one of his kids, 'Come here, you fucking moron. Yeah, you, you fucking moron.' I couldn't stop laughing. But that's the way he coaches."

Of all the coaches in the Big East, Evans is the mystery man. Part of the reason is that he's one of the newest coaches. While the older coaches have become like eccentric relatives whose idiosyncracies have become familiar, Evans is the new kid in town that no one quite knows what to make of.

An adopted child, Evans grew up an hour south of Buffalo, New York, and by the time he was in junior high school he knew he wanted to be a coach. He went to Ithaca College, then became a high-school coach. His first college job was as the freshman coach at Geneseo. Eventually, he became the coach at St. Lawrence, a Division II school near the New York-Canadian border, better known for its hockey program. In 1979 he interviewed for the Dartmouth job that went to Tim Cohane. Later he thought he had the Cornell job, until Tom Miller, a Bobby Knight assistant, got it.

Evans was crushed. He had told himself that he would get out of the business if he didn't have a head Division I job by the time he was 35. He was 34, and he had come close. Four days later, Dick Schultz, who was then the Cornell AD, called him and asked if he were interested in the Navy job. Such are the vagaries of coaching.

If this all sounds like the resume of an upwardly mobile young man, Evans had done it by himself. He wasn't part of Howard Garfinkel's Five Star camp connection, a network that is the grease for many to get into college coaching. He didn't have a "rabbi," a coaching euphemism for someone with clout who guides your career. If Evans arrived at Pitt in 1986 as a maverick, maybe it was because he had always had to make it by himself. He was outspoken, blunt, and wasn't afraid to ruffle feathers.

When in the first year of Evan's tenure Rollie Massimino accused him of cheating in getting Bobby Martin, Evans went to the press. He was quoted in the *Philadelphia Daily News* as saying that after Massimino won the national title, he "had fallen in love with himself." He later said he was misquoted, but the damage was done, intensifying the Massimino-Evans feud. That, in turn, led to Massimino and Evans refusing to shake hands with each other after the two Pitt-Villanova games of 1987. This had been rectified at the Big East meetings last spring when Evans told Massimino he didn't think either one of them was being helped by the feud.

This year Evans has been much more guarded with the media. When he was at Navy he was very accessible. Sportswriters from the *Washington Post* or the *Baltimore Sun* would periodically descend on nearby Annapolis and Evans would joke with them, be buddy-buddy. When he came to Pitt he tried the same approach. He joked. He was open. The approach soon backfired.

Last year the CBS affiliate in Pittsburgh put a live microphone on him during a practice session. Evans thought the tape would be edited. Instead, what ran was a portrait of Evans as some sort of Bobby Knight cut-out, yelling at players with language littered with four-letter words. Then, on the day the Panthers arrived in Lincoln, Nebraska, for the NCAA Tournament, an Associated Press story strung together a string of incidents that had happened over two years, painting a picture of a severe feud between Evans and Jerome Lane. In the words of one Pittsburgh writer traveling with the team, Evans "went through the roof."

So this year he's been much less accessible. He often fails to return phone calls to writers. The players are less accessible. Practice is only open to the media for one half-hour a week. But if he has become more closed with the media, there are indications he is not as harsh with his players as he was the first two years, when he and some of the veterans always seemed to be involved in a battle of wills.

Earlier in the day he sat with Dave Gavitt and Tom McElroy of the Big East office and told them he was to be more patient with this team. He knew they were young and were going to be inconsistent.

Tonight is a microcosm of that. They blow the big early lead and let Boston College back into the game, before pulling away to win, 73–64.

Afterward, Carlesimo says he has empathy for Jim O'Brien, the BC coach. He knows how difficult it is in the Big East when you have inferior talent. You have to play almost a perfect game just to be competitive, for there is never any margin of error.

It has been a tough shooting night for Barros, 6 of 20 from the floor. But when this is pointed out in the postgame press conference, O'Brien defends his player.

"I've never seen a kid play with such pressure on him like Dana Barros," he says. "There's pressure on that kid to get 25–30, night in and night out. We have to have that for us to have a chance to win, and most of the time he delivers. It's unfair to single him out. We don't have enough size and physical strength and that's it in a nutshell. Until we get that it's always going to be a struggle."

A few minutes later he starts walking down the hallway that leads back to the Boston College locker room. Someone tells him that after the first 10 minutes his team played well. He shrugs. "If we play a perfect game we're decent," he says resignedly. "If we don't we're marginal." He takes a breath. "It's been a very tough year. But I know we'll get better."

Coaches have to think that.

Especially in January.

JANUARY 23

As part of the Big East's 10th-anniversary season, Dave Gavitt is going to each one of the nine schools to speak at a luncheon. The luncheons serve a twofold purpose. First, each school is asked to nominate 10 people to receive commemorative gifts from the Big East office. They're also a chance for Gavitt to give his personal state-of-the-union address to each school. Today, the luncheon is at Georgetown.

"No one is any better at this than Dave," says Tom McElroy of the Big East office. "He personalizes each one. And it's all off the cuff."

Frank Rienzo's office is on the first floor of McDonough Gym, complete with a picture of a smiling Patrick Ewing over the doorway. Rienzo is now in his 20th year as the Georgetown athletic director, having originally come here to be the track coach after teaching English and Latin at a Catholic high school in Queens.

He shares coffee and small talk with Gavitt and McElroy while they wait to go to the luncheon. A little while later McElroy takes a visitor down a hallway to show him McDonough Gym. They are there a couple of minutes when a student comes into the gym and asks if he can help them. McElroy says no, they just want to look around. The student leaves. McElroy points to a far corner of the gym, up on the second floor.

"John's office is up there," he says. "It's nice. He's got it set up like an apartment. So when you talk to him it's like sitting in his living room."

A minute later a man walks in.

"Can I help you?" he asks, an edge in his voice.

McElroy ignores him and keeps on talking.

"May I help you?" the man asks again, the hostility evident in his voice.

"We're waiting for Frank Rienzo," says McElroy.

The other man snorts, turns around, and leaves.

"What did he think we were going to do?" asks McElroy. "Steal the gym?" Then he shrugs. It's a shrug that seems to say, What are you going to do? This is Georgetown, and things are different here.

The luncheon is across the campus at the new Leavey Center, which is attached to a Marriott hotel. It is all glass and quiet elegance, with oriental rugs and plants. Behind the dais is a large Georgetown banner. There are about a hundred people in the room, many of them behind-the-scenes people: representatives from the alumni office, the development office, minority affairs, and the two booster clubs, Hoyas Unlimited and the Hoya Hoop Club. The men are in jackets and ties, the women in business suits. It all seems a long way from the locker room.

Gavitt presents the 10 Big East awards. The first one is to Thompson, who is not there. His two assistants, Craig Esherek and Mike Riley, accept for him. Mary Fenlon gets one. She too is not there. The dean of admissions gets one. Also the director of sports marketing. Someone instrumental in forming the Hoya Hoop Club. All are people deemed by the university to be unsung supporters of the Big East Conference.

Then Gavitt turns to Rienzo, who is seated at the end of the dais to his right.

"The one major principle we had when we founded this conference," he says, "was not TV contracts. Or the number of people in the seats at Big East games. Nor the competition. Those things were addressed down the road. But the major thing was to make it better for the kids, without sacrificing admissions integrity and institutional autonomy. I can think of no other person who has done more in this area than Frank Rienzo. From being there whenever we had a problem to meeting teams at the back door of the Cap Center, Frank Rienzo has been a trend-setter."

Gavitt then turns back to the audience.

"I remember the first year we went into St. John's for a

TV game and all the lights blew out. They had never had a TV game before. Remember that first TV year? The advertisers were things like De-Con Roach Killer, acne pads, pomade for your hair. We also had something that first year called Big East ties, one of the great boondoggles of the first year. That first year the gimmick was that if you bought a ticket to the tournament you got a Big East tie. The only problem with the tie was that you couldn't wear it in the sunlight or it went up in flames."

"We've come a long way, baby," says Rienzo in a stage whisper.

"Any 10-year history of this conference has to include the Hoyas of Georgetown," says Gavitt, turning to the crowd. "They have been the measuring stick the other teams measure themselves against. They have been the standard bearer. The league has learned a lot from the leader. Imitation is the greatest form of flattery, and if you look around the league it's the Hoyas who have taught us to play 'right here.' " He puts his hand in front of his face.

"There are a lot of lessons this university has taught the Big East," he continues. "What you have accomplished in the past decade has elevated all of us."

Without question, there is a special bond between the Big East and Georgetown. A case can be made that the Big East's rapid ascension had much to do with the emergence of Georgetown as a national basketball power. Certainly the two have ridden the escalator to the national spotlight hand in hand. If the Big East gave the Hoyas the stage upon which to strut their stuff, Thompson's recruiting Patrick Ewing was the turning point.

Gavitt has always been able to deal with Thompson, no small skill if you want to be the commissioner of a conference in which Thompson is a coach. Forget the Hoyas' public-relations problem. Or their reputation for getting into fights. Or their reputation for being just plain belligerent. Rest assured, the Hoyas haven't been the easiest team in the league for the Big East office to deal with on an internal level either. They always do things their way. Everyone else has an unlimited time after games that their locker room is open. The Georgetown locker room is open for 15 minutes only. Thompson is the only coach who fails to attend the Big East coaches' meetings every spring. Georgetown's practices are always closed.

Because of these practices, occasionally there is rumbling in the Big East office about the Hoyas and their idiosyncracies. Gavitt is always their defender in these office discussions. Part of it is his personality. He is someone who avoids confrontations, someone who long ago learned the cagey politician's trick of never letting your adversaries know what you're really thinking. He's also someone who doesn't like to be a disciplinarian. When he coached, he had the ability to get his players to do what he wanted because he was able to convince them it was in their best interest, not because he carried a big hammer. His managerial style now is to delegate responsibility, not be dogmatic. He hires talented people and then gives them the room for their talent to flourish. His first method in dealing with unpleasantries is often not to act but to wish they would go away. Not in any sense of weakness, but because it's his personality not to deal with issues until he feels he has no other options.

Part of it also is that Gavitt's never forgotten the debt his conference owes Georgetown. And it's also the respect he's always had for Thompson, even if no doubt some of "Large Father's" methods have at times exasperated him.

One gets the feeling the sense of respect is reciprocal.

Earlier in the season, when asked by Billy Packer what was the first thing he thought of when Gavitt's name was mentioned, Thompson just smiled and said, "Smart."

The Capital Centre is out on the Beltway, in Landover, Maryland, in Prince George's County. Sugar Ray Leonard grew up a few miles away, as did Lenny Bias, the Celtics' first-round draft choice who died of a cocaine overdose.

Tonight it is Georgetown and St. John's, one of the Big East's magic match-ups. For years these two schools have had many heated games together. This rivalry served as a showcase for the personal battles between Patrick Ewing and Chris Mullin, the Big East's two most famous players.

It's also a showcase for John Thompson and Looie Carnesecca, two of the fixtures in the league. These two men have evolved into a mutual admiration society. What's funny is that the bond is linked to a sweater, of all things. A few seasons back, Carnesecca started wearing a sweater to games, presumably because he had a cold. It was a hideous sweater really, a garish mishmash of colors. But Looie kept wearing it, calling it a lucky sweater. One night, right before a Georgetown–St. John's game, Thompson ripped open his jacket, Superman style, to reveal his own ugly sweater. It was a nice touch, and it calmed some of the tensions that existed between the two arch rivals then.

An hour and a half before the game, Billy Raftery is interviewing Carnesecca in the empty arena. He asks him how the season is going so far for St. John's, and as Looie answers, he suddenly stops in midsentence.

"We sound like two parliamentarians," he says to Raftery. "Stiff. We're stiff."

Raftery laughs, and they roll the tape again. Again he asks Looie how the season is going.

"There hasn't been a lot of sauce on the pasta the past few games," says Looie with a sly smile. "We're trying to put a little sauce on it."

A few minutes later, Thompson calls Raftery into his locker room. He apologizes to him for the incident the year before, when Raftery had criticized the Hoyas for getting in so many fights on national television and Thompson had retaliated on his coach's show and called Raftery a losing coach. He tells Raftery he regrets the things he said about him.

An hour before the game, the building starts to fill. At one end, high in the rafters, are the Bullets banners. At the other are blue Georgetown ones, and the centerpiece is a large one that says "Georgetown, 1984 National Champs." At one end of the court the students yell "Hoya." At the other they yell "Saxa."

So what is a Hoya?

And what is all this Hoya-Saxa stuff?

Back in the days when all Georgetown students were

required to study Greek and Latin, their team nickname
was the Stonewalls. As the story goes, someone mixed his
Greek and Latin and came up with "Hoya Saxa," meaning
"What Rocks?"

The Hoya part stuck.

Georgetown gets off to an early lead. Alonzo Mourning
picks up his second foul after only four minutes and is
replaced by Dikembe Mutombo, the 7-foot freshman.
Mutombo immediately scores, then blocks Robert Werdann
at the other end. The students in "Rejection Row" underneath the basket wave and line up cardboard hands for each
block. At the half Georgetown is up by 16 and Mutombo
already has 9 blocks.

With roughly 13 minutes left to play, Georgetown's John
Turner and Jayson Williams of St. John's get into a fight,
spontaneous combustion in the heat of a rebound battle. A
little déjà vu from the old days.

The fight is quickly broken up, and both Thompson and
Carnesecca rush out onto the court trying to restore order.
Both players are ejected. The Georgetown students chant
"Bullshit, bullshit" when it's announced Turner has been
ejected. As he walks across the court, heading for the runway that leads to the locker room, he is loudly cheered by
the Georgetown students. Seconds later, Williams also leaves.
As he walks down the sideline, flanked by three security
guards, Thompson pats him on the shoulder as he walks by.
A TV cameraman tries to film Williams being escorted off,
but Georgetown Frank Rienzo puts his hand over the camera.

Later on, referee Larry Lembo calls a technical foul on
Thompson for vociferously arguing a call. The chant of
"Asshole, asshole" sweeps down from the crowd, directed
at Lembo. Lembo, a former great player at Manhattan in
the early sixties and one of the most respected officials in
the game, stares straight ahead, his face expressionless.

Georgetown eventually wins by 11, 75–64, for their sixth
straight victory. Mutombo finishes the game with 12 blocked
shots, a Georgetown school record, breaking by one a mark
set by Mourning earlier in the season. It's also a Big East
record.

It is Georgetown policy that their locker room is open when Thompson comes into the interview room and is usually closed when Thompson leaves. This puts sportswriters into a quandary. They can either listen to Thompson or they can talk to the players. Take your pick. No one ever said that covering the Hoyas is easy.

In the Capital Centre the Hoyas use the Bullets' locker room. There is a red rug and white walls, and the blue lockers have red borders with little stars on them. In front of one of them is Mourning. He is already dressed and is about to put a necktie on when a TV camera approaches him, its light on.

"Wait until your tie's done before you talk to him," Assistant Coach Craig Esherek says to Mourning.

Mourning glances at him with a perplexed look on his face, as if he didn't hear him clearly.

"You can talk to him," says Esherek. "But wait until your tie is done."

Next to Mourning is Mutombo. He was raised in Zaire, where he came of age speaking French. One of the ways he learned basketball was watching videos at the American embassy. Later, as he grew tall, his father and his high-school coach told him he had to "go to America and play ball." So he came to Georgetown two years ago and spent last year learning English.

"One day I think I will get the NCAA record for blocked shots if Coach gives me the opportunity," Mutombo says in his clipped accent. "One day I'm going to be a good player."

He is asked about his classes this year at Georgetown and begins to answer.

"Dikembe," butts in Esherek, standing nearby. "Don't talk about any classes. Talk about the game. Talk about your schedule when you're back at Georgetown. Talk about the game here."

Bill Shapland, the Georgetown sports-information director, comes into the room. "Four minutes, folks," he says loudly. "Four minutes."

Mourning is asked about the fight between Turner and Williams.

"People write about Georgetown being fighters," he says. "We're not. Other teams just get frustrated. I didn't want anything like that to happen all year, so that image will go away. Unfortunately, it did."

Carnesecca later downplays the fight, calling it a little "subway push," nothing serious. He also denies that there is any bad blood between Georgetown and St. John's. There is respect, not bad blood. Once upon a time Carnesecca was quoted as saying, "Georgetown scares the hell out of you." Now the two teams have become like neighbors who have lived on the same street for a long time.

Meanwhile, Mourning is asked about Mutombo. "I'm proud of him," he says. "Dikembe and I are friends. He helps me out in practice. He blocks my shots all the time."

Next to him, Mutombo is telling another writer about the odyssey that took him from Zaire to the Capital Centre.

"Dikembe, just talk about the game," says Esherek, still standing nearby and monitoring the conversation. "If he wants to set up a separate interview, fine. But now just talk about the game."

"Two minutes," Shapland says loudly. "Two minutes."

Mourning and Mutombo are both delightful interviews and obviously like the attention. They are so different from the stereotypical Georgetown player over the years, who spouted the company line if he talked at all. Two minutes later, Shapland is trying to shepherd the remaining reporters out as Mary Fenlon comes into the room, an agitated look on her face. Mourning is still talking. She mutters something to the effect that both Mourning and Mutombo want to be media stars. The times they are a-changing at Georgetown, even if Mary Fenlon doesn't seem very happy about it.

JANUARY 28

It's another show in the Dome. An hour and a half before the game, crowds throng the Astroturf on the Dome floor behind the screen. People are sitting on picnic benches. Hawkers are selling everything from food to sweatshirts. On the large screen are several Big East players talking about how education is their first priority, a little in-house Big East P.R. When the video ends a rock band starts playing. Another night of tailgating, basketball style.

In the small visitors' locker room, Providence coach Nick Barnes is talking to his team. He is wearing a dark suit, and the players, in their black warmups, sit in front of their orange lockers. He is going over the man-to-man match-ups.

"Eric," he says to guard Eric Murdock, "you got Stevie Thompson. Dare him to shoot. No, double dare him to shoot. But don't let him get a running start to go behind you for the alley oop."

He tells Marty Conlon to remember that Derrick Coleman is left-handed. He tells Cal Foster to keep Billy Owens off the offensive boards. He turns to Carlton Screen.

"Get all over Sherman so he can't make the entry pass. Don't give him time to throw the pass. Harass him. Get all over him.

"Matt," he says to Matt Palazzi, "you got Matt Roe. He's an excellent three-point shooter. Make him put the ball on the floor. Be aware of where he is all the time.

"The key is to handle their transition game," he tells everyone. "They will get frustrated if we handle their transition. Put a lot of pressure on the ball, and rebound, rebound, rebound. Offensively, we want to establish our inside game. Make them guard us. Go inside and out, and the offense will come. Remember to make the extra pass. Great teams make the extra pass."

He pauses. The tension is starting to build.

"We need a pit-bull mentality," he says, his voice louder now. "Go out and lay it on the line for 40 minutes. Have fun, and lay it on the line for 40 minutes. Okay."

The players leave the room. It's about an hour before the game. Barnes walks outside into an orange hallway. Down the hallway the Syracuse players are lining up, about to go into the Dome for practice. At the front of the line is Sherman Douglas. Barnes waves at him. Douglas smiles back.

"You know him?" Barnes is asked.

"Sure I know him," says Barnes with a smile. "I recruited Sherman. I spent a lot of time with that kid."

"What's a lot of time?"

"Oh, I don't know," replies Barnes. "I probably saw him play 15 times between high school and summer leagues. But that's not really that much. You know Carlos Yates, the kid at Mason? I saw him play 66 times."

Ah, the glories of being an assistant coach.

When the players return to the locker room, they clap hands and exchange high-fives. If before they were calm, like students in a classroom, now the game is only minutes away and they are all nervous energy.

"Remember," yells Barnes, "70 percent of their offense comes in transition. Make them run an offense."

Then Bryan Benhan speaks. Though a senior, he rarely plays. He grew up in Georgia, basically by himself, shuttled around between relatives, essentially on his own at 14 years old. He was all set to go into the army when Rick Pitino, having just gotten the job at Providence, offered him a last-minute scholarship. Now it's nearly four years later, and if he doesn't play much, he will always be the captain of this year's team. He will graduate in June. He is one of the kids for whom college basketball has worked, even if the stats don't say so.

"Let's just remember what we were going through last year," he says, referring to the year before when the season had turned into the winter of their discontent. "And how it felt. And for the freshmen to learn what it takes to win."

Then they meet in the center of the room for the Lord's Prayer.

The Dome is a blaze of orange. The Dome Ranger, complete with his mask, slaps palms with the Syracuse players as they run the layup line by him. The lady in the orange fright wig is knitting in the end zone. Dome Eddie is shouting to the crowd. The P.A. announcer tells the crowd to make sure they buy a program so they can take part in nine lucky drawings, the grand prize being a trip to Florida. There's an ad in the program for Jim Boeheim's Big Orange Basketball Camp. Sherman Douglas is announced as "Captain-

General Sherman Douglas." The crowd of 25,000 stands and waits for the first basket of the half. It doesn't get any bigger than this.

The game starts like a scene from Barnes's worst nightmare. Douglas breaks the Providence press and passes to Coleman, who dunks the ball. Then Coleman dunks again off the press. Then Stevie Thompson dunks off a steal. The Providence game plan is to take away the lobs and the slam dunks, the transition baskets. So far they haven't done that.

The Friars settle down, however, get a great shooting night from Palazzi, and only trail by 1 with 1:22 left to play. It is the best a Providence team has ever played in the Dome. Syracuse has played well, too. They have even made their free throws when it's counted, their traditional stumbling block. Then Billy Owens makes a great inside move, scores, and gets fouled. Syracuse hangs on to win, 100–96.

The Friars come back into the locker room, defeated. All losing locker rooms have the same funereal look. The players slump in front of the orange lockers in silence. They have played as well as they have played all year, but it just hasn't been quite good enough. Not against Syracuse in the Carrier Dome.

"I want you to hurt so bad you can't stand it," says Barnes. "Hurt so bad you can't sleep at night. Because we're good enough to win the whole thing. Syracuse? They're supposed to be national contenders. You know as well as I do that we're as good as Syracuse. But we got to go out and prove it every night. And if we do that, we'll see what happens in March." He stops. "Okay, bring it in."

They meet in the center of the room for a prayer, the players kneeling in their black uniforms. A few minutes later the room is silent, the smell of defeat everywhere. The players are still sitting in front of their lockers when Barnes comes back into the room.

"You know what bothers me?" he says, his voice rising. "We kicked their ass all over the place. But we don't have any room for error. We can't give them lobs and shit like that. This is when the mettle rises to the top. This is when the guys who can play have to come to play. But you have to bust your ass every night."

He pauses a beat, then continues. "I am upset. You know why? We should have won that goddamn game. And now people are going to say that we played Georgetown and Syracuse tough. Forget all that shit. It's not enough for me to play these teams close. I don't want that. And you can't want it either.

"Are you satisfied?"

He goes around the room. Carlton Screen, Matt Palazzi, Eric Murdock, Marty Conlon, all shake their heads.

"Cause I know what's going to happen. You're going to go back to campus and everyone's going to tell you what a good game you played." His voice rises. "And if you're men at all, you'll look at them and say, 'Fuck you. We didn't win the game, and that's what we came up here to do.' If I see one of you guys taking congratulations and you don't say 'Fuck you,' then I'm going to fuck with you.

"You guys better start playing like you're 3–15. Like you did back when you were picked for last in the Big East and everyone thought you stunk. We haven't proved anything yet."

Barnes leaves the locker room and begins walking down the hallway to the interview room.

"How'd I do?" he asks, giving a wink.

"So you really weren't that upset?"

"I'm upset," he says. "But I was just messing with them. The main thing I want is that they don't start feeling good just because they played well."

JANUARY 29

Other games from the night before:

• Seton Hall trounces Boston College in the Meadowlands 103–79. Afterward, BCY's Jim O'Brien says it was like the Pirates were playing seven on five.

• Georgetown loses to LSU by 2, 82–80, on national television in the Super Dome in front of 54,321, the largest crowd ever to watch a regular-season college basketball game.

• Connecticut clobbers St. John's in Hartford, 74–66, the Redmen playing without Jayson Williams, suspended for his fight earlier in the week with John Turner.

• Villanova beats Pittsburgh, 79–78. In a jovial mood afterward, Massimino says, "This game was the way it was supposed to be between the two teams. There wasn't any of that separation of church and state stuff." But earlier, on his television show, Massimino ran a clip of Evans and said, "There's Paul Evans. He's been quiet this year—for a change."

Evans, in turn, patted Massimino on the back. "I respect Rollie as a coach," he had said the day before the game. "He cares about his players. He's honest. I don't wish anyone bad luck who does things the right way. And Rollie does." It's as if his transition period at Pitt is over.

THE STANDINGS AT THE END OF JANUARY:

	CONFERENCE PLAY	OVERALL
GEORGETOWN	5–1	15–2
SETON HALL	5–2	18–3
PROVIDENCE	4–3	15–3
ST. JOHN'S	4–4	12–6
VILLANOVA	3–3	12–8
PITTSBURGH	3–4	10–8
CONNECTICUT	3–4	11–5
SYRACUSE	3–4	17–4
BOSTON COLLEGE	1–6	8–9

6

BIG DADDY

It's a funny place to come looking for a basketball conference.

On one side of the street are boutiques and specialty shops and theaters that show art films. A block away is Benefit Street, the spiritual home of Rhode Island old money, featuring some of the country's most impressive neo-Georgian architecture. Just down the street is Brown University and the Rhode Island School of Design, two schools with national reputations. It all seems a long way from the world of big-time college basketball.

But on the ground floor of a red-brick office building is the office of the Big East Conference.

Why?

"Because Dave Gavitt wants to live here," says Mike Tranghese, the commissioner's long-time number-two man. He doesn't mean to be flip. A decade ago the Big East was a new league struggling to spread its name. Common sense figures that the ideal place for the new office would have been New York City, right in the heart of the nation's media complex. Instead it was placed in Providence, for the very same reason Tranghese says: Gavitt wanted to live in Rhode Island. His two sons were growing up there. It was an hour and a half away from his summer home on Cape Cod. In the years before he had turned down several jobs for various reasons, one of them invariably being that he didn't want to move.

And wherever Gavitt was, the Big East office was going to be. A month ago, at an office Christmas party, the Big East's Peter Frechette had put together a video to the tune of the "Twelve Days of Christmas." The final verse was "in my very own basketball league," instead of "and a partridge in a pear tree."

It was meant as a little Christmas humor, but no one in the Big East is unaware that the Big East is Dave Gavitt's "very own basketball league."

It's a good time for Gavitt.

Recently he was profiled in *Sports Inc.* under the subhead: "Trained as a basketball coach, he learned TV and transformed a sport." He is referred to as the czar of televised college basketball. Writer Gregg Krupa says, "What set Gavitt apart, almost from the beginning, is that his mind is unlike most in sports. There is nothing narrow or unsophisticated about it. Not only is he unafraid of the ambitious and the elaborate, it attracts him. In the business world, that would make Gavitt an innovator. In college sports, it makes him a visionary."

In October he was named the president of the United States of America Amateur Basketball Association, an important job in that this is the year the issue of whether pros will be eligible for the Olympics will likely be decided. His latest idea, a series of December games between the Big East and the Atlantic Coast Conference—all for the benefit of prime-time television, of course—is being talked about for next season, the first time these two glamour conferences have come together for games in any organized way.

But the Big East is his baby. He was the one who first saw the impact a league could have. He had the contacts and influence to get it going. He had the marketing genius that propelled it into a giant. In just ten years the Big East Conference has gone from a gleam in Gavitt's eye to, arguably, the most glamorous college basketball conference in the country. It has the best television package. Its budget has grown from $175,000 to a million dollars annually. Two of its teams have won the NCAA Tournament. It has had two Wooden Award recipients, symbolic of the best player in the country, in Patrick Ewing and Chris Mullin. It plays a four-day conference tournament every March in Madison Square Garden. It has a half-hour TV show that is syndicated nationally around the country. More important, it has changed college basketball in the East forever.

"I know it sounds self-serving," say Tranghese, "but no one else could have done it except Dave. He was in a unique situation. Not only was he an administrator, but he also had been a coach, so the coaches trusted him."

Gavitt also knew people. He had been fraternity brothers at Dartmouth with Syracuse athletic director Jake Crouthamel. He had strong New England ties with Boston College and Connecticut. He coached against Carnesecca for years. He coached against Billy Raftery and Richie Regan at Seton Hall. He defended Rollie Massimino early in his career at Villanova when he was struggling and wolves were already gathering outside the door. Perhaps most important, Gavitt had once been an assistant coach at Providence when John Thompson had been a player there.

"I had a particular advantage when we started," Gavitt admits. "John has an innate suspicion of people he doesn't know. He doesn't trust people easily. But we always had a good relationship the two years we were at Providence together back in the early sixties."

Now a decade has passed since the Big East was formed and no one could have envisioned its incredible success. Attendance has skyrocketed, up 48 percent at Connecticut, 168 percent at St. John's, 216 percent at Georgetown. Television rights are worth 28 times more than they were a decade ago.

In fact, the only problem Gavitt foresees on this afternoon is that some of the schools have grown "too fat and too happy."

"It's not unexpected," he says. "There's been a certain change since the league started. How can you expect people in year eight to remember what it used to be like, especially now when people are knocking down doors to get in and all the games are on TV? But it bothers me when we don't do everything for the athletes that we can legally do. For example, every year at our various championships we give the kids a softwear gift. Lately they'd been getting chintzy, so I wanted to upgrade them. Would have cost something like an extra $15,000 to $20,000, which is really nothing. But it became a battle. I eventually won it, but I resented having to fight it. I become a little frosty with our people when we are doing so well economically and not wanting to put it back to benefit the kids.

"Because the bottom line in this conference is to make it a more rewarding experience for the student-athlete. I know that sounds like it came off a press release, but it's true. Have we done that? Absolutely. In a variety of ways. Take a Chris Mullin, for example. He didn't care how much money we made from TV or how many games were on. He cared about the challenging, rewarding competition on the floor. That's my drive: how does it affect the kid? And in every way it's better now than it was before there was a conference. The officiating is better. The facilities are better. There are more trainers, more tutoring programs, more support services. All these things have improved. Look at the minor sports in the conference. We have made it better for them than it ever was before."

He hesitates.

"But I know I make some of the people in the conference nervous. Sometimes they look at me and wonder, 'What's he going to do next?' But you know, I'm not a maintenance guy. Never have been."

Right from the beginning of his coaching career, Gavitt always seemed to be playing a few moves ahead of most of his contemporaries. From Peterborough, New Hampshire, a small town in the southern part of the state that looks like a picture postcard come to life, he attended college at Dartmouth, where his freshman coach was Al McGuire. Later he played on two Ivy League championship teams that were led by Rudy LaRusso, who later played for the Lakers. Gavitt had been the cerebral point guard, a coach on the floor, even though he hadn't been a recruited player.

"I always was intrigued intellectually by the game," he

says. "I think I played a lot because I understood the game.
But I was never the typical Dartmouth kid. I always was
working, waiting on tables, hustling. I thought I'd like to
coach when I was at Dartmouth, but the Ivy League atmosphere didn't encourage it."

At Dartmouth he first exhibited the organizational ability,
not to mention the chutzpah, that would surface years
later. He created the legend of Big Daddy. He took a
nondescript member of his fraternity, called him Big Daddy,
and created an elaborate in-joke. If the frat had a great
party, it was thrown by Big Daddy. If a stock market tip hit,
it was a tip given by Big Daddy. Big Daddy ran for student
government. Big Daddy became a campus sensation. One
summer on Cape Cod there was even a Big Daddy road race.

"Gavitt created a legend, a persona," Jake Crouthamel
told *Boston Business*. "Big Daddy was just a normal guy, a
nonathlete. But before long, every event was 'Big Daddy
presents.' It was a phenomenon. You know, even back then
Dave Gavitt was the organizer." In the same article, writer
David Granger theorizes that Gavitt left Dartmouth "with a
highly evolved appreciation of how far image can take you
in this world." People close to him now often comment on
how important perception is to Dave Gavitt.

When Gavitt graduated in 1959, he didn't go into coaching but went to work for AT&T in Washington, D.C.,
instead, because Dartmouth graduates were supposed to go
to the boardroom, not the locker room. But he quickly
discovered that he could not leave the game behind. He left
the corporate world to go to Worcester Academy in Worcester, Massachusetts, for one quarter of his AT&T salary. He
taught history and was the assistant basketball coach. He
also coached JV baseball and cross-country. "The hockey
coach got sick and I even did that for three games," he says.
"I also lived in a dorm and had dorm duty. On my nights off
I used to go to either Holy Cross or Celtics games."

In the summer of 1963, Providence College basketball
coach Joe Mullaney was looking for an assistant coach.
Even though Providence had already entered Eastern college basketball's elite, it still was being done with all the

big-time aura of a church social. So Mullaney's quest for an assistant wasn't exactly a nationwide search. All it really took was an hour ride from Providence to Worcester to lecture at a clinic. By chance Mullaney traveled to Worcester that day with a Providence College priest who had gone to school with Dee Rowe. Rowe suggested Gavitt as the assistant. The priest agreed. And as fate would have it, both Mullaney and Gavitt had played in college for Doggie Julian. All the pieces seemed to fit, and after just one year as an assistant prep-school coach, Gavitt became Mullaney's assistant.

Being an assistant coach then was nothing like it is now, when assistants are all contemporary Willy Lomans, out there hustling players with a salesman's smile. Gavitt taught a sociology course at Providence College. He coached the freshman team, including an undefeated one in 1964 that featured Jimmy Walker and Dexter Westbrook.

"It was like getting a Ph.D. in basketball," says Gavitt. "I was single at the time and always hanging around Joe's house, watching television, babysitting for the kids, et cetera. We became very friendly."

In the midsixties he went back to Dartmouth. Julian was still the coach, but he was in poor health, at the end of a long career that had also seen him coach the Celtics and win the NCAA championship in 1947 at Holy Cross. Gavitt went there as the coach-in-waiting. Julian's health deteriorated that first year, and Gavitt took over in the middle of the year. He was 29 years old.

He lost his first nine games. "My first two years were very beneficial for me as a coach," he says. "I had to weather a lot of adversity. I'd been four years with Joe and we'd won 90 games. I thought it was going to be easy. I learned a little humility."

When Mullaney left Providence in the spring of 1969 to become the coach of the Los Angeles Lakers, Gavitt returned to Providence as the head coach. He had already resurrected the Dartmouth program and been named New England coach of the year for his efforts.

It's easy now to perceive Gavitt as merely the man who built the Big East Conference. Or else see him only as one

of the most powerful men in college sports. But he was also
a very successful coach. At the time he was considered by
his peers to be one of the best in the country, though
without the national attention given a John Wooden, a
Dean Smith, or a Bobby Knight. He guided the Friars to
eight straight 20-win seasons and seven postseason tournaments. Unlike many successful coaches, whose coaching
style becomes their personal trademark, Gavitt never imposed a coaching style. He won with running teams, halfcourt
teams, teams that didn't have any right to win at all. He
believed in defense as a constant, but he was always flexi-
ble. Nor did he always have the easiest players to coach. His
best year, 1973, the two best players were local kids, Ernie
DiGregorio and Marvin Barnes, one white and one black. It
was a time of racial unrest in the city of Providence, mirror-
ing that in the country as a whole, and both DiGregorio and
Barnes were pressured not to like the other, to be rivals.
That never happened. Part of the reason was that Gavitt
never let it happen. Later, both DiGregorio and Barnes
developed reputations in the pros as being difficult to coach,
but they never were at Providence.

Gavitt also lobbied for the Providence Civic Center, a
12,000-seat arena that would not only change basketball in
New England but would enable Gavitt to see the future. At
the time the good Dominican fathers who ran Providence
College wanted to play only a few games a year in this new
arena. They had their own gym on campus, it was always
sold out, and there was strong sentiment to stay there.

Gavitt saw the tremendous opportunities of a large arena.

That first year the Friars, one of the few schools in the
East regularly playing in a large arena, played to capacity
crowds. As luck would have it, that year the Friars also
went to the Final Four, one of the few Northeastern teams
ever to do so.

Gavitt started bringing in some of the top teams in the
country to play the Friars in Providence. A few years later
he got the biggest bank in Rhode Island to sponsor a Christmas tournament, then brought in Michigan, the number-one
team in the country at the time. He was able to do this
because he had a building big enough to be able to give

opposing teams big enough financial guarantees to make it worth their while. Soon the Providence Civic Center became the spiritual center of college basketball in New England, one of the few places in the East outside of Madison Square Garden and the Palestra in Philadelphia where the top teams in the country often visited.

"Joe Mullaney built the Providence program and Dave Gavitt took it uptown," says Dee Rowe, who coached at Connecticut when Gavitt was at Providence. "He put the veneer of bigness all over it."

Gavitt had also become the athletic director at Providence, overseeing a department whose seven sports mushroomed to 24 because the school became co-ed. In order to fund these sports, he learned early on that he had to be creative in order to generate enough revenue.

He was one of the first Eastern coaches who realized the money-making potential of a college basketball coach. He had one of the first successful summer camps. He taught clinics around Rhode Island, again in conjunction with the state's largest bank. He did endorsements. He had his own coach's show on television. Joe Mullaney had been a basketball coach at Providence College. Dave Gavitt became a minicorparation. "I did those things so I wouldn't have to go to a UCLA or a Tennessee," he says. "I was getting a lot of other offers for a lot more money then, and rather than move, I felt I owed it to my family to be financially aggressive."

He was widely rumored to be the choice as Wooden's successor at UCLA. He took himself out of the running for jobs at Duke and Virginia. He also began getting himself more involved in the national basketball community. He helped prepare the Pan-American team in 1976. He was the Olympic coach in 1980.

But even with all the success, there was the feeling Gavitt was destined for bigger things. He didn't like recruiting. Plus, he was also doing two jobs with little help. So Gavitt's departure from coaching in 1979 didn't surprise anyone who knew him. Everyone always assumed he would have other worlds to conquer. How was anyone to know it would be the world of college basketball?

The vehicle, of course, was the formation of the Big East Conference. Actually, Gavitt had begun thinking about a league as early as the midseventies. But not just any old league. Something special, a conference that was going to be a showcase for college basketball in the East.

College basketball in the East had always been a smattering of good teams buried beneath the glitter of the ACC, the Big 10, the Pac 10, the SEC. Even though every once in a while an Eastern team proved it could play with anyone in the country—Providence in 1973, Rutgers in 1976—the glamour was always somewhere else.

And many of the top kids in the East went looking for it. From Lew Alcindor in the midsixties, who left New York for the southern California sun of UCLA, to scores of kids who took the "Underground Railroad" out of metropolitan New York for the South and later the Midwest, you didn't need a scorecard to know that many of the top conferences in the country were living off Eastern kids. But how could the Eastern teams compete? Kids left the cold, mean streets of the Northeast for a recruiting visit and came back bugeyed. How do you keep them in Jamaica, Queens, after they've seen the UCLA cheerleaders?

Gavitt understood all this.

He knew that the kids who put the people in the stands and warmed a coach's heart wanted the glitter. They wanted to be televised playing in big arenas, not some bandbox gym on a cold winter's night. He also knew that if a conference had teams in New York, Philadelphia, Boston, and Washington, it would have teams in four of the eight largest media markets in the country.

The problem was that, for the most part, the big arenas were in other parts of the country, courtesy of the large land-grant institutions. The other problem was that the strong independents in the East—St. John's, Syracuse, Georgetown, Villanova—were in no rush to join a league. All had formed their own niches. Why move when you like the neighborhood? Carnesecca was especially reluctant.

But in May of 1978, Jack Kaiser of St. John's, Jake Crouthamel of Syracuse, and Frank Rienzo of Georgetown met with Gavitt to discuss the idea of a new league. "The thinking then," remembers Gavitt, "was that if we four athletic directors couldn't agree, there was no sense going on."

Spurring the discussions was the realization that the NCAA was beginning to frown on teams that didn't belong to any conference. Specifically, the NCAA wanted all the Eastern teams that were not in a conference to play a round-robin schedule with other teams in their area. "That meant that Providence, who was already playing a national schedule, would now be lumped together with the likes of Maine and New Hampshire. That helped a lot of schools in the East, but it was injurious to those of us who had built up strong rivalries. It just wasn't in the direction our programs were going."

The four athletic directors continued to meet fairly regularly in a room at LaGuardia Airport in New York to hammer out the details. Eventually, the word got out, and many schools wanted in. Everyone had seen the future and it said "league." And what better league to be in than a "Super Conference" being orchestrated by Dave Gavitt, already one of the most important people in the college game, already named to coach the 1980 Olympic team?

Connecticut, Boston College, and Seton Hall were the three other schools invited to join. Boston College was asked after Holy Cross in nearby Worcester had turned down an invitation. This gave the new conference teams in all the major cities along the Northeast Corridor, with the exception of Philadelphia. Each school kicked in $15,000, and the Providence advertising firm of Duffy and Shanley was hired to promote it.

Only it didn't have a name.

There was talk of calling it the President's Conference. The Seaboard Conference. The Super Seven. Then one day, as the story goes, Jim Duffy, who worked for Duffy and Shanley, walked into a meeting, looked around at everyone scratching their heads, and said, what's the big deal? It's going to be big, right? And it's going to be in the East, right? How about the Big East?

So much for creative genius.

The next priority was to get the name known. Gavitt

knew leagues that had been around for years and no one could name the teams. Thus began the selling of the Big East. Mike Tranghese, who had been Gavitt's sports-information director at Providence, became the first conference employee. He became the conference's publicity director and moved into a small office in the back of Duffy and Shanley in downtown Providence. A logo was created. Schedule cards, banners, a Big East newspaper. All designed so that by the end of the first year basketball fans were not going to confuse the Big East with some new taste treat from McDonald's.

That summer, Tranghese and Dave Duffy of Duffy and Shanley invited several syndicators to be the first one on the television block to join with the Big East. So what if no one else in the East had ever been able to put together a prime-time package before? Tranghese and Duffy kept stressing that not only did they have the product, they were also in four of the 10 largest markets in the country. By fall they had a contract.

"That gave us instant credibility in the television industry," says Gavitt. "It forced them to sit up and take notice."

The teams did the rest. Though the teams only played each other once that first season, three of them were ranked in the top 20 in the country, and Georgetown was only one win away from the Final Four. In addition, the final game of the first Big East Tournament, held in the Providence Civic Center, was the highest-rated televised Eastern game in history. Instant tradition. The following year the Big East added Villanova, their foothold in the Philadelphia market, and the year-end tournament drew over 25,000 people in one night at the Carrier Dome. Attendance for conference games also increased 38 percent from the year before.

That spring Patrick Ewing announced he was going to Georgetown. The conference also garnered 10 out of the top 13 high-school players in the East, including Chris Mullin and Ed Pinckney. Gavitt's premise had been right; the top players in the East would stay home if you gave them reason to.

The Ewing-Mullin-Pinckney class transformed the Big East into one of the elite basketball conferences in the country.

By the time they were seniors in 1985, all three had led their teams to the Final Four in Lexington, where moments before the semifinals started, Rupp Arena rang with the chant of "Big East, Big East." That was the moment that Dave Gavitt knew that his brainchild had become a titan.

The *coup de grâce* had been the recruiting of Ewing by Georgetown. As a senior at Rindge and Latin High School in Cambridge, Massachusetts, Ewing had been the most highly publicized schoolboy player in the country, billed as the next Bill Russell. His decision where he would go to college was national news. Not only did his choice of Georgetown instantly turn the Hoyas into a national power, it also served notice around the basketball world that the Big East Conference had arrived.

"Patrick was the key," remembers Tranghese. "He gave us so much attention. When he came people started to look. It would have happened eventually, but he got the whole process accelerated. Without him, it would have taken much longer. Wherever he went that first year the building was sold out. People wanted to see him."

The rise of the Big East also coincided with the rise of television in college basketball. It's probably hard to envision it now, but once upon a time there was very little college basketball on television. But the increasing popularity of the sport and the growth of cable television joined in a marriage of convenience. Not only is basketball a perfect game for TV, complete in a two-hour time block, college basketball also attracts a young, educated, affluent audience that demographics advertisers love. Then in 1981 CBS outbid NBC for the right to broadcast the NCAA Tournament and began looking to showcase more college games.

Gavitt was there with his product and with his built-in media markets. After the 1982 season, he negotiated three-year deals with both CBS and NBC totaling $9.7 million. Three years later he made another deal with CBS for $13.3 million. The other major half of the Big East's TV strategy was its association with ESPN, the Connecticut-based cable company that began in 1979, the same year as the Big East. By their third year together, ESPN carried a Big East game of the week.

A few years later Gavitt created the Big East television network. The Big East controls the games. They pick the announcers. They determine the dates. The games, in turn, are fed only to the two home markets of the participating schools, thus keeping superfluous games off the air and cutting down on overexposure.

"You only need to read the TV listings to know there's a lot of product on the air," Gavitt told *Sports Inc.* "Rights fees are flat. Ratings have tended to be flat because they have been splintered: more people are watching it, but fewer are watching any one game. There are a lot of games on TV now for which people are getting no money, zero. And I'm not being critical of them, because many of those games, those people just want to get on. They can't get on a network, they can't get on ESPN because we're there, the ACC is there, the Big 10 is there. So they'll give their game to anyone who will give them a few bucks to produce it, and then spread it around and get it on for them.

"We're okay in terms of not being overexposed because we very carefully manage our product in terms of blackouts. Our ESPN contract carries sufficient blackout protection that the integrity of the ticket buyer is honored. I think the creation of our own network, and the unique way it's been set up, helps out too."

Now the Big East has a contract with CBS that pays them $15 million through 1991. The ESPN contract, a multimillion-dollar agreement that this year has 22 Big East games, runs through 1991. And the Big East network is turning a $1.5 million profit annually.

Big Daddy would love it.

7

IT ONLY MATTERS WHO WINS

JANUARY 30

The sports-information office at St. John's is in a tan building about 50 yards away from Alumni Hall. It is extremely small and cluttered, and several desks are all but on top of one another. It seems like an office for a tiny Division II school, not one for a Catholic school with 19,000 fulltime students, the largest in the country. In the back of the room, working away at her desk, is Katha Quinn.

She has become one of the most courageous people in all of sports. At 34, she is the only woman sports-information director in the Big East, one of the few at a major school in the country. She grew up on Old Westbury, Long Island, where much of her childhood was spent riding horses. As a student at St. John's she started out writing for the school newspaper and later became the first female sports editor. To many sportswriters who cover the Big East, she has become almost as much a symbol of St. John's as Louie Carnesecca and Alumni Hall and the cheerleaders forever yelling, "We *are* St. John's." She is blunt, caustic, irreverent, with a New York street-sense about her. She's also

always been known for going out of her way for reporters,
whether arranging interviews with the players or leading
reporters through the maze of Carnesecca's idiosyncracies.

Making this all the more remarkable is the fact she's been
doing all this for the past two years while battling liver
cancer, an illness that has left her not only emaciated but
sometimes so weak that she has trouble standing up. Yet
she continues to come to work every day. She schedules
chemotherapy sessions for days when she doesn't have games
to go to. In a sport where words like "courage" and "heart"
are thrown around as easily as bounce passes, Quinn's incredible ordeal puts everything in perspective. Last year at
the Final Four, she was honored at the annual meeting of the
United States Basketball Writers. She said that when she first
learned she had cancer, she knew she was not in a fair fight,
so she knew she couldn't fight fair herself. She went on to
say how she has used her family, her friends, her coach, and
her players as her support systems. They are what keep her
going. They have become her inspiration. Little does she
realize that she has it all backwards: she has become *their*
inspiration. When asked what keeps her going, she tells
people, "One more game, one more season, one more Final
Four."

Tonight is one more game.

Now she is in her small office telling Looie stories. Everyone around Carnesecca tells Looie stories. He has long been
one of the lovable figures of college basketball, the Italian
imp who long ago became basketball at St. John's. Gavitt
remembers coaching against him one time years ago, in the
days before the coach's box put a limit on how far coaches
could roam from their bench. Carnesecca was famous for
actually ending up on the court during games. He would
start doing his contortions on the sidelines, looking like
some puppet on amphetamines, and gradually he would
almost be able to reach out and touch the players. On this
particular night he had wandered so far from his own bench
that he was standing in front of Gavitt. Finally, realizing
how far he had strayed and fearful a referee would give him

a technical if spotted in front of the opposing bench, Carnesecca promptly sat down on the Providence bench next to Gavitt.

Carnesecca is the link between the past and the present. One of the oldest coaches in the country, his roots are in another era. He may now be coaching in the Big East under bright TV lights, but his past is a melange of small gyms and bus rides, back when the Johnnies' recruiting budget was a bag of subway tokens. Until the start of the Big East, he and the Redmen were college basketball in New York, the hometown team, the last one left. Basketball at CCNY, LIU, NYU, gone to graveyards every one. Even Fordham and Manhattan seemed to belong to the past, as did Seton Hall, stuck over in Jersey somewhere. It was only St. John's that kept the City Game alive in the city.

Every year St. John's would come into the Garden for their big games, and it became a page out of the way college basketball used to be in New York, back when the Garden was the game's big room and college doubleheaders owned the winter. Through all those years, through so many players and so many teams, Looie Carnesecca has been the guiding light.

He spent most of his childhood on 62nd Street between First and Second avenues in Manhattan, where his immigrant father ran Carnesecca's Italian Delicatessen. An only child, he grew up as New York as an egg cream.

He attended St. Anne's, a Catholic high school in Manhattan, which later moved out to Queens and became the basketball powerhouse Archbishop Molloy, and played basketball and baseball. When he graduated in 1943, he spent the next three years in the Coast Guard, serving all over the world. When he returned, he started college at Fordham in the premed program, primarily because his father wanted him to be a doctor. But he soon transferred to St. John's, where he played second base on a baseball team coached by Frank McGuire. McGuire went on to be one of the all-time great college basketball coaches, both at St. John's and at North Carolina. It was at North Carolina where McGuire

started what became unofficially known as the "Underground Railroad," which funneled New York City kids to
Tobacco Road. The man in New York who found him
players was named Harry Gotkin, known affectionately
around the schoolyards of New York as "Uncle Harry."
McGuire thus became one of the first men in college basketball to benefit from recruiting, and he won the national title
in 1957.

At St. John's Carnesecca's dream of being a basketball
player ended. But he continued to hang around the gym,
refereeing scrimmages, when one day McGuire asked him
to scout. Carnesecca loved it. In a sense he was part of the
team, going to practice, sitting with the coaches, learning to
view a game the way a coach does. It was the ideal environment for a future coach.

The year after he graduated, he got a job coaching at St.
Anne's, his alma mater. He and Mary Chiesa, a girl from
the neighborhood he had known since he was 13 years old,
got married. And he began immersing himself into the world
of basketball. For two summers he worked at Clair Bee's
camp in the Catskills, one of the first summer basketball
camps. Bee, maybe best known now as the author of the
Chip Hilton books, was the coach at Long Island University
then, years ahead of his time as a basketball mind. His
camp was one of the summer way stations for many of the
big-name coaches at the time.

"Once I had the job, it was total immersion in basketball," Carnesecca writes in his autobiography, *Looie in Season*. "I forgot about almost everything else. It became a
passion for me, a fixation, a mania. I don't think I spent one
day, or part of a day, when I wasn't thinking about basketball. If there was ever a fanatic, I was it. And it wasn't for
the money. I could have made more money cutting salami in
Pop's store. Basketball was just something I loved and
couldn't get enough of.

"Mary was great. She understood my love for the game.
Here we were newlyweds and I think I took her to every
doubleheader at the Garden. My basketball education even

extended to the summer. I attended every clinic I could get to. I took down every note, attended every lecture. It was basketball, basketball, basketball. Even after our daughter, Enes, was born, I would leave Mary and the baby and go off for a couple of weeks during the summer to continue my education, to serve my internship. I paid my dues. I spent time in the laboratory. I did work on the cadaver, so when I opened it, I knew what I would find inside. I already had been there."

In 1957, when he was 33, he became St. John's coach Joe Lapchick's assistant, primarily because he was good friends with Jack Kaiser, then the Man Friday of the St. John's athletic department. (He is now the AD.) Lapchick, who was 6-5, was called the Big Indian, one of the coaching legends in the East. Looie was his Sancho Panza, and they became together the Big Indian and the Little Looie. When in 1965 Lapchick retired, Carnesecca was named the coach. He's been there ever since, save the three years in the early seventies when he went off to coach the New York Nets of the old ABA.

Carnesecca was opposed to St. John's joining the Big East. Every year he had good teams. Every year the Redmen went to a postseason tournament. What did he need a league for? What did he need the added pressure for? He now admits he was being selfish, thinking of himself and not the school.

In the early years of the Big East, the joke was that St. John's had become Transfer Tech. Reggie Carter, Bernard Rencher, and Curtis Redding were all New York kids who left to try it elsewhere, only to come back home to St. John's.

The Big East changed all that. Chris Mullin has said that if not for the Big East, he would have gone to Duke in the ACC, as so many had before him. Mullin was the perfect example of Gavitt's thesis that the great kids in the East would stay home if they had a reason to. Mullin was from Brooklyn, and by his second season he had already become arguably the most popular St. John's player in history. He was a product of the New York Catholic league, looked like a young cop, and he was white. In a sport dominated by black players, great white players acquire a special status and are treated almost as if they were an endangered species. In four years at St. John's he became college basketball's Great White Hope, one of the all-time Big East marquee players. By the time he was a senior he had become almost a mythic figure in New York, complete with all the stories about how he had his own key to Alumni Hall so that he could spend many solitary hours honing his lefty jumper.

Besides the tradition and the Big East, the other lure for recruits has always been the extra money they can get by going to St. John's. Because St. John's doesn't have any dorms, players are allowed to be reimbursed for the amount of money they would have gotten somewhere else for room and board. This has always been a big attraction for local kids, who can live at home and walk around with some money in their pocket.

But everything else aside, St. John's has become Looie Carnesecca. Consider the record: in 20 years at St. John's he has been to 15 NCAA tournaments and five NITs. In 20 years he's only had five seasons in which the Redmen had less than 20 wins.

Katha Quinn is asked how Carnesecca has changed.

"We're in people's living rooms now," she says, her voice raspy and hoarse. "You don't have to explain to people who we are anymore. We're on TV. Who would ever have heard of two TV crews in my little postage stamp of a gym? Who would ever have heard the word 'satellite uplink truck' beaming the signal out of St. John's? We used to make maybe $400 from basketball. Now some years it's $1.5 million. And Coach has had to grow with all that. Now he has a TV show on the Madison Square Garden network. Hightech Looie. He still can't turn on a radio, but he's got a great video crew.

"But he's still Looie, the absentminded perfectionist. Off in la-la land somewhere. I always tell him he keeps his watch on Rome time. In 1979, we were coming back from winning some games in the NCAA Tournament and a big celebration was planned at the airport. I had told the team and Coach what was going to happen. The other passengers were going to get off first, then us. And I told both the team and Coach that I would appreciate their cooperation. So everyone gets off the plane, and the cameras are clicking and the band is playing and everything is going great. The only problem is that Coach somehow got turned around and went over to greet these people who had just arrived from Poland and who couldn't speak English. So there was Coach, shaking hands and thanking them all for coming. But they were the wrong people.

"But he always goes out of his way for people. At a press conference one night some guy walks in late, so afterward Looie sits with him for ten minutes. He's always asking me on the road, 'Is my room okay? Is it warm enough?' Take away the basketball. Take away the TV and all that, and Looie is a nice little man who would be selling salami if he weren't coaching. I once rode in a car with him and his wife, Mary, and I looked in the backseat and they were holding hands like two 16-year-olds. This after being married 40 years. There is an Old World quality about him. Sometimes I see him lose his temper and I think, here is a nice little Italian man? Yikes. But the bottom line is, he really is a nice man.

"And all the good things happened to him late," continues Quinn. "By that time he was seasoned. He had been through the rough times. So he was better equipped to handle them. Looie didn't get to the Final Four for how many years? Now coaches don't get to the Final Four in four or five years and people criticize them. Now coaches have to be successful right away or they're in danger of losing their jobs."

Carnesecca's always been known as a great interview for his raspy Godfather voice, his knowing smile, his assortment of "Looie-isms." But he's also always understood the media's job and his role in it. Reporters around the Big East have long been used to Carnesecca saying, "You got enough?" at the end of telephone interviews. He's also regarded as one of the truly nice people in college basketball. So when he finally went to the Final Four in 1985, he became the sentimental favorite of the tournament. Little Looie finally makes the Final Four. That was the team comprised of Mullin, Mark Jackson, Bill Wennington, Ron Rowan, Mike Moses, and Willie Glass. In retrospect, it was probably Carnesecca's greatest team. But they lost in the semifinals to Georgetown. The Hoyas then got upset in the finals by Villanova. What had started out as Looie Carnesecca's Final Four became Rollie Massimino's. Rollie became the media star. Looie went back to New York.

Back to a program that was starting to show signs of age. The past couple of years snipers have been taking shots at Carnesecca for his style of play. The theory runs that Carnesecca's great coaching jobs have been done with teams that have the least natural ability. The corollary is that he overcoaches his good teams, that his controlled offense takes players' games away from them. Carnesecca's detractors point to a time last year when he supposedly yelled out to guard Boo Harvey, a speed burner, to slow it down, and Harvey yelled back, "I'm going as slow as I can."

The school has also been criticized for its low graduation rate of basketball players down through the years. Overall, there's been the feeling that St. John's has not made the commitment the other Big East schools have in terms of support services for players. It wasn't until this past fall that St. John's hired former player Bernard Rencher to monitor the academic progress of basketball players.

Much of the storm erupted last spring when both Michael Porter and Boo Harvey, two transfers from San Jacinto, the famous basketball junior college on the outskirts of Houston, fell into the academic abyss. Harvey failed too many courses, and Porter elected to go to Bermuda with his girlfriend rather than take any final exams. He left school, then got cut this season by the Pensacola team in the CBA. Harvey remained in school, hoping to be eligible for this year's second semester, but didn't make it. But he's still in school, working out with the team and hoping to be eligible next year.

Four years ago Harvey was at Andrew Jackson High School in nearby Queens, called the best schoolboy guard in New York City. He was 5-11, cheetah-quick, and at the time seemed destined to one day run the fast break in the Carrier Dome. He signed early with Syracuse, but then he was not admitted due to poor grades. His scholarship went instead to Sherman Douglas. Harvey went to San Jacinto, where his team went 73-1 in two years and he was named the cojunior-college player of the year.

In a few days he will tell Sandy Keenan of *Newsday* that his academics were monitored more at San Jacinto than they were last year at St. John's. "They stayed on me there," he will say. "They knew we weren't the smartest guys in the world. It was always work before ball. You had to show everything you did in class before ball."

When Quinn talks about Carnesecca, you can hear the affection in her voice. She long ago became used to his idiosyncracies.

"Ah, Coach," she sighs. "What would I do without him?"

She says that Chris Mullin, Mark Jackson, and Bill Wennington are "her children," the players she was the closest to down through the years. She is not as close to this team as some of the others. For one thing it's a younger team, full of kids who are new to St. John's. For another, her illness has made her unable to travel with the team. The one exception is freshman Terrence Mullin, Chris's younger brother. If he's not as tall and not as talented, there still are distinct similarities in the way he carries himself, in the way he shoots his jumper.

"Sometimes I look at him and it's eerie," says Quinn, "and he'll look back at me and it's like he knows."

She starts to gather up her things before going to Alumni Hall to begin getting ready for a game against Pittsburgh. As always, it's a painstaking process. She takes a couple of the 30 pills she takes a day. As she walks down the corridor she says how she has to go to the doctor's office tomorrow, that she hasn't been feeling well the past few days. Her voice is weak, tired. She walks slowly, the pain visible on her face.

"Why don't you go home and get some sleep?" she is asked.

She looks surprised. "This is game night," she says.

One more game. One more season.

But she will not make the season. Shortly before the Big East Tournament in early March she will go into Sloan-Kettering Hospital in New York, where she'll die soon thereafter.

Pittsburgh comes into the game 10–8 on the season, 3–4 in the Big East. The Panthers have been inconsistent, a common weakness for a team that starts five sophomores. Evans, though, contends he doesn't think his team is inconsistent as much as it needs more depth. He doesn't have someone to put in when someone else is playing poorly.

St. John's is 12–6, 4–4 in the conference, but the Redmen have lost their last two games and must play tonight without Malik Sealy; their fine freshman forward is out with a bad ankle.

A red banner along the front of the scorer's table says, "The University is St. John's." The cheerleaders sit underneath one basket. Next to them is Chris Ratay, a St. John's senior who has become quite controversial. The traditional mascot was an Indian, a Redman. But the mascot was offensive to Indians and was dropped. Enter the Red Man, dressed in a red tuxedo, top hat, and red bow shoes, complete with white gloves and a cane. The problem is that he seems to fit in at Alumni Hall like Madonna at a Daughters of the American Revolution convention. He has gotten his share of boos all year. There are even some people who sit in the front rows with paper bags over their heads, turning down their thumbs whenever the Red Man runs out onto the floor. There are "Dump the Tux" signs. St. John's used to be known for their traditional cheer, "We *are* St. John's." Now they are becoming known for a guy in a red top hat and shoes who carries a cane. The times they are a-changing.

The Redmen lead by 3 at the half in what is another typical Big East game: intense, hard fought, close. Pitts-

"The General."
Sherman Douglas of
Syracuse. *(Credit:
Thomas F. Maguire Jr.)*

Seton Hall's Gerald
Green. *(Credit: Thomas F.
Maguire Jr.)*

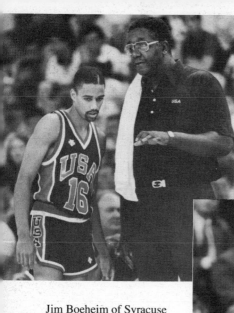

Georgetown's Charles Smith and John Thompson at the Olympics. *(Credit: Thomas F. Maguire Jr.)*

Jim Boeheim of Syracuse urging on the troops, with assistant coach Wayne Morgan (left). *(Credit: Susan Allen Camp)*

Villanova's Rollie Massimino. *(Credit: Thomas F. Maguire Jr.)*

Rebound battle between Derrick Coleman of Syracuse in white and Villanova's Doug West (42) and Rodney Taylor (35). *(Credit: Thomas F. Maguire Jr.)*

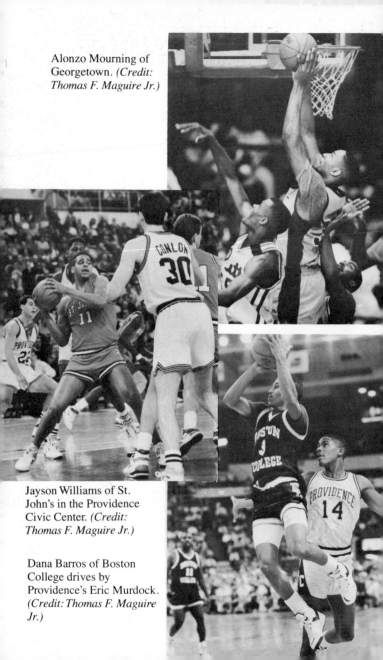

Alonzo Mourning of Georgetown. *(Credit: Thomas F. Maguire Jr.)*

Jayson Williams of St. John's in the Providence Civic Center. *(Credit: Thomas F. Maguire Jr.)*

Dana Barros of Boston College drives by Providence's Eric Murdock. *(Credit: Thomas F. Maguire Jr.)*

P. J. Carlesimo of Seton Hall, the national coach of the year. *(Credit: Thomas F. Maguire Jr.)*

Looie Carnesecca of St. John's, with Matt Brust (left). *(Credit: Thomas F. Maguire Jr.)*

Big Daddy himself, Dave Gavitt. *(Credit: Christopher Lauber)*

Mike Tranghese. *(Credit: Thomas F. Maguire Jr.)*

Dave Gavitt with Big East coaches and players in the early 1980's. In back of Gavitt—from left to right—are former B.C. coach Gary Williams, Rollie Massimino, former Connecticut coach Dom Perno, Looie Carnesecca, former Pitt coach Roy Chipman, P. J. Carlesimo and former coaching great Frank McGuire, director of college basketball at Madison Square Garden. *(Credit: Christopher Lauber)*

Pittsburgh's Brian Shorter, the Big East rookie-of-the-year. *(Credit: Thomas F. Maguire Jr.)*

Billy Owens of Syracuse driving on Providence's Cal Foster. *(Credit: Thomas F. Maguire Jr.)*

The Big East's answer to Crocodile Dundee, Andrew Gaze. *(Credit: Thomas F. Maguire Jr.)*

First year Providence coach
Rick Barnes. *(Credit: Thomas F.
Maguire Jr.)*

Pittsburgh coach Paul Evans.
(Credit: Thomas F. Maguire Jr.)

Boston College coach Jim
O'Brien.
(Credit: Thomas F. Maguire Jr.)

Jim Calhoun, Connecticut
coach.
(Credit: Thomas F. Maguire Jr.)

burgh does not shoot well, especially the guards. Keeping St. John's in the game is Jayson Williams, the 6-10 junior who has developed into one of the league's premier players. He is from Queens and went to Christ the King. Coming into St. John's as a Prop 48 kid, he didn't play as a freshman. Last year he became a starter midway through the year but gained more notoriety for an incident at the Providence Civic Center in which he threw a chair into a crowd of people behind the St. John's bench after a fight had broken out between the Redmen players and some fans. Now he is a dominating presence inside, one of the better scorers in the league, and he's being mentioned as a future pro. Tonight he will finish with 19 points and 13 rebounds.

St. John's plays much of the second half with a freshman backcourt of Jason Buchanan and Terrence Mullin. Both were considered marginal Big East players at best and were recruited by no other Big East schools. Buchanan was taken in the summer after Carnesecca looked at his backcourt and saw Death Valley. Porter and Harvey were academic casualties. Marcus Broadnax and Elander Lewis had transferred, upset with their lack of playing time. Chuck Sproling, a highly touted guard from Denver, was Prop 48. Mullin had been recruited mainly because he was Chris's brother. Now he and Buchanan are both in the game in the final minutes of a close one. Ironically, Carnesecca has traditionally been known as someone who gives younger players little playing time. This year he has had no choice.

Unfortunately, Mullin misses a breakaway layup that might have clinched the victory for the Redmen. But Robert Werdann, the freshman center who's been hobbled most of the month with a thigh injury, scores on a drive to tie the game at 73 with just 33 seconds remaining. Interestingly, his grandfather once helped build Alumni Hall. Pittsburgh fails to score on their last possession and the game goes into overtime. The Panthers eventually win by 4, 85–81.

Afterward, Carnesecca enters the old ampitheater that is used for postgame press conferences in Alumni Hall. He has a drawn look and his face is blotchy. So far he has done a great coaching job with this young team, keeping them in games they had no right being in. Tonight his team has played well again. They have played much of the second half with two freshman guards that no one else in the Big East wanted. They have played without Sealy. They should have won the game in regulation. But they lost all the same, their third loss in a row, and Looie's been around long enough to know that next week no one will care how hard his team played tonight, only that it lost.

"This is one of those games you look back on at the end of the year and know you should have won," he says in his raspy voice reminiscent of Marlon Brando in *The Godfather*. "It's the kind of a game when a loose ball here, a missed foul shot there, a missed box-out, decides things. Sometimes intensity has to be tempered with intelligence and smarts, which I'm sure will come."

This is not the Carnesecca of legend, little Looie serenading the media with his one-liners and his Old World charm. This is a portrait of Looie in defeat. He's an old coach with a young team in the middle of what is turning out to be a long season.

FEBRUARY 4

Does it really matter that it's not pretty?

The University of Connecticut is playing on this Saturday afternoon before a sold-out crowd in the Providence Civic Center. It is a basketball version of a rock fight, one of those games where intensity overshadows performance. These are two teams with visions in their heads of that prom known as the NCAA Tournament that gets underway in March. They know that you earn your invitation on cold afternoons in February like today. They are desperate for a victory, not style points.

The Friars are trying to recapture the magic that started in December when they began the season by winning 13 straight. They have lost close games at home to Villanova and Georgetown and two more on the road. In their last game they were blown out by St. John's in Alumni Hall. Not only had it been their worst effort of the season, it had resurrected all the negatives that had loomed over this team in big neon letters during the preseason: lack of inside offense, playing with a 6-3 forward in Matt Palazzi, lack of defensive presence inside. Rick Barnes is concerned that another loss would start nullifying what has already been accomplished.

The Huskies come in here today 3–4 in the Big East, desperately trying to live up to all the hype that had them ranked in the preseason top 20. Jim Calhoun knows that he just has to win, period. Although unjustified, there are too many expectations hanging over his team. That's the price tag for winning the NIT.

Adding to the drama is that these two teams don't particularly like each other. They were old New England rivals long before the Big East. Back then it was the Friars who carried the region's banner for years, while the Huskies stalled in the shadows, lost in their New England schedule. After the first game between the two schools a month ago in the Hartford Civic Center, Calhoun took a swipe at the Friars, saying his kids had to go to class and couldn't practice three times a day. Barnes hadn't liked the remark. Number one, his kids did go to class. Number two, they rarely practice three times a day.

At the first timeout, with Providence leading 6–4, Connecticut assistant coach Howie Dickenman greets the team enthusiastically as they run over to the bench. "Hell of a zone defense," he says, enthusiastically clapping his hands.

He is the only holdover from Dom Perno's tenure at Connecticut. He is in his early 40s, one of the seemingly career assistant coaches. He is also the designated "tough guy" of the Connecticut staff, part of an unofficial good cop-bad cop strategy. Dickenman is the one that gets all over the players in practice, while Dave Leitao is the one who befriends them.

Calhoun kneels in front of his bench in a dark suit. He has a reputation for being tough on officials during a game. The night in Hartford when the Huskies upset Syracuse, he spent much of the second half yelling at a small group of fans behind his bench. Near the end of the game, when it was apparent Connecticut was going to win, he turned to them and yelled, "Fuck you."

As Providence goes up by 6 midway through the first half, Calhoun gets more and more upset. "What the Christ is going on out there? We're goddamn choking." A couple of minutes later Cliff Robinson is called for traveling. Calhoun jumps in the air. "No way!" he yells. "I guarantee you he didn't travel."

The game gets closer. But with two minutes left in the half, Robinson hurts his foot and limps off. It is a major blow to Connecticut. Without Robinson they no longer have an inside presence. Shortly thereafter the Huskies' Lyman DePriest is whistled for a foul, and Calhoun rips off his jacket as if he's going to throw it.

"Easy, Jim," warns referee Joe Mingle.

"What the hell is that?" yells Calhoun. "What the hell is that?"

The half ends with both teams tied at 33.

It has become a Connecticut kind of game, played at their pace. The Friars want to run but are not able to. Connecticut continues to walk the ball up the court, deliberately working for a shot. It's as if the game is just hanging out there, waiting for someone to take it. The tension builds. Dickenman screams at his players to "get on the glass, get on the glass," like it's some form of mantra.

With just under 10 minutes to play, Connecticut's Tate George and the Friars' Eric Murdock stop and stare at each other. The building erupts. Calhoun runs out onto the court, while the people seated behind the Connecticut bench yell at him.

"Home job!" yells Calhoun, appearing on the verge of being out of control. "Home job again. Fucking home job!"

In the final minutes, Providence clings to a slight lead. Calhoun is up on every call, admonishing his players, urging them, all but pleading with them. His face is flushed. He looks ready to punch somebody. Referee John Moreau runs by the Connecticut bench and says to Dickenman, "You'd better get him under control."

With 15 seconds left and his Friars leading by 2, Carlton Screen makes two foul shots as calmly as if he were in a practice session in Alumni Hall. Ironically, it was two foul shots by Screen that beat Calhoun the first game in Hartford.

"I'll tell you what," says Calhoun to no one in particular when Screen's second free throw goes through, assuring Providence of the game. "That's the first time I've been fucked by an official all year. The first time."

But afterward in the press conference, Calhoun is composed and says all the right things. He congratulates Providence and refuses to use Robinson's departure as an excuse, even though it was probably the story of the game. Because when it gets time to send out the bids to that big dance in March, Calhoun knows it doesn't matter if Robinson played in the second half or not. Or whether or not the game was pretty. Doesn't matter if the game was a rock fight or "Masterpiece Theatre."

It only matters who won.

Save the style points for figure skating.

They may play in a new arena, but the strain of losing takes its toll no matter where you play. Ask Boston College coach Jim O'Brien. A few hours before tonight's match-up with Seton Hall, he sits behind his desk discussing the disappointing season. What makes it worse is that he's always wanted to coach at BC. It's his alma mater.

He was a fine player himself. In fact, he was a backcourt star for first Bob Cousy, then Chuck Daly. After he graduated in 1971, he played for a while in the old ABA. He was a rookie along with Artis Gilmore and later played for Wilt Chamberlain in San Diego, living what was, for him, a fantasy existence. Then his pro career ended and for six months he did nothing, living off some money he had saved from pro ball, trying to figure out what to do with his life. It had always revolved around basketball, and now basketball was over. He began selling computer products, but after a year he realized that he had left a piece of his heart behind.

Using some New England connections, he got a job as Dom Perno's assistant at Connecticut. In 1982 he went to St. Bonaventure as a head coach. He was happy there and had no real desire to leave, but when BC offered him a job, he had to take it. His wife was from Boston. Many of his college friends still lived in Boston. Then, too, here was the home of so many of his memories.

"I knew when I came here, it was going to be a struggle," he said. "It's a delicate situation, because you don't want to criticize the kids you inherited, but we just don't have the talent the other teams have, especially inside. Gary Williams was under .500 in his last year, then I got hired too late to recruit that first year. Then last fall I had neck surgery and didn't go into one house in September. We made a personalized video of me talking to every kid, but it's not the same thing.

"My most difficult problem is the academic fallout from Jay Murphy attending night school here. Admissions has really tightened up. We haven't taken a Prop 48 kid in what, five years? We can't touch a lot of the kids who other schools in the league are taking. When I got hired, Theron Mayes, the kid from New Haven, wanted to come. He would have been my first recruit. We couldn't take him. Now he's doing great at Florida State.

"But I don't mean to say it's a bleak situation. This is still the place I want to be. Sure, Syracuse and Georgetown are in their own world, but we should be able to compete with everyone else. And you don't have to win this league. All you have to do is come in fourth or fifth, and you go to the tournament and everything's great. But the Big East is unforgiving. If you don't play to your potential every night, you can't win. When we played Seton Hall the first time, we were just physically overmatched.

"And it's tough on everyone. It's even getting to Dana Barros. He was listless in practice yesterday, and I got on him very hard. I don't usually get on him, because he plays so hard. But I did yesterday. I told him that he didn't care anymore, and he was letting everyone else down. To stop worrying about the tight rims and all that other shit, and to start putting the ball in the basket. The worst thing you can say to Dana is that he doesn't care, because he cares so much. And I can't let him start feeling sorry for himself, because if he does, then we have no hope.

"This is my most difficult season. The incident with Barros's father. Stovall quitting, then coming back. It's been one thing or the other all year. And when you're not winning, it's easy for the team to say, 'Fuck this, this is really getting old.' So I told them yesterday that there is light at the end of the tunnel. There are games we can win.

"I feel I can coach with anyone. The thing you have to avoid is saying that if I had the players they had, I could do just as well. No one cares about that. They just want you to win. That's like saying, 'Well, all my kids graduate.' Who gives a shit? And the answer is, nobody. They want you to win. Nothing else. Like when Stovall wanted to come back. I had people telling me that if I took him back, it would look like we had no discipline. But if we don't win any games, are people going to say, 'Well, at least they had discipline'? Of course not. They're going to say that guy didn't win any games. Unfortunately, that's the bottom line in this business.

"So recruiting is my number-one priority. We got to get good players. You know, when I was an assistant at Connecticut with Dom Perno, he was great with me. He told me I could be at every game, and the games are what's fun. Now I'm telling my staff that if they have to go see a kid, screw the game. We can't afford the luxury of them being at every game anymore. I never thought I'd say that. You get into this profession because you like to coach. And 30 nights a year out of 365, you get a chance to do what you went into the profession for. But the reality is we need players.

"Sometimes I wonder where all this is going. When you lose, you're as down as down can be. And when you win, you're relieved. Not so much that you won, but because you didn't lose. And that's a sad way to be. You can't allow the highs and lows to govern your life, because then you're on a roller coaster all the time, and that's no way to live your life. But now guys are in the business for the money. It wasn't the same way ten years ago. It's become so much bigger than it was supposed to be."

O'Brien laughs.

"You know the old joke. This would be a great business, if it wasn't for these fucking games."

Like the one tonight.

Seton Hall comes into Conte Forum 5–3 in the league, 18–3 overall. The Eagles are 1–6 in the league, cemented in the basement. Two weeks ago the two teams played in the Meadowlands, and it was never close. The mismatch inside was so great that O'Brien didn't even play his big men in the second half, so disgusted was he by the way they'd played in the first half.

It is a sold-out Saturday-night crowd. There is a pep band. There are banners in the rafters. All the trappings are here. What is not here is a game. Seton Hall scores the first 10 points, all inside, and eventually go ahead 16–2. Inside is again a complete mismatch, and Ramon Ramos and Daryll Walker beat up the smaller, less physical Eagles. In the first half the Hall only scores one basket outside of the paint, a medium-sized jumper from John Morton. At the other end of the court, Boston College starts the game by making one out of their first 14 shots. In what has become their signature this season, Seton Hall again plays aggressive man-to-man defense, and BC never gets into their offense. Gerald Greene hounds Barros, and when Barros does get a shot off, it's either rushed or deeper than he'd like. Every time he tries to cut through the Seton Hall defense, he is bumped, hit, knocked off balance, as if lost in the middle of some elaborate pinball game.

As O'Brien kneels along the sidelines, the frustration shows all over his face. He sends in different players. He changes his defense. He gets a technical foul from referee Jim Howell. Nothing works. The final score is 105–82.

Carlesimo is extremely gracious after the game. He believes the Boston College program is moving in the right direction, "just as I thought we were moving in the right direction a couple of years ago, even though a lot of people don't understand that when you don't win games.

"I know what it's like. BC reminds me of what we were like a couple of years ago. We used to get our heads handed to us the same way. There are very good players in this league, and not too many freshmen and sophomores can play against them. We have juniors and seniors now, and that's a big, big part of the story. We should be a good basketball team. Jimmy has sophomores. I look at our kids and I look at their kids and, physically, the difference strikes me. Three years ago Morton and Greene were getting the shit beat out of them. It's night and day how much stronger they are now."

All the same, it is another lost night for Boston College, Dana Barros, and Jim O'Brien. "For me to get shots I have to commit homicide," Barros says dejectedly in the locker room. Down the hall, O'Brien says how his team is "really caught between a rock and a hard place. We just can't defend people inside. It's not very tricky, and there's really not a whole lot of answers."

FEBRUARY 8

Bill Shapland, the Georgetown sports-information director, is sitting behind the basket in the Hartford Civic Center an hour before Georgetown is to play Connecticut. He is a huge man, maybe 300 pounds, and sometimes he is referred to as Georgetown's sports noninformation director. There are easier jobs than being John Thompson's publicist.

Several years ago, when the job was handled by Jim Marchioni, Hoya Paranoia was at its height, and too often Marchioni found himself right in the middle of it. He was followed by Zachary Smith, who had played for Thompson in high school, and he was the ultimate obstructionist. For the past few years it's been Shapland, who's been better able to walk the narrow balance beam between the media and his role as the basketball team's publicist.

Now Shapland is enthusiastically discussing Charles Smith.

"He was a late recruit," he says, "and Thompson told him, 'You will never play any significant minutes. You will never score. You will play defense and be a role player.' And that's essentially what happened during Smitty's freshman year. The next year we were playing Ohio State in the NCAA Tournament and we were down 18. Smitty came off the bench and scored 22 points in 24 minutes. That summer he went on the Big East trip to Australia that was coached by P. J. and led the team in scoring and assists. P. J. made Smitty his go-to guy and Smitty responded. But if you look at the other Georgetown recruits, the typical Georgetown body types, Smitty doesn't fit the body type."

In a sense Charles Smith has created himself. A slight six-footer, he looks more like a sideman in a blues band than one of the best point guards in college basketball. Yet he is quick, poised, and has mastered an assortment of driving, off-balance, swooping shots that seem prayers until they fall in the basket. He is also supremely confident. This past fall, during Honor Olympians Day at Georgetown, Smith was asked by someone in the audience if it was an honor to be able to play his senior year with such great players as Alonzo Mourning and John Turner. "They're freshmen," Smith said. "Why don't you ask them if they feel honored to play with me?"

They should be. So far this year it's been Smith who's delivered in the clutch. In December he scored Georgetown's last 16 points in a win against DePaul. His five-footer in the lane with five seconds left was the winning basket against Providence. Against Connecticut in the first game in the Capital Centre it was his two foul shots with two seconds remaining that clinched a 4-point win.

"Alonzo is great and has been everything anyone expected him to be," says Shapland, "but this team rises and falls with Charles Smith."

The conversation shifts to Thompson—specifically, the type of high-school player Thompson recruits.

"The player has to have a desire to succeed academically," Shapland says. "Not some kid who has to be convinced that's important. He has to have a respect for authority, and someone who got along well with his high-school coach. Someone who doesn't need ticker-tape parades and doesn't need constant reinforcement all the time. Someone who's not looking to be pampered in the recruiting process. Coach Thompson is not going to kiss some 17-year-old's ass. Certainly, he looks for quickness, a certain body type. But he gets involved very little in the recruiting process early. Craig Esherek and Mike Riley do the evaluating."

"Has Thompson changed since you first met him?"

"Not really," says Shapland. "If you are loyal to Thompson, he is loyal to you. When I first got this job, I told him that I really had a problem with some of the language that he uses." Shapland smiles. "It's no secret that sometimes he uses strong language. Ever since then he has never used it around me. I have been at Georgetown in one capacity or another since 1973, and he is the single smartest person I have met there. Without question. I wouldn't work for anyone else. I'd get out of the business first."

Thompson appears in dark slacks, gray jacket, a red tie, and white towel. Always the white towel. The Hoyas enter the game on top of the Big East, ranked number one in the country in the CNN poll and second by the Associated Press. They quickly go out in front, 11–2.

Thompson spends most of the early minutes away from his seat in the middle of his players, walking up and down the sidelines.

"Thompson, will you sit down?" someone eventually yells from behind the Georgetown bench.

Thompson turns around with a smile and throws a kiss to the crowd.

Even with Smith held to just one shot in the first half, the Hoyas are up by 4. Their defense dominates the game, and with just under eight minutes left, the Huskies are down by 17 and only have 39 points. They make a little run after that, but it's a false one, and they eventually lose, 70–58. It is the Hoyas' eighth straight win, the most they've had in a row in the Big East since they won nine straight in 1984, the year they won the national title.

Minutes after the game, Shapland escorts Thompson into the interview room.

"Stand back," says Shapland brusquely, surveying the scene. "Give Coach Thompson some room."

At first glance this is typical Georgetown. Walk in, say something confrontational, immediately establish the ground rules. But Thompson quickly diffuses it.

"We don't feel comfortable unless we create a little intimidation," he says with a wide smile. Then he puts his arm around Shapland. "Especially my little brother here."

This is one more example of Thompson's new attitude this year around the media. Since media day in early November he has been downright charming. Gone are the intimidating stares, the belligerence. He has joked. He's answered all questions, even the stupid ones, with patience. He has been friendly. He has seemed relaxed. He has dropped some of his defenses. He has even at times played off the old Georgetown image, as he has tonight.

Maybe this is because he's perceptive enough to know that if he had come back from Seoul and adopted his usual antagonistic "us versus them" mentality, he would have been crucified in the press all year. Maybe it's because he lost the biggest game of his life, the one against the Russians in the Olympics, and discovered that life went on just like always. Maybe he is now intent in being a spokesman on national issues. Or maybe, after all the years and all the battles, John Thompson has come to realize that he doesn't have to prove anything anymore.

"I don't think we played well at all," he says now, as Mary Fenlon comes into the room and stands in the back. "Charles didn't have one of his better games. I told him on the sidelines, 'I'll lose with you taking shots and making plays.' Don't forget what we got Smitty for. All his shooting is extra. But this is the tough part of the schedule, and the kids are not machines. They're under a lot of pressure."

"Do you mean the pressure of being ranked number one?"

"Our program never has been geared to that, especially in February. Our program is geared to playing well in Febru-

ary. All that number-one stuff is good for the alumni and
the sportswriters. But I think if you focus on that, you make
a mistake."

A few minutes later Jim Calhoun follows Thompson into
the interview room and says how the Hoyas are awfully
good. He looks drained. His Huskies are starting to run out
of games.

"What's the difference between you and them?"

"What's the difference?" says Calhoun. "They have better players."

So much for the mystery of sports.

• Two nights ago, Syracuse held off a late-game Seton
Hall rally and won, 85–79, in the Meadowlands for their 17th
straight win over the Hall. It is Syracuse's sixth straight
victory, and it's their 20th victory of the season, the seventh
year in a row the Orangemen have won at least 20 games.
Sherman Douglas led the way with 28 points, and Stephen
Thompson added 23.

• Last night Villanova beat Boston College, 77–69, in
Villanova. The Wildcats placed five players in double figures, led by Doug West's 16 points. The Cats are now 4–5 in
the Big East and 13–10 overall. Dana Barros countered
with 28 for BC, including five for five from three-point
range.

• Also last night, Providence beat Pittsburgh 88–78 in the
Providence Civic Center. For the first 30 minutes Pitt looked
more like the team that lost to Sienna and Duquesne than
the one that beat Oklahoma and Syracuse. The Panthers
had all kinds of trouble with the Providence press and were
down by 25 with 10 minutes left in the game. All year Paul
Evans has looked for consistency from his young team. He
is still looking. He doesn't have to look at his bench. He
knows he doesn't have one.

"Look around," Evans said before the game. "Most teams
don't have all their starters play well at one time. We don't
have a bench. We need all five starters to play well. When
we do, we can play with anybody."

The only bright spots last night were the continued scoring of Brian Shorter, who had 27, and the continued emergence of Jason Mathews as one of the fine young players in the league.

• Yesterday, Syracuse's Derrick Coleman pleaded guilty in Syracuse City Court to harassment and disorderly conduct stemming from a fraternity brawl and a break-in on the Syracuse University campus in December. He was sentenced to 50 hours of community service and restitution of damages he caused during the incident.

THE STANDINGS:	CONFERENCE PLAY	OVERALL
GEORGETOWN	8–1	18–2
SETON HALL	6–4	19–4
SYRACUSE	6–4	20–4
PROVIDENCE	6–4	17–4
ST. JOHN'S	5–5	13–7
VILLANOVA	4–5	13–10
PITTSBURGH	4–6	11–10
CONNECTICUT	3–6	12–7
BOSTON COLLEGE	1–8	8–11

8

THE BIZARRE WORLD OF RECRUITING

Last Saturday night, an hour after Seton Hall beat Boston College in Conte Forum, Seton Hall assistant Rod Baker was standing in the empty gym. Workmen were already in the process of dismantling the parquet floor, taking it up in sections and transforming the building back into a hockey rink. A few yards away from Baker was a slender black high-school kid from Boston named Trent Forbes. He's considered to be one of the best point guard prospects in the East, a senior at Dover-Sherburn High School outside of Boston, where he is bused every day. Back in the fall he had verbally committed to the University of Maryland, but now the word in the internecine world of recruiting is that he is reconsidering.

"We're still alive and kicking," said Baker, who has known Forbes from two years ago when he worked the Providence College summer camp and Forbes was a camper. "It's us and Maryland, and the longer it goes, the more it's us. We've told him he can come in and start right away. That we need someone next year to replace Gerald Greene and we think it can be him."

Baker looked over at Forbes.

"We just want him to visit," he said, "because our guys are great when kids visit. They are fun to be around, and they never big-time anybody, because our guys are not big-time guys. But it depends on what you promise guys when you recruit them. If you promise them the moon, how you going to discipline them? You can't. P. J. doesn't promise them anything other than a chance to play."

Thirty years ago, recruiting was a part-time affair. Most coaches only had one full-time assistant to help run practices and often coach the freshman team. This was before the days of scouting services and the showcase summer camps. Coaches relied upon either personal contacts, or alumni, or luck, to discover high-school talent. Much of it was happenstance. Consider Providence College, for example, in the late fifties, when Joe Mullaney was the coach. The main reason the Friars landed Lenny Wilkens from Boys High in Brooklyn was that Mullaney knew his priest. They got Johnny Egan from Hartford because he couldn't get into the University of Connecticut. They got John Thompson because of the NBA's 50-mile territorial rule. They later got Jimmy Walker, then in obscurity at a black prep school in North Carolina, because his cousin was already at Providence. Walker brought Dexter Westbrook with him. Two years later, in 1965, Walker and Westbrook led Providence to the Eastern regionals. The point is, their recruiting success was in large part good fortune. They had no recruiting strategy.

The ACC schools were good because they had a pipeline into the metropolitan New York area. Most of the Southern schools all had contacts in New York called "bird dogs," Damon Runyon characters who prowled the New York playgrounds and youth leagues looking for talent. Of the most famous examples, Harry Gotkin worked for Frank McGuire's North Carolina teams in the late fifties, and Howard Garfinkel scouted for Everett Case at North Carolina State.

By the early seventies, recruiting was changing. Most schools now had two full-time assistant coaches. Freshman teams no longer existed, so assistant coaches basically had no other responsibilities other than to recruit. Popping up were showcase summer camps modeled on Five Star, Garfinkel's camp in the Poconos, where much of the top talent was paraded around like so much prized livestock. There were recruiting services, again spurred by Garfinkel, that rated virtually every schoolboy who could hit two jumpers in a row. It was all becoming much more specialized.

Lefty Driesell, the former Maryland coach, is regarded as one of the founders of the modern recruiting era. He made his reputation at Davidson, a small Division I school outside of Charlotte, North Carolina, where he would periodically jump into the station wagon and travel throughout the South, sometimes sleeping in the back of his car. One of the first things he did when he got the job at Maryland was to take out a full-page ad in the *Washington Post*, complete with the names of four D.C.-area players, that said "Maryland wants you." One of them was current CBS analyst James Brown.

Driesell understood one thing: great players make great coaches. He was extremely organized, and he believed in the old maxim of hard work. Send your assistants out on the road and tell them to come back with players. One of his assistant coaches was Dave Pritchett.

Pritchett, now an assistant at Oral Roberts, used to brag that he only came home for a change of clothes. "Pit-Stop" Pritchett he called himself. He says he always parked his rental car in a no-parking zone, so that when it was towed he'd always know where to find it. He also, as the story goes, once rented seven rental cars in a 24-hour period. In a time when guys began making their reputations not on what they knew about the game but on how well they could sell, Pritchett was one of the early cult heroes.

Tom Abatemarco is another of the all-time recruiting cult characters. While at North Carolina State as Jimmy Valvano's assistant, he once met Pearl Washington at the airport, and as he drove out of the parking lot he ripped open his shirt to reveal a T-shirt that said "Welcome Pearl." He also used to howl like a wolf into the phone to let recruits know just how much the Wolfpack wanted them.

Just about everyone agrees that college basketball has almost become divided into two halves: the games and the recruiting. And more often than not, the recruiting has nothing to do with coaching. In this surreal world, promising high-school players often begin receiving letters from colleges when they are still freshmen, high-school coaches often wield more power than a Tammany Hall ward boss, and no one seems to think it's weird that you almost have to move in with a kid if you want to recruit him.

"There is no way to do it with dignity," says Gary Walters, who coached at Providence in the first two years of the Big East and is now a Boston stockbroker.

In Walters's second year he was recruiting a 6-9 kid from Elizabeth, New Jersey, named Stanley Wright, who was going to a Catholic high school in Maine. One Saturday afternoon in February he and the Providence academic advisor went to the kid's apartment to have him and his mother sign a letter of intent. Into a red-brick housing project they walked, through a courtyard strewn with broken glass. Grafitti scarred the walls. The hallways smelled of urine. The apartment was small and dark. The kid sat on the couch, his mother on the arm of the couch. Every once in a while she would pat him on the head. In the corner of the room was a guy from the neighborhood, who said he was there "to translate for Mrs. Wright."

The Providence academic advisor talked about the special tutoring Stanley would receive. Walters talked about all the special attention Stanley would receive because the school was small and created a family atmosphere. Outside, late-afternoon shadows lengthened across the gritty courtyard. Inside the apartment, it was getting darker. The mother kept periodically patting her son's head. The kid never spoke; he just looked straight ahead with a blank stare on his face. Walters continued talking, about ready to close the deal.

"Excuse me," the mother asked, a perplexed look on her face, "are you people from a college?"

"I think that's when I knew it was all bullshit," says Walters. "And you know what the kicker was? We couldn't get the kid into school. The whole process has become absurd."

Nevertheless, recruiting is the lifeblood of any college basketball program. The average Big East school spends about $100,000 a year on recruiting, which is now mostly computerized. This money covers airline tickets, hotels, rental cars, the endless mailings, postage, telephone calls, and glitzy recruiting videos. Recruiting films are the newest craze, and some are as costly as $30,000. And just to make sure that everyone is in step, the Big East office also periodically sends a confidential survey of each school's athletic budget to all of the schools' presidents and ADs. It is done to make sure that the bottom schools in the league keep up with the top ones in terms of expenditures.

What's more, there are a great many assistant coaches who employ any strategy to land a recruit. One of the more common is known as the "bump," the coaching euphemism for a meeting with a kid that is a neat little shuffle around the NCAA rules. If you're an assistant coach who just happens to find himself at a high-school game in the Bronx, wouldn't it be rude not to ask the kid how his family was? Surely this couldn't be counted as an official visit, could it? After all, you're in the neighborhood and just happened to bump into the kid. Some kids get more bumps in a season than an amusement park dodge-em car. Maryland supposedly used to have assistant coaches stationed at both doors of Washington, D. C., summer league games so a kid couldn't get out of the gym without getting bumped. And the coach at the wrong door would then run around the building and get the kid after the first coach had paid his respects. A double bump.

About a decade ago assistant coaches started going to all of a recruit's high-school games, not to do talent evaluation but to woo, a recruiting version of a marriage that needs fresh flowers every day. When Harold Presley was a senior in Uncasville, Connecticut, several winters back, Villanova supposedly saw every one of his high-school games. Back in the early eighties when he was a Syracuse assistant, Brendan Malone spent so much time in Newark recruiting Rafael Addison that the guys in the neighborhood started calling him "Syracuse." It's known in the trade as "baby-sitting," and the reality is that often it's all for nothing. Former Providence coach Joe Mullaney remembers the winter he was recruiting David Wingate, then a senior at Dunbar in Baltimore. Providence saw Wingate play 15 times that winter and thought they had him, only to have Thompson, who hadn't gone to one of his games, come in and swoop him up in the last minute. So much for hard work.

One of the unpleasant but all too common plays is negative recruiting. Big East coaches say the conference gets them in the door with the best kids. It also often gets them recruiting against each other, which is where the process of tearing down the other school comes in. Even the best programs have negatives attached to them: Syracuse recruits too many great players and you'll get lost in the shuffle, as happened to Earl Duncan and Keith Hughes last year, two highly recruited players who both transferred to Rutgers because they weren't comfortable with their playing time. Basketball is the third sport at Boston College, behind football and hockey. Connecticut is out in the boonies. St. John's is a commuter school, and Looie walks the ball up the court. There is no stability at Providence: four coaches in the past five years. John Thompson shuttles players in and out of games, so you will never find your rhythm as a player. No one goes to the games at Seton Hall. How close any of this is to the truth is irrelevant; it is all part of the ammunition schools use against each other.

Two years ago a story circulated that Pitt assistant John Calipari told a recruit who was also considering St. John's that Carnesecca was dying of cancer. That story spread through the league like spontaneous combustion, and it became a topic of discussion at the Big East coaches' meetings.

"Everyone talks about cheating," says Jim O'Brien of Boston College, "but the biggest thing going on is all the negative recruiting. Schools are really being critical of other schools. That happens much more than cheating. We don't do that, and I'm afraid we're being hurt because we don't. I'm not sure we're killers enough. You almost have to be a killer nowadays."

On top of all this, everyone knows recruiting is an inexact science. This year's senior class in the Big East is a great example. The top three point guards in the conference—Douglas, Barros, and Smith—were not considered great prospects coming into the league as freshmen. All are examples that evaluations of 18-year-old kids shouldn't be chiseled in stone, not even by men whose job it is to make them.

Still, recruiting is now the way that young coaches make a name for themselves. One who did is the new Providence coach Rick Barnes. His career as an assistant coach is such a fine illustration of the new world of recruiting that it's worth exploring in some depth.

He grew up in Hickory, North Carolina, a sleepy little town in the foothills of the Blue Ridge Mountains. His parents divorced when he was four, and his father left his mother with four children to raise by herself. While his mother worked, Barnes was raised mostly by his grandparents and his older sister, Sandy. Two days after her high-school graduation, Sandy was killed in an automobile accident.

"That was a tough time for me," he says. "I was going into the eighth grade and I had a hard time understanding why she was gone. I had somewhat of a bad attitude."

Basketball became his way of defining himself. One day he had gone to the local community center and befriended an older kid whose father ran the community center. Barnes soon became a fixture there. That summer a friend of his mother's gave him $56 to attend a summer basketball camp. He returned to school as the best player on the eighth-grade team, but even then he was a long way from knowing about such things as being a member of a team, and working hard, and not giving up when adversity hits you in the face—all the clichés sometimes taped to locker room walls, the clichés upon which he fashioned his life.

Eventually, his ability got him a scholarship to Lenoir-Rhyne, the local NAIA school. The dream was to one day be a great player in the ACC, maybe even a pro, and Barnes worked at it. He got up early and lifted weights. He worked day and night. But none of it ever happened. Barnes now thinks that, in a sense, he became a victim of his own intensity. Success was something he wanted so badly, he became afraid to fail and was never able to fully relax as a player. It is a lesson he has carried with him into coaching: you can never create a situation in which your players are afraid to fail.

"I was always too hard on myself," he says. "But what happened was that the work ethic I established as a kid has carried over to my coaching career."

He knew early on that he wanted to coach, mainly because the biggest role models in his life had been some of his coaches, but the original goal was to be a high-school coach. So his first year after Lenoir-Rhyne he worked at UPS from four in the morning to eight, then at a local hosiery mill, then was an assistant coach at North State Academy in Hickory. At the end of the year he decided he wanted to get into college coaching, but he didn't have any contacts. In fact, he didn't know how to go about it at all.

"We started at the bottom," says his wife, Candy.

He and Candy wrote dozens of letters and sent them out. All came back with standard rejection form letters, except for a handwritten one from Denny Crum of Louisville, saying there were no openings now but he'd keep him in mind. This gave Barnes hope. A friend knew Bobby Cremins, then at Appalachian State, so one day he drove to the mountains of Boone, North Carolina, to talk with Cremins. Cremins said he had nothing, but he did tell him that the only way to get into college coaching was to "volunteer."

One thing led to another, and through a friend he got an interview with Eddie Biedenbach, the new coach at Davidson, Lefty Driesell's old school. The interview was for eight in the morning. Barnes, who was working all night at UPS at the time, showed up two hours early in his only suit and sat outside Biedenbach's office. And sat and sat and sat. He had been there for 11 hours by the time Biedenbach walked in and realized he had forgotten their appointment. He felt so bad that he hired Barnes. The job title said part-time assistant. The salary was $3,000. The job description was to help Biedenbach run his summer camp. To supplement his income, Barnes worked part time in a nearby lumber mill.

If it was a fringe job, it was a fringe job in basketball. Plus he joined a staff that knew the value of recruiting at a time when recruiting was becoming not only sophisticated but almost a profession in itself.

Into Davidson's rich tradition Barnes immersed himself. Legendary "Pit-Stop" Pritchett had been the coach at Davidson the year before, and his legacy endured. The staff included John Kochan, later to work for Driesell at Maryland. There was Jeff Bzdelik, now the assistant coach of the Washington Bullets. There was Bob McKillop, now the coach at Lutheran High School on Long Island. And the year before there had been Tom Abatemarco, one of the all-time recruiting cult figures.

"It was a great environment for me," says Barnes. "I learned so much just from sitting around listening to those guys talk. Biedenbach had been the assistant at N. C. State when they recruited David Thompson, Tom Burleson, and Monte Towe, the team that later won the national title. Kochan and Abatemarco had been with Dave Pritchett at Davidson. Pritchett wrote the best letters to recruits that I ever saw. I learned from Kochan that when you recruit you've got to ask the tough question. He used to say, 'We don't want any guys in three-piece suits working here. You got to get down in the gutter. You got to get it done.'

"Candy and I lived in a house behind the all-night 7-11. Every time John Kochan wanted me he would come by and shine his headlights into the window. To this day he calls me the '7-11 kid.' But early on I learned the value of recruiting. You can't always outcoach people, but you can outwork them."

The next year Kochan went to Maryland and Barnes became the part-time assistant. Mostly he recruited. "I was all out," he says. "I was gone. Up and down the East Coast. I mean, I'm *getting after it.*"

One of his trips was to Tuscaloosa, Alabama, trying to recruit the son of Coach Wimp Sanderson. On the surface it was nothing out of the ordinary. But he had hitched a ride from North Carolina to Birmingham in a 12-wheel truck driven by his brother. He didn't get the kid, but he did meet Sanderson. Seven years later he would work for him at Alabama.

He was at Davidson for a year before going to George Mason in Fairfax, Virginia, just outside of D.C. Joe Harrington, who had once been Driesell's assistant, had just gotten the job and he was looking for a young go-getter. Kochan kept telling Harrington he had to hire Rick Barnes.

One day Harrington was at the University of Maryland with Kochan. It was seven in the morning.

"Call the office at Davidson," Kochan said, "and I bet you he'll be there working."

Barnes was. Harrington offered $12,500. Barnes, who was making $5,600, held out for $15,000, afraid of the cost of living in suburban Virginia. He got the raise and got the job. But three months later Biedenbach came back after him. A full-time assistant's job had opened, and Biedenbach wanted him back. He offered him $18,000.

"I was going to go back to Davidson," he says, "but one day I came outside in the apartment complex where we were living and Candy was lying by the pool. I was wearing a Davidson T-shirt, my way of telling her that we were going back. But she said to me that if I went back there, I would always be thought of as the volunteer coach, the part-time coach, the kid. You know what? She was right. It was the best decision I ever made. And you know what? A year later Eddie Biedenbach got fired."

It was at Mason that Barnes earned a reputation as a great recruiter, someone who would, in his parlance, flat-out get after it. He was out every night at Mason. It was before the NCAA had changed the recruiting rules, creating "dead periods," when no recruiting is allowed. This was a free-for-all time when being an assistant meant all but living on the road. He went to high-school games. He went to camps. He went to summer-league games in D.C. He had come of age in a recruiting environment, and now he was applying the lessons he'd learned.

It was also at Mason that he quickly learned how recruiting works. His first year there he was recruiting a kid named Andy Bolden from Granby High School in Norfolk, where Driesell had gotten his coaching start. He and Harrington brought Bolden in for a visit, and afterward Bolden said he was coming. It was Barnes's job to call the kid when he got home after the recruiting visit and make sure he hadn't changed his mind.

"But when I call him, he says he has a problem," Barnes remembers, "and he puts this older friend of his on the phone. His friend says Andy really loved his visit and wants to come, but there's a problem. Seems he already has told another school that he's going to sign with them, and seems that this other coach is due at the house any minute to close the deal, and seems that there is this party already scheduled to celebrate. So I ask him what the other school is and he says Appalachian State. I can't believe it. It had only been three years ago that Bobby Cremins had helped me. So now I don't know what to do, but Bolden's friend says he really wants to go to Mason and what should he do? I tell him to tell Bolden not to sign anything. He says he's not sure he can tell him that. I tell him he has to be strong. So that night I'm on the phone to Bolden for an hour and Cremins is downstairs in the living room. Then when Bolden hangs up, he tells me to call him every ten minutes. Eventually, Cremins gets tired of all this, leaves, and we get the kid. But I didn't feel good about it, and I told Joe Harrington this. He says to me, 'Hey, baby, that's recruiting. That's getting it done.' "

Five years later Barnes went to Alabama to work for Wimp Sanderson, then to Ohio State with Gary Williams, before coming back to Mason for his first head coaching job. A year later he was in the Big East.

It's widely assumed within the conference that Syracuse and Georgetown start off with the biggest advantages in the quest for players. Syracuse has the Carrier Dome, college basketball's biggest stage. No longer do they only recruit kids in the Northeast, like in the old days. The Dome and the incredible power of television have made them a national team.

Many believe that Syracuse doesn't really have to recruit that much, that the presence of the Dome and the fact the Orangemen sometimes seem to be on television more than the "Cosby Show" have created a situation where all Boeheim has to do is select who he wants. Everyone tells the story of how Stevie Thompson used to come home from school in Los Angeles and there were the Orangemen on ESPN, playing in front of 30,000 people in the Carrier Dome.

But the perception is not true, says Bernie Fine.

Fine, the long-time Syracuse assistant coach, was the student manager on Syracuse teams Boeheim played on. A former high-school coach in Syracuse, he had no intention of ever coaching in college until Boeheim got the job. Now he's in his 13th year as an assistant. In the beginning he recruited in New York and drove everywhere. Now Wayne Morgan covers metropolitan New York, Baltimore, and Washington, D.C., and Fine essentially covers everything else.

"We look for players who want to get out and go," he says. "We go to the big camps and subscribe to the scouting services. Our style of play and the fact that we're on TV a lot really help, but we really have to work at it, too. I recruited King Rice, the kid who went to North Carolina, since he was in the eighth grade. But no one cares if you come close with a kid. Close only counts in horseshoes and grenades. But we don't negatively recruit. We tell the kid why we think he should come to Syracuse: we have mandatory study halls, we monitor the kid's academic progress, and 34 out of 36 kids have graduated. But you never know why a kid selects the school he does. He'll tell you that he went somewhere because he liked the color of the uniforms, or that he went for a visit and met a certain girl, or that he went somewhere for a visit and didn't like the food. Even after all these years, you never know."

The other national team in the Big East is Georgetown. In a sense they have become black America's team. Thompson can seemingly get any black kid in the country, and he has a tremendous advantage when he goes on a home visit because, in the words of a fellow coach, "He can tell black mothers what they want to hear."

Not that anyone is really too sure just why Thompson gets involved with the kids he does. As with everything else, Georgetown is very guarded when it comes to recruiting. Usually, everyone in the league knows who everybody else is dealing with. Except Georgetown.

One theory about Georgetown recruiting is that Thompson spends little time these days personally evaluating high-school talent, and relies on his assistant coaches to make evaluations. The other theory is that Thompson refuses to woo anybody. The kid either wants to come to Georgetown or he doesn't. There is no seduction process. Another theory is that Thompson puts a lot of stock in a kid's background. If it's unstructured, he gets wary.

This approach has its drawbacks. This year the big fish that got away is Kenny Anderson, a senior at Archbishop Molloy in Queens, where he played on the same team as St. John's Robert Werdann. He's generally considered to be the best guard in the country. New York City superscout Tom Konchalski calls him the best guard to come out of the city in 30 years. Not bad when you consider that in the past decade New York City has produced Mark Jackson, Kenny Smith, and Pearl Washington.

When he was in eighth grade, Anderson envisioned himself going to Georgetown and playing for Thompson. Like many black kids across the country, he had adopted the Hoyas, just as Mourning had as a kid growing up in Virginia. Later, it was assumed Anderson was going to North Carolina, following in the footsteps of Kenny Smith, a Molloy alumnus. Adding to this theory was that Smith's older brother has been a sort of unofficial advisor to Anderson.

At the start of his senior year Anderson's potential choices came down to five schools: three from the ACC—North Carolina, Georgia Tech, and Duke—and Georgetown and Syracuse of the Big East. When John Thompson didn't come for a visit, Georgetown was eliminated.

"Georgetown was the main interest six months ago," Jack Curran, the long-time coach at Molloy, told the *New York Times*, "but then the Olympics got in the way of his recruiting and Kenny really wanted to be recruited."

On the other hand, Jim Boeheim believes that over a four-year period he saw Anderson play more than any other head coach. As the school year started in September, he thought he was going to get him. Anderson had told Wayne Morgan, Boeheim's assistant, that he was coming. The Syracuse coaching staff wanted his mother to accompany Anderson on his visit to the Syracuse campus, and she said she didn't have the money. Then she showed up on her son's visit to Georgia Tech, where he later signed, causing the Syracuse staff to think something strange was going on.

"Everybody dreams of playing in front of 30,000 people," Anderson said in the *Times*. "That's very tempting. But you have to look beyond that. You have to think about your life after college."

The other great guard in the Northeast that got away is Bobby Hurley, from St. Anthony's in Jersey City. Seton Hall thought they had him locked up. They planned for him to come in and start next year, taking the place of Gerald Greene. Instead, he signed with Duke, sending the Hall's recruiting year into almost a crisis situation.

If it hasn't been a recruiting year like last year, that doesn't mean it's been bad. Pittsburgh, for one, is well on its way to having a great recruiting year, one of the best in the country. Last year they got shut out. With a great freshman class, Paul Evans decided to recruit only four great players. They all went somewhere else. Now they've already signed three potential great ones: Jamaal Faulkner, a 6-7 forward from Christ the King in Queens, one of the most highly recruited players in the East; Chris McNeil, a forward from Oak Hill Academy in Virgina; and 6-7 forward Danny Griffin from Los Angeles. They are also supposedly leading with Eric Mobley, from New Rochelle, New York, considered to be the best schoolboy center in the Northeast. The only drawback is that they could all be Prop 48 kids and would have to sit out their freshman year.

Villanova has also done well, having won James Bryson from Largo, Maryland. Interestingly, as of now Bryson is a projected Prop 48, and if his test scores don't improve later in the season he will be the first Prop 48 kid Massimino has taken. Syracuse has signed Conrad McRae, a 6-9 center from New York City, and St. John's has corralled two local guards, David Cain and Carl Beckett.

And how has Rick Barnes fared?

He has received word from the NCAA that Orlando Vega will not be penalized for leaving Arizona after signing a national letter of intent. (The fear was that he would only have one and a half years of eligibility left if he had enrolled at Providence.) Now he will have two and a half years and he already has enrolled in school. Barnes considers him a player with big-time potential and envisions him as his go-to guy, the game's new euphemism for a guy who can get his own shot at the end of games and score, not someone who needs an offense to get him shots. Vega is also a prize catch in that he's the type of player who Providence has never been able to recruit coming out of high school, someone who has a lot of offers from big-time schools. The overwhelming majority of their stars through the years have been kids who made their reputations at Providence, not in high school.

They have also heard that Trent Forbes, the Massachusetts schoolboy guard who was supposedly deciding between Maryland and Seton Hall, wants to come to Providence. But not without ruffling a few feathers within the conference. It seems that two summers ago, when Forbes attended the Providence College camp, he was befriended by Pop Lewis, a Providence player at the time. Lewis and Forbes have remained friendly, to the point that Lewis occasionally visits Forbes. It was during one of those visits that Forbes told Lewis he wants to come to Providence. So Lewis asked Barnes if he were interested. Barnes said sure. The problem is that Lewis is employed by Providence College as a minority recruiter and he visited Forbes during one of the NCAA's dead times, when coaches are not allowed to have any contact with recruits. So Seton Hall and Boston College hollered foul. Barnes said no foul: since Lewis is not a coach, it is just one of those flukes, another example of the vagaries of recruiting.

"Most of the time you work your butt off and get nothing out of it," says Barnes, "and then there's something like this when you do nothing and it falls in your lap."

Making the Trent Forbes case even stranger is that not only did Forbes never make an official visit to Providence, he seems to be one kid who was lured by the thought of less playing time, not more, almost unheard of in this day and age.

"Seton Hall was telling him that they wanted him to come in and play the point right away," Barnes says, "but I don't know if that's what the kid really wanted. I think he thought that might be too much pressure on him. We told him we wanted him to come in and play behind Carlton Screen for a year. To play against Carlton every day in practice and maybe play eight to ten minutes a game next year. He liked that. He knows he's coming out of a weak high-school league and isn't ready yet to play in the Big East. But I like him. He's got great quickness, he's an athlete, and he can pass the ball. I think he can be a great defensive player for us."

This comes on the heels of Barnes's involvement with Arron Bain, a 6-7 forward from Flint Hill Academy in Fairfax, Virginia. All year long Bain has been one of the most highly recruited players in the East, especially after he failed to sign with anyone in November. The word around the league is that he will sign with Villanova in the spring, but Barnes has become involved. He is friendly with Stu Vetter, the Flint Hill coach, and when he discovered that Bain's father had New England roots he started recruiting him in earnest.

"I want to make sure I see him at least once a week," he says.

"For how long?" he is asked.

Barnes smiles that little-boy smile, and when he speaks you can hear the backwoods in his voice.

"Until I get it done," he says. "I don't know if I can out-coach anybody in this league, but I'll tell you what: I'm going to get players. You can count on that. We are going to get it done."

9

THE CREAM RISES TO THE TOP

FEBRUARY 13

There is nothing better in the Big East than a Syracuse-Georgetown game. Since the beginning, they have been the league's two glamour teams. St. John's has had their moments, going to the Final Four in 1985. Boston College had some good teams in the early years of the league. Villanova was the national champ in 1985. Providence came out of nowhere to the Final Four in 1987. Pittsburgh won the league title last year and shared it the year before. But Syracuse and Georgetown have been the two patriarchs for 10 years now, and when they play, it's always an event. Tonight there are 123 accredited reporters, from as far away as Dallas, Denver, and San Diego.

It is also a game with all sorts of plots and subplots.

Not only has Georgetown won the last five games in a row against Syracuse, the Orangemen have lost their last eight here in the Capital Centre. The game features a match-up between Sherman Douglas of Syracuse and Charles Smith of Georgetown, two point guards who grew up on the D. C. playgrounds and now are leading contenders to be the league's player of the year. There is the drama of Douglas's last game in the Capital Centre, the same Sherman Douglas from Springarn High School in nearby Washington, who dreamed of going to Georgetown but was not recruited by John Thompson, who supposedly considered Douglas too undisciplined. Douglas has always played down any potential controversy and has often said everything turned out for the best. "If I was at Georgetown, I'd probably be rotating with two or three other guards. Here it's just me." And this is the first meeting between Alonzo Mourning and Billy Owens, the two celebrated freshmen.

It has become their fate to be linked together, in the way Bird and Magic have been. Who is better now? Who will one day be better? The arguments started back in high school and they still continue.

Mourning entered the Big East as the glamour player, mostly due to his summer experience with the Olympic team. His star billing has left Owens less than thrilled. "We never played head to head, so how could anyone tell?" he asked before the season.

Mourning has been an impact player since the first game of the season, as advertised. The Hoyas needed an inside presence, and he immediately filled the bill. Owens's progress has been slower. He joined a team with four veteran starters, and on nights earlier in the season he seemed an afterthought in the Syracuse offense. Douglas runs the team. Derrick Coleman is the first inside option. Stevie Thompson gets the ball in transition. Matt Roe is the designated shooter. Owens gets the leftovers. But over the past several games he's been getting more shots and averaging 15 points.

Syracuse arrives ranked ninth in the country, 21–4 overall and tied for second in the Big East with Seton Hall at 7–4. Since their atrocious 1–4 start, they have won seven in a row. One reason is that Douglas's back is better. Since the night a few weeks ago when the Orangemen lost to Connecticut, he has been the Douglas of old: 25 points in a win over Notre Dame and an unbelievable 22 assists against Providence, a performance that garnered him Big East player-of-the-week honors. The Orangemen have all five starters averaging in double figures, with Thompson at 18.6, Douglas at 18, and Coleman at 17. Coleman has also broken Rony Seikaly's all-time Syracuse rebounding record and is ranked fourth nationally in rebounding and blocks.

Georgetown is ranked second in the country, 18–3 overall. They are now 8–2 in the Big East, after being upset in the Pittsburgh Civic Arena two days earlier by Pitt in a game in which Mourning fouled out. The Hoyas are led in scoring by Smith with 19 points a game, Jaren Jackson with 15, and Mourning with 13. Mourning also continues to lead the country in blocked shots with 6 a game.

The Capital Centre is sold out. The ESPN team of Mike Gorman and Billy Raftery are in place. Rejection Row, the group of Georgetown kids who hold up cardboard hands to indicate blocked shots, are in a line under one of the baskets. With only a couple of exceptions, they are all white.

The starting five are introduced and meet at center court for the perfunctory slapping of palms, then go back to the foul-line area. It is the season of the "low-five" in handshaking etiquette, and all players give quick, perfunctory handshakes. Few of them show any emotion.

Georgetown starts Mourning at center, Jackson and John Turner at the forward positions, and Smith and Dwayne Bryant at the guards. They are in their gray uniforms with the dark blue trim. Virtually every team in the country that plays at home wears white uniforms. Not the Hoyas. Syracuse is in their orange uniforms. They start Douglas and Roe in the backcourt, Coleman at center, and Owens and Thompson at the forwards.

In what has become a commonplace, Roe is the only white player on the floor. In fact, he is one of the few white starters in the Big East. There is Sean Miller at Pitt, Matt Brust at St. John's, Tom Greis and Marc Dowdell at Villanova, Marty Conlon and Matt Palazzi at Providence. And there's Australian Andrew Gaze at Seton Hall.

This is not an issue that's discussed openly. The delicate topic of race is one that no one really wants to talk about in big-time college sports. Instead, people tend to talk in euphemisms and buzz words. For instance, when coaches talk about recruiting more "athletes," they are usually referring to "blacks." Certainly, college basketball coaches realized long ago that you can't win without black players, but there's also the feeling that as more of the players have become black, the game has become more athletic, at the expense of fundamentals.

Some of this is evolutionary, of course. Every sport goes through subtle changes over a period of time. What remains is the theory that there are two ways to play the game: the "white" way, the traditional textbook basketball with its emphasis on fundamentals; and the "black" way, which is more playground oriented, emphasizing style and flair. The "white" game relies more on perimeter shooting and setting a series of screens to open up the jump shot, while the "black" game tends to be more individually oriented and drives to the hoop. One of the traditional reasons given for the difference is that white players often practice their shooting by themselves in their backyards, while black players learn the game in the playgrounds, where you must take the ball to the hoop.

The complications arise when the two ways of playing the game clash. Jim O'Brien says he often thinks how much the college game has changed since he played it nearly 20 years ago: though the players are quicker, more athletic, he has seen a deterioration of passing skills and certain fundamentals that were once taken for granted. This is one of the reasons why pressing defenses are so successful nowadays: they take advantage of a lack of passing skills.

Much of coaching is an attempt to establish a structure to the team so that the individual is subordinated to the team, making the whole stronger than the sum of the individual parts. The common complaint of players, from biddy leagues to the pros, is that the coach "won't let me play my game." But every coach has his own style of play. When Carnesecca is criticized at all, it is for taking playground kids and trying to make them play the style of ball he learned long ago: walk the ball up the court, run a pattern, take the good shot. In other words, play "white." Massimino plays the same way, and so does Calhoun. Evans and Carlesimo tend to give their teams more offensive freedom, but their teams would never be classified as running teams. The two teams in the Big East with an offense that gives the players the most freedom are Syracuse and Providence. And Georgetown? Thompson also plays "white" on offense. One interesting theory holds that he's well aware of the stereotype of blacks as undisciplined playground players, and he wants to show that blacks can play as well fundamentally as whites.

"Undisciplined—that means nigger," Thompson once told Bil Gilbert of *Sports Illustrated.* "They're all big and can jump like kangaroos and eat watermelon in the locker room, but they can't play as a team and they choke under pressure. It's the idea the black man doesn't have the intelligence or character to practice self-control. In basketball it's been a self-fulfilling prophecy. A white coach recruits a good black player. . . . He puts him in a free-lance, one-on-one role. Other black kids see this and think that's how they're expected to play."

So Thompson's teams are always disciplined offensively. It's his way of battling the stereotype.

Both teams begin the game playing man to man. Georgetown also begins in a press, and Syracuse's strategy is to throw over it for the layup. Midway through the first half the Hoyas lead by 8 and the Capital Centre is bedlam. Before the end of the half Syracuse changes into a zone, and the Hoya offense suddenly seems to downshift. At the half the Orangemen lead by 2, and Coleman already has 16 points.

But Coleman never seems to get the ball in the second half, and the Hoyas gradually take control of the game. At one point Mourning dunks, then runs back down the court, throwing his fist in the air. This is a rare show of emotion for a Georgetown player, for the Hoyas traditionally display all the facial expressions of accountants at tax time. Mourning's passion for the game is always evident, though, his emotions all over his face. A few minutes later he wrestles an offensive rebound away from Owens and dunks it backwards over his head. With a little under six minutes to play, the Hoyas are up 49–43, and the vaunted Syracuse transition game is stuck in first gear. The Orangemen cut the lead to 4, but Smith hits a big jumper over Douglas on the right side, then blocks a Douglas drive in the lane before scoring again to put the game out of reach, 61–54.

In the individual match-up with Douglas, Smith has won this round. Smith has scored 16 points, shooting 6 of 9 from the field. Douglas has struggled from the field, going 5 of 15. Mourning has also won his personal battle with Owens, with 14 points, 9 rebounds, and 5 blocked shots. Owens, who fouled out with 32 seconds remaining, scored just 5 points, shooting 1 of 9 from the floor.

Afterwards, Mourning is asked about his ability to block shots.

"It's not something you go into the gym and practice," says Alonzo, who once had 27 blocks in a summer-league game. "I think blocking shots is a God-given gift. Bill Russell made shot blocking into an art. I'm still learning, I'm still working, for Russell blocked a shot, but he also kept the ball in bounds. Coach Thompson talks about him all the time. He tells me Bill Russell was a great defensive player because he took advantage of all the things that he knew how to do. And he never tried to do the things he couldn't do."

"Did you ever see him play?" he is asked.

"I'm too young," he says. "But I've seen a great deal of film clippings on him."

In a narrow locker room on the other side of the Capital Centre, Billy Owens sits in front of his locker. A group of reporters hovers around him. A year ago he was finishing one of the most glittering careers in high-school basketball history, leading his team to four Pennsylvania state titles in a row. He had scored over 3,000 points, second in state history. (This year, with Owens gone, Carlisle High School lost 18 of its first 19 games.) He was so good last year as a high-school senior that Dick Vitale called him the next Magic Johnson—on national TV, no less—and Howard Garfinkel called him the high-school player of the decade.

Boeheim has told him to forget about the comparisons, to just go out and be Billy Owens, but he has not been allowed to be that, and Owens sometimes seems affected by it.

Earlier in the season he told David Ramsey of the *Syracuse Herald Journal* that he didn't like people yelling things at him in the Carrier Dome before games. "They ain't my friends and I ain't their friend," he said. "They're trying to put pressure on me. They yell at me when I warm up: When are you going to score? When are you going to do something? I just block it out because they don't know what's going on. They're probably just drunk anyway."

He has said his situation is different from Mourning's because he joined a veteran team, while Alonzo came to a team that needed an inside presence. Mourning is a great shot blocker, and that's what Georgetown needed.

"I never had any doubts that he was a great player," he says now. "I was looking forward to playing against him. I think I was a little too pumped up to play. There was too much made of the match-up. I tried to do too much. I was moving too fast. Any time he blocked one of my shots I was just thinking, Shit, I know everybody's talking. Everybody's saying he was the better senior coming out of high school."

"When did you first meet Alonzo?"

"At the Nike camp when we were juniors in high school. Then we played on the same McDonald's team. He didn't used to be able to block my shot. When we used to play, like at practice for the Dapper Dan, he could never get my shot. Tonight he timed it well. Anytime I beat my man he was there to block my shot. He got my first two shots."

Owens shakes his head at the memory of it.

"We even visited Syracuse the same weekend together. We used to talk a little bit about going to the same school. We started talking about that at the Nike camp. But Georgetown never came after me. So I just picked Syracuse."

"Would you have gone to Georgetown if they had come after you?"

"I might have. But I'm happy at Syracuse. The program is great. The social life is great for me, and the academics are going well."

He starts putting his uniform into an equipment bag, seemingly oblivious to the reporters jockeying for position to hear him.

"Can you say that now he's one up on you?"

"You can say that," says Owens. "I'm 0–1 against him. We used to talk about it when we were juniors in high school, about who was going to be number one next year."

"Do you think you and Alonzo are going to be competing with each other for the next four years, the way Ewing and Mullin did?"

"It's going to be that way every time we play," he says softly, his voice devoid of emotion. "Every time we play, that will be the big match-up. We came off great high-school careers. Everyone expects a lot from both of us. But the Big East Conference is tough, and I'm finding that out early. And I'm going away from the game remembering one thing: Alonzo Mourning is going to be in the middle for George-town for the next two or three years, and I've got to go against him every time if I want to be champion of the Big East."

Back in the interview room, Boeheim is at the podium, and he is testy. Late night with Jimmy Boeheim.

"I thought we played very good defense, but everyone ignores that and says that Syracuse just runs up and down the court and doesn't play defense. Everyone says we never win any big games. We have won 76 percent of our games for years, but we supposedly never win any big games. I get tired of defending our team. Is there something wrong with alley-oop passes? I think it's a good play. UCLA used to throw them and no one ever criticized John Wooden for being flashy. I think we play pretty good defense and that's why we win games."

When asked about Owens, he looks even angrier. "Billy has played great all year. He's been excellent defensively all year. He passes well. He hasn't been releasing the ball well the last three or four games, but he was an off-and-on outside shooter in high school, too. There are not many 6-9 guys making 17-foot jump shots in college basketball. Un-fortunately, he's coming off a senior year in high school where he scored a lot of points, but if you look at what he did the other years in high school, you'll see that he didn't score a lot. This year he joined a team with three top scorers, so he shouldn't be expected to score a lot of points. He's done everything we have asked him to do."

He pauses and looks around the room at the few reporters who are left.

"I don't defend Billy Owens, I just state the facts. I get tired of defending our whole team."

FEBRUARY 14

The Villanova team has gathered for another pregame meeting in the student union. In the front of the room, behind a table that is being transformed into a makeshift altar, is the Reverend Bernard Lazor, a silver-haired man in a white robe over his priest's black. He has been the Villanova team chaplain for 10 years now.

There is a knock on the door. Massimino answers it. Two guys in dark suits have come to deliver a Valentine Day poem to freshman David Miller. With a devilish gleam in his eye, Massimino tells Miller to stand up. When he does, the two guys in the suits start reading the poem. The rest of the players are all but rolling in the aisles.

"Is this from your girl back home?" Massimino asks, and the players laugh louder.

Miller tries to avoid the question, but Massimino has already caught on. "Oh, I see," he says. Miller tries to explain, but his defense is drowned out in hoots and catcalls from his teammates.

You would never know this is a team struggling.

A few minutes later Massimino reads a short passage from the Bible. Then the Reverend Lazor delivers a short sermon about having the strength to go on when things are not going well. The truly courageous are the ones who fight through adversity. His sermons are always different, usually based on a passage from the Bible linked to what the team is going through. For the Wildcats are now 4–6 in the Big East, tied for seventh. If Seton Hall is the big surprise, Villanova is the flipside.

The players file into a large auditorium next door and go

over the scouting report on Providence. Twenty-three pages long, it has been devised by Massimino's son, Tommy. Each assistant coach prepares for certain opponents and takes charge of going over the report to the players. Tonight's game plan is to control the tempo, find their three-point shooters early, and make it a "one-shot game." The scouting report contains pages of Providence's offensive formations and extensive information on each of the Providence players: their tendencies on the court, where they like to shoot from, et cetera.

"We knew what Seton Hall was going to do better than they did," mutters Massimino, referring to Villanova's recent loss to the Pirates. "But you still have to execute, or what good is it?"

Half an hour later, Doug West is in his dorm in the middle of the campus, just up the walkway from the Connelly Center. He knows tonight's game is vital. The Wildcats need some wins or they can forget about a return trip to the NCAA Tournament.

"In the beginning of the year when we weren't playing well, our attitude was that it's a long season and we can't get down on ourselves," he says. "Now it's not a long season anymore."

Throughout the preseason there was talk that this team was similar to the 1985 team: a senior team, experienced, poised for a great season, ranked in everyone's top 15. That hadn't happened. No one is really too sure why. Too soft? Not enough perimeter shooting? No real leaders? All of the above? Take your pick. But now the Cats are 13–11 and have all but been written off, especially after losing to Georgetown in the Spectrum by 15. The following day in the *Philadelphia Inquirer*, columnist Bill Lyons wrote that this year's team no longer responds to the Massimino magic. Rollie has reached the bottom of his psychological bag, and now there's nothing left.

"It's little things," says West, shaking his head. "I think we just let some things slip away. We're disappointed in ourselves. I don't really know what it is."

In a sense, Villanova's year has mirrored West's personal

year. He has not shot well consistently from the perimeter. He also hasn't gotten much help. Though he has heard people say his individual game has suffered in Massimino's patterned halfcourt offense, he says his coach's emphasis on defense and fundamentals has definitely made him a better player.

"When I first came here, I couldn't guard that fire hydrant over there," he says, looking down the hall.

Now he's starting to think about getting a chance to play in the NBA next year. He knows his career at Villanova is winding down, even if he's not quite ready to see it end just yet.

"This has become my home," says West. "Coach Mass told me when he recruited me that coming here would make me a better person, and that's what happened. I'm more mature. I deal with people better. It's been great. I wouldn't trade these past four years for anything."

Before the game Dick "Hoops" Weiss sits in the press room of the Spectrum. He works for the *Philadelphia Daily News*, and in a sense he's the dean of Eastern basketball writers. There might not be another sportswriter in the country who sees more games every winter than he does.

At 41, he has grown up with Eastern basketball. He grew up in Drexel Hill, a Philadelphia suburb, back when the Big Five—Temple, Villanova, LaSalle, St. Joe's, and Penn—was one of the biggest rivalries in college basketball. As young as 10 years old, he was going to the old college doubleheaders in the Palestra, the old hoop house on the Penn campus that is the spiritual home of college basketball in Philadelphia.

When he graduated from Temple he became a sportswriter, essentially because "I liked being at the games, and writing about them was the price you had to pay." He started at the *Trenton Times*, then went to Camden, and eventually ended up with the *Daily News*.

In 1969 he began going to a high-school all-star game in Scranton, in which the best players in the state were showcased. In the early seventies he started going to Five Star, the showcase summer camp run by New York superscout

Howard Garfinkel. The camps were starting to change the
game, although no one really knew it then. It was here that
he got to know the coaches, talk to them, drink with them,
and he began seeing the game through their eyes.

"That's where I got to know everybody," he says. "Guys
like Rick Pitino and Pete Gillen and Mike Fratello worked
the camp then. Those guys loved to teach. You really learned
the game watching them work. And when I was growing up,
you could go out, have a beer with all the coaches, and sit
around with them all night. Now you can't have a damn
drink with them without going through their agent. Now
everyone wants a piece of the TV pie. It used to be that
people went into the game because they wanted to coach
children, not make money off them. That part has really
changed. That really stings a bit. But to really understand
the game, you have to look at the way things used to be,
not the way they are now. Because the roots of the game are
in the fifties and the sixties, not the eighties.

"My passion for the game has never changed. My palms
still get sweaty before the doubleheader at the Final Four.
But now it's become very corporate. The essence of the
game is still there, but it's radically different than it used to
be. Recruiting is the most important part of the game now.
There are no geniuses anymore unless you have the players
to go with them. Everyone now wants to recruit the best
team, not coach the best team. Every radio talk show I go
on, 70 percent of the calls are about recruiting."

Weiss began to see basketball change in the East with the
formation of the Big East.

"It's almost created a pro-style atmosphere," he says.
"The New York papers used to cover St. John's and nothing
else. Now most of the major papers cover the Big East.
That was unheard of in the old days."

Weiss is asked about Massimino, since after the scene in
the Hartford Civic Center several Connecticut writers blasted
Massimino for being pompous and arrogant.

"With me he's been terrific because I knew him when he
was an assistant," says Weiss. "You have to understand that
as late as 1979 he was only making $21,000. It's been like a

rocket. He built the program for the most part with kids who weren't that good, and he's a very proud man. He's very protective of what he's accomplished. But I'll tell you what. His kids love him, and isn't that the bottom line for a coach? Does it really matter that there are people who think he's arrogant? He's not a good loser, and I've learned to avoid him in postgame interview situations. But would you rather have him be plastic and say everything's fine, or have him be honest? He's a high-strung, emotional man who rides the crest. The bottom line is he's great with his kids, and I've never heard him publicly hurt a kid. Harold Presley and Harold Jenson had awful freshman years for him, and he never said a thing about it. He made a call to get Gary McLain a job in Holland when he could have blackballed him and everyone would have understood. But he didn't."

The John "Jake" Nevin Field House is named for the legendary long-time trainer who died of Lou Gehrig's disease shortly after Villanova won the Final Four in 1985. Throughout the last years of Nevin's life, Massimino always had him travel with the team as part of the family. Sitting in his wheelchair at the end of the Villanova bench, Nevin became the unofficial good-luck charm of the Villanova team. The field house is the infamous "Cat House," once one of the biggest homecourt advantages in college basketball. In back of it rises the sleekly modern duPont Pavilion, the $15 million complex that opened in 1986.

A large blue banner proclaiming Villanova University the 1985 national champions hangs in one corner. The students, all fresh scrubbed and overwhelmingly white, sit in a long section of bleachers that extends out from behind the basket near the Villanova bench. On the bench next to Rollie is Mario Andretti, the race-car driver. This is the second time Massimino's designated an Italian-American on the bench as an honorary coach. Nine days earlier in the Spectrum, in a national TV game against Georgetown, he included Dodger manager Tommy Lasorda, in direct violation of Big East rules. Before the season Gavitt had sent a confidential memo to all the coaches, the gist of which was that if they criticized the officials or a fellow coach, they could be suspended for the next game. Included in the edict was a notice that only university personnel could sit on the bench during games.

So much for Big East rules.

Massimino and Lasorda first met at an Italian-American affair and became fast friends. Lasorda invited Massimino to Los Angeles for a Dodgers game, later followed by a dinner with Frank Sinatra. Massimino was even a celebrity bat boy for a Dodgers game. Afterward, Lasorda gave Massimino the telephone number of the Dodgers' dugout, and last summer Massimino would occasionally call and talk to Lasorda in the middle of a game. He also helped Massimino get his Rolaids commercial.

After the Georgetown game, Thompson said he was astounded when he looked over and saw Lasorda on the Villanova bench. He told Massimino, "I don't believe it. You brought another one of those Italians with you. Who are you going to have next, the pope?"

Tonight it's Mario Andretti. The rumor is that next week when Villanova plays Pitt in Pittsburgh, wrestler Bruno Sammartino will be on the bench. There are a couple of theories why Massimino is doing this. One, it's a way of showing his AD, Ted Aceto, that he will do anything he wants, rules or no rules. Another is that he's going to do what he wants, period. Rollie's defense is that in the past, he's had people who were critically ill on his bench. When asked what people may think of this extended basketball family, he said, "I really don't care, quite honestly. I worry about my shop. I worry about what we do and how we do things. That's the critical part."

Massimino's public stance is that he will not discuss his team's chances of getting into the NCAA Tournament. But certainly this is a vital game for the Cats.

Providence is another team fighting to get into the tournament. After beginning the season with 13 straight wins, they are now in the middle of the Big East season, and the wins come slowly. They have not been slumping as much as playing better teams. They are now 6–4 in the league, 17–4 overall. The consensus is that two more wins will make them a shoo-in for the NCAA Tournament.

This is another hard-fought, defense-oriented game in which nothing comes easy. Villanova leads by 1 at the half, 34–33, but the game goes back and forth in the second half. Kenny Wilson, the Villanova point guard, gets in foul trouble, forcing Massimino to play two freshmen, Chris Walker and David Miller, against the Providence pressure defense. It is a bad match-up for Villanova, since the Friars' strength is in their backcourt of Carlton Screen and Eric Murdock, certainly one of the best backcourts in the Big East. They are the focus of the Providence press and lead the league in steals.

Providence leads by 3 with 47 seconds left, but the game goes into overtime when Rodney Taylor makes one of two foul shots in the dying seconds to force the game into overtime. Villanova has escaped.

They are in serious foul trouble, though, during the overtime period. Wilson has fouled out. Greis has fouled out. Freshman starter Marc Dowdell has fouled out. Taylor fouls out. The Cats are now playing with Miller and Walker in the backcourt, West, Massey, and freshman Greg Woodard. The tallest player is West, a stringy 6-6 and normally a guard. Even so, they hang on to win by 3, 86–83.

Massimino is elated. He comes into the postgame press conference complete with his omnipresent postgame cigar. His blue shirt is stained with sweat.

"For a team that's supposed to be on the bubble, our kids really responded down the stretch," he says. "Especially our three freshmen. That was a great college basketball game."

Like any great motivator, he always believes that if the right buttons are pushed, the right words said, mountains can be moved. It is at the core of his coaching philosophy, and history bears him out. A few years ago, dissatisfied with his team's play in a late-season game against Pitt, he told the starters at halftime they had three minutes to play better or they were coming out. After three minutes of the second half, he pulled everybody and lost by 30. Six weeks later he won the national title.

"Did you know that at one point in the game West was 1 for 10?" he is asked.

Rollie looks surprised. "One for 10, huh? I should have sat him down. That's how smart I am."

Half an hour later Barnes is sitting in the front row of the bleachers in the now-empty gym. Out on the court, Providence's Eric Murdock and Villanova's David Miller are having a family reunion, surrounded by about a dozen of their extended family. Second cousins, Murdock and Miller grew up in a mostly black section of Bridgewater, New Jersey, called Hobbstown. Murdock was just a few months old when his mother was hit by a car and killed. For the first few years of his life he lived with his father. When he was five he went to live with his grandmother in Hobbstown. The Millers lived down the street. So he and David, and David's younger brother, Lance, one of the better schoolboys in the East and who's already committed to Villanova, grew up together. It was all one big extended family.

When Murdock went to Bridgewater-Raritan High School, the coach was a white man named Vaughn Stapleton. Stapleton and his wife, Gerry, befriended Murdock. They owned a farm about 20 miles away, and Murdock would sometimes stay there in the summers, working around the farm. In the Providence College media guide Murdock lists the greatest influences in his life as his grandmother and Vaughn and Gerry Stapleton.

"I guess he felt sorry for me, not having any parents and all," says Murdock. "But he took special care of me. He took me to games. He made me think I could be somebody. He made sure I graduated from high school. Even now, he keeps telling me that the most important thing is to graduate from college."

Murdock is representative of the Friars. He arrived in the Big East unheralded. He had been all-state in New Jersey, but he had not been to the prestige summer camps and he hadn't been invited to the Nike camp at Princeton University, the camp where the best 200 players in the country are invited every summer, though it was only half an hour away from his house. Besides Providence, the only other Big East school to show any genuine interest was Connecticut, with a late sniff from Seton Hall.

So when he arrived in the Big East he had something to prove. He was the lone bright spot in the Friars' disastrous 1987–88 season, averaging 11 points a game, the best of all Big East freshmen, and ending the season with 55 steals, 4 off the Big East record. But in the following November when he was invited to media day in New York, he sat in the corner most of the morning, like the guest at the party no one ever talks to.

"I saw everyone around Derrick Coleman and the other big names, and I was upset," he says. "It was like we weren't getting any respect."

They do now. So does Murdock.

Barnes is still coming down from the emotion of the game. He doesn't look happy. Every once in a while he puts his head down, as if off somewhere in a private moment.

"We should have won," he says, almost to himself. "A possession here or there. I knew it would be that kind of game. But we had the game won. We just didn't execute in the offensive end to keep the lead."

His Friars are now 17–5, but Barnes knows he needs at least another win to get into the tournament, maybe two. In a sense he has now become a victim of his success. The Friars' 13–0 start has increased expectations, and if the Friars don't get into the tournament, the year will be considered some sort of failure. Barnes knows that even his team would see a trip to the NIT as a failure; just as their fans' expectations have been raised, so have theirs. Once again, Barnes's team has played well on the road. Once again it hasn't been enough.

FEBRUARY 15

On this Wednesday night Seton Hall is here to play Connecticut, but the big news is the fallout from last Saturday-afternoon's game in the Hartford Civic Center against Boston College, a bizarre game won by the Huskies, 86–47.

Connecticut played Dana Barros very aggressively, trying to keep him from getting the ball. They trapped him, played a box-and-one for a while, kept a revolving succession of people taking turns guarding him. At the half Connecticut led 35–15, and the game was essentially over. Still, Connecticut continued to play Barros aggressively, and Calhoun continued to coach as if this were a Final Four game. The more BC coach Jim O'Brien saw of it, the more he didn't like it. For all practical purposes, the game was in garbage time and it was time for Calhoun to call off the dogs. He particularly didn't like the way the Huskies continued to play Barros. With about 10 minutes left to play, Barros hit his first three-point shot of the game, extending his streak of at least one three-pointer to 61 straight games. O'Brien then got off the bench and yelled down at Calhoun, "Hey, Jim, you can take off your fucking press now."

Later in the game, O'Brien yelled at Connecticut's Phil Gamble, "Go tell your coach he's a fucking asshole."

While this was taking place Calhoun was being booed for not putting in Dan Cyrulik, a freshman seven-footer who has become a favorite of the Civic Center crowd. As the score mounted, many students began screaming for Calhoun to play Cyrulik. When he didn't, Calhoun began to hear the boos. The result was a home crowd booing a home coach who was up by 30 points. Unbelievable.

Afterward, O'Brien told a few of the Connecticut writers that he resented Calhoun running up the score on him and that there would be other days. He also said he resented Calhoun for basically playing his top eight players throughout the game, even though the issue had long been decided.

Calhoun later said the reason he only played eight men was that John Gynne was on a one-game suspension for a practice incident, and Cyrulik, "who I think is going to be very good, has been soft in practice, so I didn't want to play him more than four or five minutes."

He also said he forgave O'Brien for bad-mouthing him.

"I like Jimmy. I've known him for 10 years," said Calhoun, "and I know he's frustrated, but he should be worried about the maroon and gold, not the blue and white. He should be worried about why his team quit on him, not what my team is doing. Afterward, he went around the corner with some of the writers who were his friends when he was here as an assistant and says that I'm a motherfucker, and I put the boots to him. Fucking Calhoun this, and fucking Calhoun that. It's like he broke the code you have with your fellow coaches. If he had a problem with what he thought I did, he should come up to me afterward instead of going to the writers. I always coach the same way. If it had been reversed, I would still have been up coaching. I only have 60 hours a year to coach, 60 hours to do what I like to do best. But I'm not pissed at Jimmy. I just think he used me to deflect the fact he was down by 30. Jimmy has to worry about his team, not mine. Because the last thing I was worried about was Jimmy O'Brien.

"But I get along with him. I get along with just about everyone in the league. John Thompson has been like a big brother. Looie's been like a father to me. I get along with Boeheim. Evans is crazy, but I get along all right with him. There only one guy I don't get along with."

Calhoun is in his early 40s. He grew up in Braintree, a Boston suburb, and played basketball at American International in Springfield. Upon graduation, he spent two years as an assistant there, a year as a Connecticut high-school coach, then went back to Massachusetts to coach a few high-school teams. The Northeastern job opened in 1972. At the time Northeastern was a Division II school in Boston, a large urban school with a concrete campus and little basketball tradition. What little it had stemmed from its inner-city commuters. There were so many of them, in fact, that they were known unofficially as the MBTA team, a reference to the Boston subway system. Suffice it to say, that kind of job was not in demand. Calhoun was able to parlay a great record at Dedham High School, plus a recommendation from Red Auerbach, whom he knew from working at Auerbach's camp, and got the job.

"What I wanted was eventually to be competitive in New England," says Calhoun, "but both the school and myself weren't too sure just how to go about it."

So began the arduous process of trying to build a program. Back then getting a name school like Colgate or one of the Ivies on the schedule was a major coup. Going to the Brown Tip-Off Tournament one year was a major coup. In the beginning Northeastern went anywhere it was invited: to the Palestra to play Penn, three times as a designated patsy to Manley Field House to play Syracuse. Calhoun became known as a master at recruiting kids who fell through the cracks of the recruiting process. The outstanding example, of course, was Reggie Lewis, who had been the sixth man on the great teams at Dunbar High School in Baltimore. In addition, Calhoun spent about five years acting as a coach/information director, forever on the phone and trying to convince people his team was good. Eventually, it began to work. Then, just when the basketball world began discovering Northeastern, along came the Big East.

"In the beginning I couldn't understand why we couldn't get people interested in us," he says. "But by the time the Big East came, I was tired of it. I realized the worst thing was to waste energy on things you couldn't control. If I was constantly comparing us to the Big East, I'd go crazy."

Until he got the Connecticut job, Calhoun was always one of the names paraded about every time a coaching job opened at a major school in the East. He had built a program from the bottom up without much help. He was aggressive, and his teams always seemed better than anyone thought they were. The unfortunate result? Connecticut was ranked in the preseason top 20, and everyone thinks his team is better than it is.

Welcome to the Big East.

"He said he's not responsible for the intensity of both teams," says Randy Smith of the *Manchester Journal-Inquirer*, "but he definitely buried BC with all the zeal of a defrocked priest. This is very much a coach's league; they're all bigger than life. But there's also a certain respect for the other guy. I think he made Boston College bleed. Calhoun says that he'd like to relax on the bench but he can't, but I think when you're up by 30 you'd better show some compassion for the other guy."

Smith is in the runway between the press room and the court.

"I think people are disappointed with the Huskies. What else is new? Peter Gammons once called the Red Sox fans Calvinists. That's what UConn fans are, too. But you are starting to hear an undercurrent of dissatisfaction. People are tired of 10 years of always being the also-ran in this league. They saw Providence go to the Final Four two years ago. They see Seton Hall being good now. They want it to be them. So I think Calhoun's slipped some in their eyes since the NIT nirvana. It was probably inevitable."

Like most Big East games, this one is attended by several NBA scouts. Representatives from the Denver Nuggets, the new Minnesota Timberwolves, and the Boston Celtics have all requested seats for press row. Before the game Rick Weitzman, who scouts for the Celtics, says he likes Connecticut's Cliff Robinson and Seton Hall's trio of Ramon Ramos, Daryll Walker, and John Morton. Robinson is rumored as a first-round pick, even though he's had an up-and-down career at Connecticut: flashes of brilliance some nights, unfulfilled potential the next.

"I don't look at the game," says Weitzman. "I look for athletic ability. How someone runs. How they shoot. Raw talent. And Robinson's got that."

Calhoun is not enamored of Robinson's play this season. He won't come out and say so, wanting to protect his player, but the feeling around Connecticut is that Robinson doesn't like pressure situations, that in crucial times in the game when he's expected to take the game over, he doesn't. For the Huskies to get to the NCAA Tournament and live up to their preseason hype, they need a great senior season from Robinson. So far they haven't gotten it. Certainly, he's been good, but not great. Calhoun said before the season that Robinson was the difference between being a good team and a great team. The crucial stat is that in the last eight minutes of the eight Connecticut losses, Robinson has had only eight points. If the Huskies are going to get to the NCAA Tournament, the Huskies are going to need more crunch-time production from him.

Robinson has had a strange career at Connecticut. He arrived as a highly touted, 6-11 freshman who could run and shoot. You looked at him then and saw the NBA in his future. That year, the last year of Dom Perno's tenure at Connecticut, though, the team went nowhere, 3–13 in the Big East. Robinson did not respond well. In one game, after being taken out by Perno after a near fight with a Central Connecticut player, he stood in front of the bench the last eight minutes of the game. He made an obscene gesture to the crowd. And at the end of the game he had to be restrained from going after the Central Connecticut player. That, and the fact that he played with a perpetual scowl on his face, didn't endear him to Connecticut fans. Not only that, says SID Tim Tolikan, but "The writers here never really liked him."

Enter Calhoun.

Soon after he got the job, he met with Robinson and essentially struck a deal. If Robinson did what Calhoun told him, he could be a pro. He had heard about Robinson's attitude, how he'd been influenced by Earl Kelley, who "was a punk here." But the next year he and fellow sophomore Phil Gamble were declared academically ineligible midway through the season, victims of a lack of tutorial support. Nevertheless, both players persevered and became symbols of the new era at Connecticut. Last year Robinson averaged nearly 18 points a game, and he began this year as a pre-season all-Big East selection. Now Calhoun waits for him to play like one.

Tonight is Connecticut's ninth straight sell-out.

They are 13–7 overall, 4–6 in the Big East, but their season is starting to run out. "We never show up bad, we always show up to play. I don't know what it is," says Calhoun. "Maybe there's too much Ghost of Christmas Past around here. I remember in the NIT last year at West Virginia someone said to me that they thought our crowd was surprised when we won. We are overscrutinized here. It's a very tough place to play. We had kids my first year here who hated to play in the Hartford Civic Center because the crowd was so negative.

"But we've made our fate very difficult. We've had quality wins against Syracuse and Pepperdine, and on the road at Virginia, but we need at least two or three more wins."

Tonight is not an easy time to get one of those wins. Seton Hall is rolling along at 20–4, 7–4 in the Big East. The Hall goes up at the half by 10, the beneficiary of four Andrew Gaze long-range bombs. Connecticut fights back, though, making it another of those Big East games that can go either way. The Hall is leading by only 1 with 1:08 to play. Then John Morton makes two key free throws, Gaze hits a leaner in the lane with just 11 seconds left, and the Pirates hang on to win by 3, 72–69. Gaze finished with 22 points, shooting 6 of 8 from three-point territory.

It has been one of his better games of the year.

Gaze is only averaging about 13 points a game, but he has been better than advertised. He came from Australia with the reputation of a proven scorer. The plus is that he also passes well and really works at playing aggressive man-to-man defense. His only negative is a lack of speed, which he compensates for with great court awareness and a wonderful feel for the game. His biggest difficulty has been adjusting to the realization he isn't going to score like he did when he was back home playing for the Melbourne Tigers. The folks Down Under look at his 13-point average and wonder what's wrong. They aren't overly impressed when Gaze tells them his team has been ranked in the top 10. After all, there are only 14 teams in the entire country. So what's the big deal about being in the top 10?

"When I first came here, I thought my biggest attribute was scoring," he says. "I had never had a problem scoring before. But at first I wasn't scoring consistently here and at times I worried about it. I finally reached the stage when I realized that scoring was not the do-all and the end-all in assessing my performance."

Ramon Ramos, the other half of Seton Hall's international duo, scored 27 and was unstoppable inside. It was his fifth straight game with double figures in both points and rebounds. He is from Canovanis, Puerto Rico, a small town in the middle of a rain forest near San Juan. Carlesimo, who began coaching summers in Puerto Rico back when he was at Wagner, first saw him when Ramos was in the ninth grade. He'd been told about him by Herb Brown, the brother of Larry. So every summer Carlesimo would see him play, then write him letters.

Ramos didn't start playing organized basketball until he was 13, and then only because he was already 6-4 and self-conscious about his size. When he first arrived at the Hall he was clumsy and awkward. Every year he got better, but for a while no one really noticed. Last year he started, averaging 10 points a game, but he played in the shadow of Mark Bryant, who had a great second half and carried the Pirates to their first NCAA Tournament appearance.

Then when the season ended, he went to the trials for the Puerto Rican Olympic team and spent most of the spring playing for the Puerto Rican national team in South America. During the summer it was more games and more practice, before spending September at the Olympic games in Seoul. After that, his life seemed to change. He became, if not a national celebrity, at least someone who was no longer anonymous. He is also an excellent student, and he wants to be a CPA. He might be one of the few players in big-time college basketball who, when asked what their career aspirations are, does not say the NBA. Ironically, he is playing more and more like someone who might be an NBA second-round draft pick. Tonight he has certainly outplayed Cliff Robinson.

Carlesimo once again says his team is very good. He's been saying it all year, and yet no one ever seems to hear him. People go through the laundry list of great players in the Big East, and no Pirates ever seem to be high on it. Yet they have inside scoring in Ramos and Daryll Walker, a deep threat in Gaze, plus the one-on-one brilliance of John Morton. Gerald Greene has given them strong leadership at point guard all year. Coming off the bench, Michael Cooper always seems to make an impact on the game, and Franz Volcy brings size and quality. Everyone in the league believes that Anthony Avent is going to one day be a dominant player in the Big East. No team in the league has as much quality depth, with the exception of Georgetown. Still, feeling lingers that the Hall is not as good as their record.

Carlesimo is followed into the interview room by Calhoun, who looks spent. It has been a tough year emotionally for him. His team has been under siege throughout the Big East season, and tonight he bears signs of the struggle. He runs his hand through his brown hair and lets out a sigh. You can almost see the emotion seep out of him, like steam from a manhole cover. His team has battled back, has played hard. It just hasn't been enough. When Calhoun speaks, the words all but tumble over themselves. He says Seton Hall is as good as any basketball team in America, and there are good reasons why they are 21–4 and ranked 12th in the country.

"I can't ask any more of my basketball team," he says. "We need a break once in a while. Right now I'm very emotional. I don't think we can play any harder than that. I'm proud as hell of this team and I told them that. We have six games left and I can't ask any more of our basketball team."

He hesitates.

"I know one thing: teams can play better than us. But no one's going to play Seton Hall any harder than us."

It is a good exit line, and Calhoun goes out of the room, followed by several of the Connecticut press corps, the infamous "Horde."

Games from Saturday night, February 18:

• Pittsburgh upsets 12th-ranked Seton Hall, 82–76, in Fitzgerald Field House on the Pitt campus, getting 26 points from Brian Shorter and 22 from Jason Mathews. It is the second time the Panthers have beaten the Hall this year, and it moves the Panthers into fourth place in the league standings, where Seton Hall is tied for second with Syracuse.

Since beating St. John's in overtime back in Alumni Hall on January 30, the Panthers have been back on a roller coaster. They were blasted in Pittsburgh by Syracuse, lost by 10 in Providence, then came back to upset Georgetown in Pittsburgh. That caused Paul Evans to say he thought his team could still get to the NCAA Tournament if "we reach 16 or 17 wins." The victory over the Hall is a step in the right direction, another win against a nationally ranked team.

It is another great performance by Shorter, who is now on course to be the most productive rookie in Big East history. The 6-7 Shorter is now averaging 19.5 points and 9.8 rebounds a game. Earl Kelley of Connecticut holds the mark with 16.7 points a game as a freshman in 1982–83. He is followed by Chris Mullin, Charles Smith of Pittsburgh, Pearl Washington and Ed Pinckney of Villanova. If Shorter were to keep up his rebounding pace he would better Smith's 8.0, which is followed by Pinckney and Patrick Ewing.

Shorter's Big East debut has been overshadowed all year by the arrival of Alonzo Mourning and Billy Owens. Mourning's averages are 13.0 and 7.6, while Owens's are 11.3 and 6.6. Mourning also continues to lead the country in blocked shots.

• St. John's holds on to beat DePaul in Chicago, 67–64, after the Blue Devils stormed back from a 17-point deficit. It is a great win for the Redmen. Not only is it on the road against a glamour team, but it stops a two-game slide for the Redmen. After beating Providence in Alumni Hall, they were hammered in the Carrier Dome by Syracuse and lost by 10 to Pitt in Fitzgerald Field House. The Redmen had three freshmen in double figures—Malik Sealy, Robert Werdann, and Jason Buchanan—along with junior forward Jason Williams.

• Villanova beats Connecticut 78–67 in duPont Pavilion. The Cats place five players in double figures, including 14 points from freshman Marc Dowdell.

• Georgetown, the fourth-ranked team in the country, roars by Boston College in Conte Forum, 80–69. Alonzo Mourning led four Hoyas in double figures with 19 points. Dana Barros had 23 for the Eagles, who also got strong games from Steve Benton and Doug Able.

• Fifth-ranked Syracuse beats Providence, 87–80, in the Providence Civic Center. It is the Orangemen's 20th straight victory over the Friars since the Big East started. Syracuse pulled away from a 72–72 tie in the final seven minutes. Once again, as they have done many times this year, they

shot foul shots down the stretch. Derrick Coleman led the
Orangemen with 22 points and 13 rebounds, followed by
Stevie Thompson with 19 points. Sherman Douglas and
Matt Roe were also in double figures. Marty Conlon had 29
for the Friars.

THE STANDINGS AS OF FEBRUARY 18:

	CONFERENCE PLAY	OVERALL
GEORGETOWN	9–2	19–3
SETON HALL	8–5	21–5
SYRACUSE	8–5	22–5
PITTSBURGH	7–6	14–10
PROVIDENCE	6–6	17–6
VILLANOVA	5–6	14–11
ST. JOHN'S	5–7	14–9
CONNECTICUT	4–7	13–7
BOSTON COLLEGE	1–9	9–12

FEBRUARY 28

Seton Hall has become one of the surprises of the college
basketball season, the school that no one ever heard of west
of Pittsburgh.

Monty Hall? Tammany Hall? Fawn Hall? Robert Hall?
Certainly. But Seton Hall? Just who are these guys? And
just where is Seton Hall, anyway? Delaware, right?

Tonight, the Seton Hall basketball team has just arrived
in Providence for its game tomorrow with Providence College, and they're having a late dinner at the Players' Corner
Pub in the shadow of the Civic Center in downtown Providence. The walls of the pub are covered with photos of
various sports figures and the pennants of many colleges.
They are all here: the Big East, the Ivies, Notre Dame, the
biggies from around the country. And the one for Seton

Hall? It's probably the smallest pennant in the dining room, hung way up high near the ceiling so you have to look long and hard to even find it.

"Hey, Daryll," says P. J. Carlesimo to Daryll Walker, pointing to the pennant. "Look where they put our pennant."

The players are sitting at three tables in the middle of the dining room. Sitting with Carlesimo are Mike Tranghese, Peter Frechette, Chris Plonsky, and Linda Bruno from the Big East office. Bruno got her start in sports as Jim Valvano's secretary at Iona, and before long she was also functioning as a volunteer academic adviser to the players. After becoming an assistant AD there and at Yale, she was hired by the Big East, where she is now an assistant commissioner in charge of running the conference's various tournaments and interpreting the NCAA's innumerable rules for the nine schools.

She first met Carlesimo when she was at Iona and he was at Wagner.

"He used to do everything there," she says. "You'd show up there for a game and he'd be the one who unlocked the locker room for you. Then you'd ask about tickets and he'd take you into the ticket booth. He even used to count the money at his games. One night we came in there and he was actually in the ticket booth selling tickets before the game. So I told him that I would sell the tickets for him so he could go talk to his team.

"He's exactly the same now as he was then. Success hasn't changed him at all. He always was one of those people you thought, 'Something good is going to happen to him.' Because of the way he was. You didn't know it would be coaching, but you always knew he'd end up somewhere."

At the moment Carlesimo is worried about the size of the Seton Hall pennant. "Hey, Jody," he yells at owner Jody DiRaimo. "The kids are upset at both the size and the placement of the Seton Hall pennant."

"The way you guys used to be, you're lucky you have a pennant at all," counters DiRaimo.

An hour later the team heads back to the hotel. Carlesimo stays behind with the Big East people. Relaxed, self-deprecating, he talks fast, like a New Yorker.

"Sure, I'm more relaxed now," he says. "When you're winning, you don't have to be snapping at people all the time."

His father, Peter J. Carlesimo, retired this year from running the NIT, the tournament he has been credited with saving. His name is synonymous with college basketball in New York. But when P. J. grew up, his father was the long-time football coach at the University of Scranton. P. J. is the oldest of 10 children, and some of his earliest memories are of going to his father's games, hanging around the practices and coming of age with sports. The Carlesimos lived two doors away from the youth center, a building that became P. J.'s second home. He went to Scranton Prep. Afterward, he considered the Naval Academy but went instead to Fordham, which offered him a combination basketball-baseball scholarship. At Fordham he took sociology and classics, but he knew he wanted to coach. It was the late sixties, a time of student protest and the counterculture. P. J. wanted none of it. He was in ROTC for two years. For four years he was in the gym. At the time Fordham was going through three coaches: Johnny Bach, Ed Conlin, and Digger Phelps. Carlesimo sat for all four years. During his sophomore year his father became the Fordham AD.

In his senior year he was accepted at law school, but the next year Phelps left to go to Notre Dame, and Hal Wenzel became the new Fordham coach. He offered P. J. a chance to be the freshman coach for $500 a year. He was also put in charge of concessions. The next year he became the full-time assistant and stayed for four years. Then one day he saw an ad in the *New York Times* for a coach and AD at a small school in New Hampshire. It was New Hampshire College in Manchester, and Carlesimo grabbed it. The school was going Division II. He was going to be his own boss. And he was going to have his own team.

"I thought I'd be there for a long time," he says.

Instead, the head job opened at Wagner, and the Staten Island school was looking for a young coach from the metropolitan area. There for six years, he went 21–7 in 1979 and was named the Eastern coach of the year. His record plummeted after that—Wagner is one of those places where winning is an accident—and went 3–23 his last year.

Then the Seton Hall job opened. Billy Raftery, the popular coach, had had enough and resigned the year before; his assistant, Hoddy Mahon, had been the interim coach. The Big East was two years old, and all the Hall had to show for it was Danny Callendrillo and a lot of losses. The gym was an antiquated relic. There were no support services, no money, not even a coach's office. Just a location 14 miles from New York City and a basketball tradition that hailed back to the early fifties, when the Pirates won the NIT (back when that was considered in many circles winning the national championship). But everything about Seton Hall seemed past tense. The only thing the job seemed to have going for it was that it wasn't Wagner, and it was in the Big East.

"Richie Regan called me about the job, and we met in a Staten Island restaurant," says Carlesimo. "The word was they were getting desperate. I told him I thought Hoddy should get the job. The next day I got it."

He was coaching in the Big East.

Sort of.

"You couldn't believe how screwed up it was," he says. "There were no side baskets in the gym. It took two men four hours to set the gym up for a game. There was no weight room, no training table. It was mind-boggling. It was like the league had started for everybody but us."

He was also the lowest-paid head coach in the league.

At the time the Hall was the joke of the league. Tom McElroy of the Big East office remembers a time early on when he was supervising a Big East golf tournament on Long Island. The Seton Hall team was comprised of four guys in sneakers, two of whom had antiquated clubs with wooden shafts. Supposedly the coach had gone into the cafeteria earlier in the day and asked for anyone who wanted to go play golf in the Big East Tournament. Linda Bruno remembers the time she was at a women's cross-country meet and two of the Seton Hall runners, both wearing makeshift uniforms, got lost on the course, and the coach had to go looking for them in a golf cart.

So when he got the job, Carlesimo knew the program had a long way to go. Sure, the Big East was a great recruiting tool. Playing on TV. Playing a postseason tournament in Madison Square Garden. But all too often he found himself recruiting against other Big East schools, a not uncommon practice in the Big East.

In these situations when the Hall was competing against other league schools, all the advantages of the Big East were nullified. What did he have to sell? The other Big East schools had additional advantages to throw into the pot, and Seton Hall had Walsh Gym. He knew his team was getting better, but how much better were they getting in relation to the rest of the league?

The first signifigant recruit was Mark Bryant. He was a local kid, the first sign that maybe the Hall could keep the good ones home. The next year Carlesimo went after Walker, Greene, and Morton, all from New York. All were all-city, the kind of kids who used to either go to St. John's or take the underground railroad south. He told them that if they went to Seton Hall, their families could see them play. They were only 17 miles from the Garden, on a campus that even had some trees on it. And, of course, he sold them on the Big East. That was the first time he thought he might be able to go head to head in the recruiting war against St. John's. But even then it wasn't easy.

"Two years ago we were 4–12 in the league, but we were competitive with everyone," he says. "It was the first year we really had been. We knew we were getting better, but people don't want to hear that when you've only won four games in the league."

He went to the annual coaches' conference at the Final Four two years ago in New Orleans, not knowing whether he had a job or not. He had one year left on his contract, but there were rumors the school was going to buy it out. Gavitt stood up for him repeatedly, telling Monsignor John Petillo, the Seton Hall president, that Carlesimo should not be fired. Thompson also supposedly called in support of him.

Then last year, just when it seemed his contract would not

be renewed, his team got hot down the stretch and his career was reborn. He was signed to a new five-year, $1.2 million contract, a sizable increase and a salary that put him in the middle of the Big East coaches' pack.

Even in the bad times he was always considered a good interview, and Carlesimo is secure enough to admit his relationship with the media helped him through some of the tough times. When his team was bad, he was happy to be interviewed—anything to get some recognition for a school that seemed like the bargain-basement team in an upscale league.

It is getting late, and the party's breaking up. Carlesimo is asked what time his team will have its walk-through tomorrow. He shrugs and runs one hand through his beard. He started growing his beard two summers ago, when he coached the Big East team that was scheduled to tour Australia. The team was training at Seton Hall, and he just didn't shave. He continued not shaving throughout the tour. When he came back to school that fall, he still didn't shave. But the first real test was media day in November, the annual coming-out party for Big East coaches. The second test was the first game.

"I was a little nervous about it at first," he says, "but then I realized that if we didn't win some games, it wasn't going to matter anyway. Now it's a big recognition factor. There are a lot of people who don't know my name, only that I'm the coach with the beard."

The Hall has a short break in the schedule after the game tomorrow night, and Carlesimo is all set to go to Florida, then Chicago, in search of a juco point guard. He says the one thing the success of this season has already accomplished is to attract kids the Hall never had a chance with in the old days.

"Our perception nationally is 180 degrees different than what it used to be," he says.

"How about yours?" he is asked.

He shrugs. Carlesimo shrugs a lot.

"I guess it's changed," he says. "Winning's done that. But the other day I left my name with a secretary and it was obvious she had no idea who I was. So just when you start to feel important, people put it in perspective for you."

But he keeps on winning. The next night Seton Hall beats Providence 80–68. It is the second time in five days that the Hall has beaten the Friars.

MARCH 2

Everyone loves Carlesimo, one of the great stories of the season. But how about someone who has won year in and year out? Listen to Jim Boeheim.

It is one of the ironies of college basketball that he feels a need to defend both himself and his program. He is one of the winningest coaches in college basketball. In the great tradition of Syracuse basketball, Boeheim is the one constant through all the years, first as a player, then as an assistant, and now as the coach. Everyone else has come and gone. Boeheim is still here. His teams play an exciting style. In this day and age, when college basketball has become more and more a coach's game, Boeheim is known as a player's coach. He never puts the reins on his players' creativity. Instead, he creates an offensive environment in which a Sherman Douglas can throw alley-oop passes and a Stevie Thompson can run and dunk to his heart's delight.

The Big East's Mike Tranghese believes Boeheim is the most misunderstood person in the league. "He's a flat-out good guy," he says. "People say he wins because of the Dome. Well, he also got great players before the Dome. He does a fabulous job of recruiting."

But when the Billy Packers and Dick Vitales of the world sing hosannahs to the great coaches in the country, they are usually not crooning about Boeheim. Bob Snyder, a Syracuse writer who's covered Boeheim for years, thinks he's more concerned now with his reputation as a coach than ever before. He wins as many games as the so-called great coaches do, and he makes as much money as they do. The only goal left is to be reverently lauded as they are, a genius with a clipboard.

"Sure, I think it bothers him that he is not perceived that way," says Snyder. "I don't think he's perceived as a bad coach. He's just not perceived as a great coach."

This year Boeheim has been featured in several ads in Syracuse newspapers modeling different eyeglass frames, complete with a caption that reads, "I found a whole new me." In one he's dressed in a tuxedo. In another he looks like he's auditioning for a role in "Miami Vice." Not that anyone believes Boeheim is going to change. Not even Boeheim himself.

"People have been watching us play for years and really don't see," he says. "There's a misconception that all we do is run. You know, we practice the fast break, it doesn't just happen. It's a skill.

"The fans are very supportive. People think I'm a god in Syracuse. I have an hour-long radio talk show, and the three lines are always lit up. Last year I never got one call criticizing me. Same thing this year, even when we were 1–4. But with the media, no matter what we do it's never enough. The things we do well are ignored. They talk about all the talent. Where is it? Everyone says Villanova doesn't have any players. Hell, they have a roster full of high-school All-Americans. Not one coach in the league wanted Sherman Douglas. No one wanted Matt Roe. Coleman was the 87th-ranked player in his class."

He laughs ruefully. "I'm either a hell of a recruiter or we're very lucky. We've beaten Seton Hall six straight times, but no one writes that. If Sherman hadn't gotten hurt, we probably would have lost only two games. If I were doing as badly this year as Rollie, it would be the end of the world."

Boeheim takes off his glasses and rubs them for a second before going on.

"It's all gotten way too big. I just want to coach basketball and forget all that other stuff. We have 32,000 people in the Dome? I just try to ignore it. I never look up in the stands. I make seven or eight times more money than I did when I first started, but it doesn't mean anything to me. The fact that every game is on television doesn't mean anything to me. It doesn't change what I do. We've always had to win. I've known that all along. You learn early on that you either win or you're not going to be in coaching very long."

He pauses.

"I tell people how good my players are; some coaches tell people how bad their players are. I'm not nice to writers, I don't make small talk with them. That's just not me. And I'm not going to be phony. I see some coaches going over and talking to writers. Fuck that. I'm not going to do that.

"Look, I understand we're the pro team in Syracuse. There is nothing else. Every day there are three TV stations. There are eight different people that cover us and they all want to talk to me every day. That's 56 interviews a week.

"But I'm not a tough individual. People think I am. They see me always bitching and complaining. A lot of coaches do that, but I get the credit for that. I'm a private person. I don't like to be the center of attention. I'm the same guy I always was, shy and quiet. The only problem is that when you're a coach, shy and quiet becomes aloof and arrogant.

"But I'm not happy when we win. I'm just unhappy when we lose. Because when you win, you have to win again and again. Everyone wants you to be in a tough league. They want you to play tough games outside the league. And they want you to win every game. But the trouble with playing in the Big East is that you're going to lose some games. We lost at St. John's by two in the game that Sherman got hurt early in. We lost at Connecticut—which is a tough place to play—with Sherman playing at 20 percent. But nobody accepts that. And hey, it doesn't even matter what I do anymore in the regular season. The whole thing now is the NCAA Tournament."

He goes on to say that Syracuse is still a football school. Everything revolves around football. His basketball program makes nearly $6 million a year, $350,000 in ticket sales for one game alone, but still football comes first. He gives a shrug that seems to say that's just the way it is. After all, no matter how far he's come, he's still a guy from upstate New York who's never wanted to coach anywhere but his alma mater.

"In the beginning I used to get calls about other coaching jobs, but no more. People know I'm not going to leave Syracuse."

It is the last home game for Dana Barros.

He is one of the all-time great players in Boston College history. He has led the Big East in scoring the past two years. He has been one of the great success stories in all of college basketball. The kid from nearby Mattapan who was given a last-minute scholarship has made all of his playground dreams come true.

The flipside is that he has never been on a good team. He has always been the recipient of doubleteams and box-and-one defenses designed strictly to stop him. Opposing coaches didn't have to spend too many hours figuring out elaborate game plans on how to stop the Eagles. It was simple: stop Dana Barros. Barros has never had the luxury of being surrounded by teammates who could take some of the pressure off him. He was never surrounded by players who could have made him look better, as Sherman Douglas and Charles Smith have had. How good could he have been with a strong inside game that would have freed him up on the perimeter?

We'll never know.

Tonight is also senior night, and Boston College is honoring its four seniors: little-used players Tom Hjerpe and Mike Corcoran, Steve Benton, and Barros. One by one, Hjerpe, Corcoran, and Benton walk to centercourt, escorted by their parents, as long-time Boston College AD Bill Flynn presents the mothers with red roses. Then it is Barros's turn. "One of the greatest Eagles of them all," the P.A. announcer says.

He is escorted onto the court by his mother and grandmother. The crowd rises in tribute. Among them is his father, who has been a constant fixture at Boston College games, sitting in the first row alternately screaming encouragement to the players and yelling at the referees in his incredibly booming voice. The last couple of years, when the games were played in the Boston Garden, he often ran around under the basket. Last year he became such a nuisance that he was told that if he didn't stay in his seat he would be thrown out. Earlier in the season he and Jim O'Brien had gotten into an ugly shouting incident outside the BC locker room, though he downplayed the incident afterward, saying that he has a voice that carries and sometimes he gets frustrated because it's his son's senior year and he wants him to go out in style. The irony is that he has not lived at home since Dana was a young child, and so now he stands on the sidelines and watches the ceremony for his son.

The tribute seems to spur Dana on.

Syracuse is flat, and the Eagles go up by 10 at the half. The air smells of upset. Syracuse comes back in the second half and takes the lead with about nine minutes left on a Douglas breakaway layup. Still, the game seesaws back and forth, the Eagles trying to hang on, before Barros hits a jump shot from the right side, giving BC a three-point lead with 36 seconds to play. He throws his right fist into the air as he comes back downcourt. He then hits two free throws with six seconds left, and the Eagles hang on for a 90–86 upset victory.

Afterward, Barros is interviewed on the court as several hundred fans remain behind to watch. There has been so little to cheer about this year, and this has become their moment. It is also Barros's moment. In a frustrating year when the good times have been few, the Eagles have beaten Syracuse, and he has scored 31 points in his last home game. When the interview is over, Barros turns and runs across the court back to the locker room. The people in Conte Forum give him a rousing hero's farewell.

MARCH 5

Syracuse will hardly go out of the season without a show, however.

Today, on national television, Georgetown comes into the Carrier Dome to play before the largest on-campus crowd ever to watch a college basketball game, 32,683. The pregame news speculates on whether Charles Smith and John Turner will play for Georgetown. Rumor has it that Thompson will keep both out of the game while they nurse minor injuries and prepare for the Big East Tournament. The Hoyas have already clinched the Big East title and the number-one seed in the tournament, so the game is of no real importance to them. In fact, if he plays without two of his starters, Thompson can use the game as a psychological ploy. Losing to the Hoyas in the Dome without Smith could be devastating to Syracuse, especially coming in the wake of their loss to lowly Boston College. On the flipside, losing to Syracuse on the eve of tournament season might be the best message Thompson could give to his team: you're not invincible, there's still a lot of hard work to be done.

"You got to love the Hoyas," says Chris Plonsky of the Big East with a smile. "No one knows whether Smith's going to play."

Not even he doesn't. Nor does Turner.

Today both Georgetown and Syracuse are unveiling new uniforms. Both Thompson and Boeheim have contracts with Nike that require their players to wear Nike sneakers and the two coaches to make a certain number of appearances a year. Georgetown's new uniforms are supposedly made of light denim, what representative Sunny Vaccaro calls Nike's "force line" uniforms, to be worn by "schools that are strong and powerful like Georgetown or Michigan." The new Syracuse uniforms are one-piece unitards, the so-called "flight line." Vaccaro says these are for schools that are flashy, like Syracuse and UNLV. So not only is this the last game in the regular Big East season, it's also a sneak preview of a sartorial future.

Even without Smith and Turner, the Hoyas are up by 14, with 15 minutes remaining in the game. The game has been played at the Hoyas' pace, but with six minutes to go, their lead has been sliced to 3. The game is tight, the Dome crowd in a frenzy. The momentum has shifted. As he's done so many times in the past, Thompson elects to back the ball out and play deliberately, trying to milk the clock and regain a paced tempo. Boeheim counters with a press, standing in front of his bench, frantically waving his arms, trying to get his team to get into the press sooner. Throughout the second half he has been a sideline show, and the CBS camera has constantly panned his pained expressions and contortions.

With about four minutes left in what is still anyone's game, some oranges are thrown on the court. An enraged Boeheim asks for the microphone.

"No more stuff thrown on the court," he yells, like a principal admonishing his rowdy students. "Anymore, and I'm going to ask the referees to call a technical foul on us."

Syracuse goes on to win in overtime, 82–76. Afterward, as people stream onto the Carrier Dome floor as if the Orangemen had just won the national title, Boeheim and Thompson hug at midcourt.

In the individual match-ups, the little minidramas that run throughout the game, Mourning has had 16 points, Owens 19. Sherman Douglas, playing his last game in the Carrier Dome, finishes as Syracuse's all-time leading scorer and as the all-time career NCAA assist leader.

The regular season has ended, and the standings look like this:

THE STANDINGS AT THE END OF JANUARY:

	CONFERENCE PLAY	OVERALL
GEORGETOWN	13–3	23–4
SETON HALL	11–5	24–5
SYRACUSE	10–6	24–6
PITTSBURGH	9–7	16–11
PROVIDENCE	7–9	18–9
VILLANOVA	7–9	16–14
CONNECTICUT	6–10	15–11
ST. JOHN'S	6–10	15–12
BOSTON COLLEGE	3–13	11–16

10

THE REGULAR SEASON WRAP-UP

The walls of the Big East office are like a shrine to the conference's tradition. Inside the front door are framed, blown-up pictures of three *Sports Illustrated* covers. One is from 1985, the year the league placed three teams in the Final Four in Lexington, and shows three pictures of Ewing, Mullin, and Villanova's Dwayne McClain, under the heading, "The NCAA's Is a Big East Feast." One is a picture of Georgetown's Michael Graham dunking against Houston in the 1984 Final Four. The third is a picture of Villanova's Ed Pinckney against Georgetown in 1985, under the heading "Top Cats."

The office is one main room with several smaller offices off it. The main room is where Lisa Silva, Gavitt's executive secretary, sits, as well as the interns and secretaries. Large framed pictures of the conference's players of the year stare down from the white walls, Big East icons: John Bagley in 1981, Dan Callendrillo in '82; Mullin in '83; Mullin and Ewing in 1984, again in '85; Walter Berry in 1986; Reggie Williams in '87; Charles Smith of Pittsburgh last year.

As usual on Sunday, Chris Plonsky is in her office. As usual, she will talk to all the SIDs in the league and the beat writers. Then again, it's the start of a big week in the Big East. Today the coaches will vote on the three All-Conference teams that will be announced tomorrow. A luncheon of all the players and coaches will be held at noon, followed that evening by the Big East Tournament in Madison Square Garden.

On the surface, picking both the All-Conference teams and the player of the year seems like a simple enough procedure, but it's not without its potential for controversy. Since coaches are not allowed to vote for their own players, a few years ago John Thompson voted for Pearl Washington, then a freshman, instead of Chris Mullin, allegedly to protect Patrick Ewing, who was competing with Mullin for player of the year. Ewing and Mullin were later named coplayers of the year.

"Dave will supervise the tabulation of the votes, and if there is anything that's totally out of whack he will fix it," says Plonsky.

The next day the first team will be annnounced. It includes Charles Smith of Georgetown; Sherman Douglas and Derrick Coleman of Syracuse, Brian Shorter of Pitt, and Ramon Ramos of Seton Hall. Shorter, who averaged 20 points and 10 rebounds a game, is also named the league's top rookie, no small feat in a year that's unveiled Alonzo Mourning and Billy Owens.

Mourning, named the league's defensive player of the year, anchors the All-Big East second team that includes Dana Barros of Boston College, Connecticut's Cliff Robinson, Stevie Thompson of Syracuse, and Jayson Williams of St. John's. The third team is comprised of John Morton and Andrew Gaze of Seton Hall, Providence's Eric Murdock, Doug West of Villanova, and Jason Matthews of Pitt.

The All-Rookie team includes Shorter, Mourning, Owens, Malik Sealy of St. John's, and Marc Dowdell of Villanova.

Also on this Sunday the *Providence Journal* begins a four-part series on the finances of the Big East. Written by sportswriter Mike Stanton, it covers four areas of the conference: television, coaches' salaries, recruiting monies, and the question of whether the pressure to win pushes academics into last place.

Recruiting, understandably enough, is portrayed as an endeavor without a budget, where the bottom line is to get the players who can make you competitive in the conference; there's no pinching pennies. Whether it's travel, recruiting videos, or mailings, the idea is not so much to outdo opposing schools as to make sure you don't fall behind. Stanton writes that Connecticut's basketball budget is $580,000 this year, with $75,000 allocated to recruiting, plus another $40,000 for postage and mailing. Compared to the other schools in the league, this is not considered extravagant.

Perhaps the biggest reaction comes from Stanton's disclosure of the coaches' salaries. Once upon a time, of course, no one went into coaching to make money. That's no longer true. In the Big East, even the lowest-paid coaches in the conference are in the $200,000-a-year range, what with the sneaker contracts and the camps and the radio and TV shows. Or as Jim O'Brien, who came from St. Bonaventure, says, "Coaching in the Big East puts you in a different tax bracket."

One who saw it all change was Joe Mullaney, who coached at Providence in the late fifties and sixties, went to the pros for a decade, then came back to coach at Providence in the early years of the Big East. He remembers his first trip to the annual Big East coaches' meeting held every spring. He was used to the old days, back when coaches would sit around late at night and talk about the game, about strategy and tactics and stories. But this was different.

"All of a sudden guys are talking about money," he says. "They're asking, 'What kind of deal you got?' They're asking about this shoe deal and that shirt deal. I couldn't believe it. It was THE topic of conversation. They never talked about the game, or what's good for the game. Guys today basically talk about money. They want to get rich."

For those not privy to late-night chats, though, the figures are astounding. The article lists four categories for the coaches: school salary, sneaker contract, camp gross, and TV-radio shows. Thompson is listed as having the highest school salary, at $362,575, while Barnes and O'Brien are the lowest, both listed at $70,000. Calhoun is at $79,000, while Massimino, Boeheim, Evans, Carlesimo, and Carnesecca are all listed in the $100,000 range. The sneaker contracts range from $60,000 (Carlesimo and Calhoun) to Thompson's $200,000.

Massimino is said to gross approximately $400,000 a year from his camp, with Boeheim not far behind. Other big moneymakers in this category—approaching $200,000—are Calhoun and Evans.

Boeheim is listed as the leader in the TV-radio category, with $45,000, followed by Massimino and Carnesecca. The big winner here, though, is Carlesimo, who supposedly makes $50,000 for a TV show he doesn't have. It seems the figure was guaranteed in his new contract, but then Seton Hall couldn't arrange the show.

Stanton estimates that Thompson makes as much as $700,000 a year, while Massimino and Boeheim are in the $500,000 range. Barnes and O'Brien are at the bottom of the salary structure, in the $200,000-a-year range.

"I saw our coaches start to get big in 1982, the year John Thompson first went to the Final Four," says Mike Tranghese. "We were just on TV so much."

What has dramatically increased coaches' salaries, though, are the sneaker contracts, a relatively new phenomenon. Twenty years ago Converse, then the leading sneaker company in the basketball world, used to give away sneakers to various college and pro teams as a way of promoting their product. Later Adidas, trying to cut into Converse's stranglehold on the market, also started giving their sneakers away. Then Nike started paying coaches. First it was just a few thousand a year. Now in the big conferences it is tens of thousands, and it's usually figured into the overall package when a Big East coach is hired.

But unlike other professions, where success often means that you can slow down the pace and profit from all the work you did before, that is not true in coaching. Continued success requires a continual assembly line of players. Or as the old coaching adage goes, you can't make chicken salad out of chicken shit.

"Everyone recognizes that you have to work," says Tranghese. "You have to have good coaches who are going to work. And if you are at Seton Hall or Connecticut or Providence or Boston College, at no time can you be outworked. If you do, you will pay a price for it. Even when you are successful, you have to keep working. Look at Boeheim. You can't get involved with the people he gets involved with and not work. His ability to work has been expected, not appreciated."

Tranghese, 45, has been Gavitt's right hand for years. And the irony is that it all began as an accident. In the spring of 1972 Tranghese was working as the sports-information director at American International College in his native Springfield, Massachusetts. The summer before he had gone to a meeting of SIDs at Dartmouth College, where by chance he was paired up to play golf one morning with Vin Cuddy, who worked with Gavitt at Providence College. The two got along well and spent most of the three days together. At the end of the meeting, Cuddy said there was a job open at PC the following year, and Tranghese had to come down and talk to Dave Gavitt.

"Dave and I went for a walk around the campus," Tranghese says. "That was the interview. It was the strangest conversation I ever had with anyone. He never mentioned what he wanted me to do, or the job description, but rather talked the entire time about responsibility.

"Dave told me he would call me the following Friday at 11 in the morning," he recalls. "He did. But it was from the 10th tee at some golf course in New Jersey. That should have been my first clue that things were always going to be done a little differently."

Since then he has, in a sense, become Gavitt's alter-ego. If Gavitt is the visionary, Tranghese has always been the one to make sure the vision gets actualized. Their closeness started developing in that fall of 1972, just six weeks after Tranghese went to work at Providence College. Marvin Barnes, then a PC star, was charged with hitting a teammate with a tire iron in a postpractice fight, and Tranghese got a phone call at home from Gavitt.

"I think you better come in," he said. "You're about to begin earning your money."

Tranghese became an integral part of Gavitt's inner circle. Gavitt called him Iron Mike, later shortened to Iron. In a way the name is symbolic of their relationship. Tranghese is unwaveringly loyal. Unlike many working relationships in which the protege either outgrows his mentor or eventually wishes to change the dynamic, Tranghese has never chafed in his role. In turn, Gavitt kept giving Tranghese more and more responsibility. In a way Gavitt and Tranghese are like a long marriage that still works, each aware of the other's idiosyncracies but never bothered by them.

"We really are not very much alike," he says. "Dave is married with two kids, and I've been single for a long time. And we fight all the time. Dave is a great idea person, and I am always telling him why his ideas can't work. But in the 17 years I've worked with him we have never had a major philosophical difference over a major issue."

Gavitt echoes this, then takes it a step further.

"If Mike Tranghese were to leave, I would have to seriously reconsider my decision to be here," he says. "Many of the things I do, and many of the things I do for the conference, I don't think I would be able to do without him. He permits me to do a lot of the blue-sky and creative things, then he comes along and implements them. And implements them in the same way I envisioned them. I don't think people understand Mike's ability, because he's not visible. If I left here tomorrow he could step in and we wouldn't miss a beat."

For someone who's been so successful, Tranghese's never been someone who has needed his ego massaged. He's seemingly been content to stay in Rhode Island as Gavitt's understudy, play golf, hang out at the Players' Corner Pub, and help run what is, arguably, the most glamorous college basketball conference in the country.

"One of the reasons is that with the exception of being the commissioner of the ACC, Big 10, Pac 10 and SEC, there are very few jobs any better than I have now. If you thought about what are the most interesting things to work on in this office, you'd probably come up with the basketball scheduling, the TV schedule, and managing the money. And those are the three areas I deal with. The only thing I really don't get from being the associate commissioner of this conference is my name on the top. And with that comes being imposed upon in ways that right now I'm not. The other great thing about this job is that our office is not run like any other commissioner's office in the country, and that's because of Dave's personality. Our office is very informal. People are given responsibilities and expected to perform them. There is no such thing as punching in and punching out."

Tranghese continually stresses how Gavitt's coaching background has influenced how he shaped the league.

"Dave took the game away from winning and losing because of environmental factors," he says. "There are no more bandboxes, where long winning streaks are common. Dave passed a rule that you have to play in a building that seats at least 6,000 people. Officials are answerable to both coaches. I remember in the early years Dave and I would go into Pittsburgh to play Duquesne, and the refs would be two guys from Pittsburgh wearing ripple shoes. Dave just thought you couldn't win there. The officials weren't going to let you. That kind of thing doesn't happen in this league. Dave's coaching instincts always come out. If it's not good for the teams, we don't do it. And remember, people turned their basketball lives over to him. Georgetown understood from the beginning the necessity of a league. They also made the biggest sacrifice in going to the Capital Centre, which they did on their own. We never told them to do it. Then again, we never had to tell them how to run their basketball program. They've always understood how to do that. So did Syracuse, who knew they needed the league for scheduling. Looie? Looie was apprehensive. Dave said, Trust me. Rollie understood it, trusted Dave. Pittsburgh later understood it. Providence was in because Dave said they were in. BC,

Connecticut, and Seton Hall just wanted to be in with the big boys.

"With just a couple of exceptions, these are small Catholic institutions without major football programs, where basketball is the lifeblood. They aren't state universities with their vast resources. Georgetown, in concert with John, took their program and built it by design. They would have won the national championship in 1984 without us. But Villanova never would have won without the conference.

"There's no doubt that in the beginning we didn't know how good we could be, but there was a plan. Once we formed, there was no such thing as a school telling reporters they couldn't get in, as they did at Syracuse and St. John's the first year. There was no such thing as doing things second class, as they had been done in the East for so long."

Tranghese also was there when the Big East was faced with its greatest challenge, the specter of a new league in the East, one that would have dramatically changed what is the Big East of today.

In the spring of 1982, Joe Paterno, the Penn State football coach, wanted to enter the league. He was also the AD and he wanted a home for his basketball program. After he had met with Gavitt in Hartford, Gavitt sounded everyone out on the sly, and the basketball people—St. John's, Villanova, and Georgetown—said no. So Paterno wanted to form an Eastern football league, one that would include Pittsburgh and two schools in the league, Syracuse and Boston College. Gavitt knew that Paterno needed Pitt to have a football conference, so if he could get Pitt into the Big East, the idea for a football conference would be diffused.

"We met in Boston," says Tranghese, "and there was an element within the conference that wanted Pitt and an element that didn't. Some saw them as a football monster. We saw them as a new city, a school with a certain basketball tradition, and that playing at Pittsburgh was better than playing in State College. It was a higher comfort level. Coming back from that meeting I never saw Dave so mad. We both knew that if Pitt didn't get in, they would side with

Penn State, and there would be two leagues. When Dave got back, he called those three schools opposing him and said he wanted to see both the AD and the basketball coach in his office the next day. What he said was that if Pitt didn't get in, there would be two leagues. The talent would get divvied, so that while both leagues would be good, neither would be able to compete with the ACC. John Thompson was at that meeting. He understood just what Dave was saying."

Enter Pittsburgh through the back door.

One of the keys to the Big East's success has been television coverage, and Tranghese cites two unsung stars in this respect. "We knew from the beginning that we had to get on television. That's why Lenny Berman doing our games those first few years on Monday nights was so important to us. Lenny gave us immediate marquee value, and he also knew a lot about TV production. Because in the beginning Dave and I were doing games without any clue to what we were doing. Lenny was our expertise. And Billy McCoy was our director. Then in our seventh year when we began the Big East TV network, it was Billy McCoy who ran it for us. Then he taught us how to do it ourselves. If you talk about the most important people in the 10-year history of the Big East, two of them have to be Lenny Berman and Billy McCoy."

Tranghese talks about how the threat of a scandal is always a concern. For unlike some of the other major conferences in the country, there is the feeling that the presidents of the Big East would say it's not worth it and close the conference doors down. But he thinks the next major crisis in the conference will be when Gavitt leaves "his very own basketball league," whenever that will be.

Assistant Commissioner Tom McElroy agrees with Tranghese that the Big East will undergo its first significant crisis when, for whatever reason, Gavitt decides he's had enough. He is 37, blunt, with a native New Yorker's ability to cut through the pretense. He remembers being surprised when he first joined the conference office in 1981.

Gavitt was still the AD at Providence then and wouldn't join the Big East full time until the following year. So the Big East office was Tranghese, McElroy, and secretary Diane Woods.

"The attitude was that this is your job, now go out and do it," McElroy says. "I remember the first year I did something different on the cover of the media guide, and I wanted to show it to Mike first. He didn't even want to see it. He said it's your guide, do it the way you want. I could have had four coaches on the cover in the nude for all he cared."

McElroy also soon learned Gavitt's style. He is a strategist, not a detail man. He's someone who has grand visions, then surrounds himself with people who can carry them out. He's constantly coming up with new ideas, whether it is the Big East TV network a few years ago or next year's December series with the ACC—both to keep the Big East growing and to keep the Big East office stimulated, to prevent them from merely becoming managers. And McElroy learned that Gavitt is always trying to be two steps ahead of people he's playing with, no matter what the game.

"But Dave's first commandment, and the one he stresses to us all the time, is to make things better for all the kids that play our 16 sports in this conference. Sure, basketball gets all the attention and makes all the money, but Dave believes in the trickle-down theory: some of the money basketball makes should go to making it a better experience for that girl who plays tennis at Connecticut, or that golfer at Boston College. And that if we stop doing that, then it's time to close the doors, turn out the lights, and get out of the business."

MARCH 9, MORNING

It is a Thursday morning in the Grand Hyatt hotel on 42nd Street in midtown Manhattan, the site four months earlier of the Big East media day. The regular season is over, the Big East Tournament starts tonight, and in a few minutes the coaches are going to have another media session, the only time since that November morning that all nine coaches will be in the same room.

The surprise team, of course, has been Seton Hall, and the coaches have voted Carlesimo their coach of the year. It is the second straight year he has won, and he joins only Thompson and Carnesecca as multiple winners of the award. His selection is to be announced to the hundred or so media in the room by Dave Gavitt, who later says, "Personality-wise, P. J. hasn't changed a bit since he came into the league. As far as his coaching philosophy and style, that hasn't changed much either. The only perceptible difference is that his players play better defense now. Their man-to-man defense is outstanding."

Carlesimo stands before a bank of TV lights and cameras and speaks into a group of microphones. "I thought John deserved the award," he says, then goes on to praise the coaching jobs Evans, Carnesecca, and Barnes did as well. "But people don't understand how good our players are. I'm not being flip about it, but when you have great players and great assistant coaches, you're going to be successful."

Gavitt and Carlesimo then pose with a guy from Chrysler. Carlesimo holds the trophy, they smile, and the cameras click.

"That's the same dopey picture that's in the media guide this year," whispers Tom Luicci, in the back row of the reporters. Luicci, from the *Newark Star-Ledger,* has covered the Big East since the beginning. He has seen the evolution of Seton Hall first-hand. "I think P. J.'s wearing the same suit from last year, too. I think I liked it better when he was 6–23 and no one wanted to talk to him. The locker room was always open. He was always accessible. Listen to him now. He's so serious."

The ceremony is over, but Carlesimo remains in the front of the room, surrounded by reporters. Back in November he was a guy just happy to be there at all, someone whose career had been saved. Now he's one of the hottest coaches in the country, complete with a team that's going into the

NCAA Tournament for the second straight time. Last year, even after he had been named the Big East's coach of the year, the perception lingered that he hadn't really proved it. That's all changed now. All year the Hall has been one of the better teams in the country, and Carlesimo's been duly recognized for his resurrection of the Seton Hall program.

"Can you go further in the NCAA Tournament this year than you went last year?" he is asked.

"It's too early to say," he replies, "but this team is better than last year's. I didn't know too much about seeding last year, but then we had to play Arizona in Arizona in the second round, so now I got a little better appreciation of just what it means."

Seton Hall is a far different place than it was when he first went there, he says. There are new dorms, a new recreation center, more support services for his program. As he fields more questions, Luicci slowly shakes his head, as if remembering all those times in the past seven years when Carlesimo was just someone to say hello to before going somewhere else for the real interview.

"P. J., was your being named coach of the year a popularity contest?"

"I hope not," he says. Then he reflects for a moment. "Perhaps more so last year, to be honest about it."

"I'm wondering if Paul would do better if he ran harder," says a sportswriter from Pittsburgh.

Carlesimo laughs.

Evans has had a very good year. The Panthers come in having won five of their last six games, not only salvaging their season but making a strong statement that they belong in the NCAA Tournament.

"I think we have met the criteria of the NCAA," says Evans.

He won't find too many people to disagree with him. The Panthers have beaten Oklahoma, Syracuse, Georgetown, and Seton Hall twice. They also have what is generally considered to be the best recruiting class in the conference already lined up.

"You've seemed less controversial this year," he is told.

Evans looks up. He is wearing tassled loafers and a stylish black-weave sport jacket. "I had some things to say and I said them," he says. "I'll pick my spots." He pauses a beat, before adding, "The officiating still sucks."

Vintage Evans.

Next to him is Jim O'Brien. He is upset that Dana Barros didn't make first-team All-Conference. Not that he has many people to tell it to. O'Brien has finished last in the league, and that means the media crowds are always somewhere else. In that regard, little has changed since media day in November. You don't need much data to understand coaching status in the Big East: the number of reporters around each individual coach is a clear indication.

"It's hard for me to imagine that the guy who led the league in scoring and is 32 points shy of being the conference's all-time leading scorer can't make the All-Conference team," says O'Brien, an incredulous look on his face. "Did the other guys who made it deserve it? Certainly. But so did Dana."

It is not, of course, the first snub of Barros. Last spring, he had not been invited to the Olympic trials by Thompson, though he had led the Big East in scoring. In the triumvirate of senior guards—Douglas, Smith, and Barros—Barros has been the afterthought this year. Everyone acknowledges his ability; then they forget about him as soon as Boston College leaves the gym.

Across the room is Rollie Massimino. In November he was riding high. He was coming off a trip to the final eight, and he had four starters coming back. He started this year telling people this team reminded him of his title team. Now it's four months later and he knows he needs a miracle in the Big East Tournament, or he's destined to end the year in the NIT.

In tomorrow's *Daily News*, CBS basketball analyst Billy Packer says Massimino is the "kind of guy who becomes more dangerous when he thinks he's the underdog and convinces his kids they can overachieve." But Packer goes on to say he doesn't think Massimino is going to conjure up any magic in this tournament. "At this point I think he's frustrated. He thought his team was a top 10 club. He has to wonder why things aren't working. When Villanova hit the halfway point of the season, he had to be wondering what the hell happened. Kids can feel that stuff. Whenever they feel hesitancy on the part of the coach, they become hesitant themselves."

Not that Massimino is going to admit this. When asked about the mood of the team, he says, "The mood has been great. We've had great practices. Everyone's upbeat."

"Do you still feel you have a chance to make the tournament?"

"We don't delve in those things. We just go out and play. If we win, great. If we don't, we're not going to jump off any bridges. That's the approach we take, this year or any year."

But this hasn't been like any other year. In the nine years it has been in the Big East, Villanova has missed only one NCAA Tournament. In the past decade only North Carolina has been to the final eight of the NCAA Tournament more than Villanova. So now Massimino sits with a defensive look on his face. It's the look of someone who would rather be anywhere else than sitting here having to answer questions he doesn't want to hear.

Massimino is not the only coach here who needs a miracle. But Jim Calhoun is approaching it differently.

Standing near Calhoun is Tim Tolikan, one of the most respected and well-liked SIDs in the league. Always well versed, he is equipped with all sorts of stats to support the argument the Huskies belong in the NCAA Tournament. They played 16 games against top 50 teams. They were 4-0 against teams ranked anywhere between 50 and 100. If it's truly the NCAA Selection Committee's goal to have the 64 best teams in the tournament, the Huskies deserve to be invited. But even with the ammunition, one senses Tolikan knows Connecticut is a longshot.

"We think we're an NCAA team, but I think we're going to have to prove it and get Seton Hall tomorrow," he says.

Calhoun seems more concerned with what happens if the Huskies don't get invited. He is known for being extremely accessible to the media, to the point that some people within the conference think Calhoun talks too much. Now he's ticking off plusses in the season. Connecticut has had back-to-back winning seasons for the first time since the Corny Thompson teams of the early years of the Big East. The program is ahead of schedule. There's a reason he was given a seven-year contract three years ago, for rebuilding the Connecticut basketball program was not going to happen quickly.

For all his heartiness, though, he has to be disappointed. Yes, the Huskies are better than they have been. Yes, they have played everyone tough all season long. Yes, they undoubtedly are ahead of schedule in Calhoun's rebuilding plan. But not only are they still some distance away from being among the Big East's elite, one suspects that Calhoun has come to believe the job is a lot tougher than what he envisioned back when he was at Northeastern.

In the back of the room Carnesecca, in a camel-hair sport jacket, looks at a group of writers around him.

"I'm amazed at how many people are over here," he says softly in his raspy voice. "I thought I'd have to come to you guys."

Carnesecca is not used to this. Since the league began, his teams have always been in the first division. He has always been in demand. Now his team has finished eighth in the league, and he's in the tournament's qualifying game, the so-called game of shame. But he handles it well. Looie always handles adversity well, talking about how hard it is every year to put the balls away. He's part old coach, part philosopher, part neighborhood butcher reminiscing at the end of the summer about where the season went.

The faces in front of him keep changing, and Carnesecca continues to sit with his arms folded, talking basketball. He notes that some years he hasn't liked the chemistry of his team, for reasons that have nothing to do with wins and losses. This year's team, though, he's enjoyed.

Back in November he was faced with a young team with-

out a backcourt, a built-in recipe for failure. But this
season can't be viewed as a failure. Jayson Williams has
emerged as a genuine Big East star. Werdann and Sealy, his
two touted freshmen, have already been through the Big
East wars, their red badges of courage already earned. Add
Boo Harvey to this lineup, mix in a few more talented
young players, and this becomes a first-division Big East
team next year. "Rebuilding years" often are euphemisms
for bad years, but not this time.

"If you told me back then we'd win 15, I'd have been
happy," he says. "Now you'd like to win some more. You
get greedy."

Nearby is Rick Barnes, and much has changed for him
since media day back in November. No longer is he just the
new coach, the guest at the party nobody knows. No longer
is he just another name that only recruiting junkies know.
Now he is one of the season's success stories, and his national reputation is growing.

He came into the season inheriting a team that had limped
to the finish line the year before, riddled with dissension. So
his primary goal was to bring some stability to a turbulent
program, and he did that before he even played a game. By
the end of December the Friars no longer looked like they
had Pitino's ghost hovering over them. A month later they
had become one of the surprises of the Big East. Last
Saturday night his Friars won their 18th game of the season,
virtually assuring them of an NCAA bid. So now he sits
here and talks about tomorrow's game with Syracuse and
how important it is for his team, but deep down he surely
knows that it's all frosting. The real work of the season
already's been accomplished.

At his own table Jim Boeheim has gathered his own
crowd, once again defending his program. Ever since November there was the feeling that if Syracuse didn't go to
the Final Four somehow their season would be disappointing.
That perception still remains. Maybe that is always to be
Boeheim's fate.

In many ways he has become a victim of the Carrier
Dome, where, in many ways, the show is more important

than the actual game. To routinely fill the Dome, it has to be a show. There have to be dunks. There has to be flash. Would 30,000 people come to watch Syracuse every night if they played the same patterned style as Villanova, for example? And like all shows, the show that is Syracuse basketball has always to top itself; it constantly needs an assembly line of showmen who are going to keep putting people in the seats.

The offshoot of all this is that success is now expected. Syracuse has become one of those few programs in the country where the measure of success has become so unrealistic that only a Final Four appearance will satisfy its fans. Boeheim gets no credit for his remarkable achievements. He only gets blamed when his team fails to measure up to the near-impossible expectations. Is it any wonder he always seems on the defensive?

"The NCAA is a turkey shoot," he says. "The year we went to the Final Four, we went through the toughest schedule in the tournament we ever had. In the preseason, Seton Hall was picked seventh in our league, but if they get beat in the first round, their fans will think they had a bad year. I guarantee it. The bottom line in college basketball now is the NCAA Tournament. If you don't make that, you've had a bad year. Last year we won 26 games, but we lost to Rhode Island in the second round of the tournament. People were not thrilled."

The talk turns to last Sunday's game against Georgetown in the Carrier Dome, one in which many TV shots showed Boeheim seemingly out of control on the sidelines.

"That's an actor," he says. "The Jim Boeheim you see during a game is an actor. That's not me."

He hesitates, and when he speaks again his voice is softer.

"I didn't realize I was coming across as so hostile. I would be afraid of that guy on the sidelines. I don't like that public image, even if I wasn't aware of it. But I'm not going to change. I just want to coach and block everything else out."

Nearby is John Thompson, "Large Father" himself. Mary Fenlon sits behind him. Bill Shapland is close by. So is AD Frank Rienzo. Team Georgetown.

At media day in November, Thompson was the center of attention. He had been friendly, charming, as relaxed as if he were sitting around his living room. He had just returned from the Olympics, and during the preseason practice he had taken his own kind of leave. He stopped answering the phone. He stopped answering his mail. He stopped giving interviews. Essentially, he stopped doing the things he doesn't like to do and just coached his team.

Now it's four months later, and Thompson seems to have grown in stature. The Olympic loss seems to be behind him. At the beginning of the season there was speculation he would be greeted with a lot of abuse in arenas around the country. That has not happened. He has become one of the game's ombudsmen, someone who now has the stature to speak out on issues that affect the game. One suspects the Prop 48 controversy was only the beginning. We will hear more from John Thompson, for he's transcended being a basketball coach and has become a national figure. Certainly, he has conducted himself that way throughout the year.

People close to him say Thompson doesn't do anything differently this year than he's always done.

"I don't think John's changed as much as he's received differently," says Michael Wilbon of the *Washington Post*. "Starting in the '82 season when Patrick Ewing was a freshman, people became more aware of John and the way he did things. He really had never been on the national stage before. But he always had the same rules: freshmen couldn't talk to the media until the first of the year, closed practices, players being less accessible than in most other programs. But it never was a local problem, because it had always been that way. The feuds with the media were never local.

"After 1982 John definitely tightened up, but I don't know if you can say he was needlessly uptight. He took a lot of shots. After all, some guy from Utah wrote that he was the Idi Amin of basketball. That's pretty strong stuff."

Wilbon, who is black and started covering Thompson in 1981, the year before Ewing arrived, also knows a side of Thompson the public rarely sees. A few years ago, when

Wilbon's father died on the day the Hoyas were in a NCAA Tournament game, it was Thompson who sent the biggest wreath. When Thompson heard one night that Dave Kindred, a sports columnist for the *Post,* was leaving for Atlanta, he showed up at the paper with a bottle of champagne. When he found out Katha Quinn had cancer, he always went out of his way to send her notes and call her, though the two of them had never been particularly friendly.

"He is one of the most control-conscious people I have ever seen," says Wilbon. "And he's always demanded the right to do things his own way and has gotten upset when his personality was not respected. But I don't think he's changed this year as much as in 1986. That was the year that Reggie Williams was a senior, a time when the pressure was off. For the first time in years Georgetown was allowed to be an underdog, and I didn't see the same bluster. Plus, he had already won the national championship. This year is just a continuation of that."

Wilbon also believes some of the basis for the attacks on Thompson over the years is racial. "When people say he is 'intimidating,' that is a code word. Here's a guy who has a soft, fleshy face and wears bifocals. How intimidating can he be? He doesn't do anything other coaches don't do, but because he is 6-foot-10 and black, he gets called intimidating."

Certainly, the issue of race has always complicated the public perception of Thompson. White coaches can be dictatorial and do things their own way, while Thompson's never been given the same leverage. And there's no doubt that Thompson's someone who defies labels. Nationally, he's been perceived as a racist because all his players are black and the Hoyas have become black America's team. Yet in D.C. he's been called an Uncle Tom for, among other things, sending his own two sons to Princeton and Georgetown, and for never sending any of his players to a black agent. Outside of his players, he lives in a white world. One minute he can be as charming as he wants, the next he can throw the word "motherfucker" around as easily as Alonzo Mourning dunks a basketball.

"He is full of contradictions," says Wilbon, "which is why

he's so fascinating. He is one of the greediest people I know, and he makes no bones about it. John is much too bizarre to figure out with code words."

A political columnist has written in the *Washington Post* that Thompson should run for mayor of the District of Columbia. "What Washington needs is a leader who has overcome disadvantage to succeed through discipline and determination, who can inspire young people, who embodies genuine values and who is categorically his own man," wrote Mark Shields, a Georgetown season ticketholder.

"Can you envision me a politician?" Thompson laughs. "You have to be concerned with public perception. How would they like it if I told them my office was closed? Can you see it? Reporters wanting to see the mayor, and the office is closed?"

He sits at a small table in a dark suit and dark tie, the microphones in front of him, reporters clustered around him. He is still the center of attention, and many of the questions concern his third-place finish in the Olympics. Rest assured, Thompson has heard all the criticisms: how he didn't select the right players, how he stressed defense when he should have stressed offense.

"And it hurt him deeply, it had to," says Rienzo. "But John is a strong guy and it's amazing how he's able to put things in perspective. He never got too high over winning, so this wasn't going to defeat him either."

Early in the season Thompson told Thomas Boswell of the *Washington Post* he had come back from Seoul a depressed and frustrated man. Now he says coaching in the Olympics was all part of his philosophy of taking risks in your life.

He goes on to talk about how he deplores the recent development in basketball of making stars out of high-school players. He dislikes the climate in which schools have to keep seducing high-school kids. Wilbon believes that Thompson's displeasure with the recruiting process will eventually make him leave coaching, probably about the same time Mourning leaves Georgetown. He says that he once heard

Thompson rant and rave about the indignities of recruiting. ("The motherfuckers want me to write them 15-page letters about my program, but the motherfuckers can't read them anyway.") It's no secret that Thompson spends little time at high-school games, leaving the job of talent evaluation to his assistants. Supposedly, he never even saw Mourning play in high school.

"Are you tired?"

"I'm aware that I've been working for a long time," he says. "But what puts the stress on you is what happens off the court, not on it. And in respect these kids have been great, because they've allowed me to concentrate on basketball and not all the other things you sometimes have to worry about."

Media day is drawing to a close. Most of the coaches have already headed upstairs to the luncheon, and the only two left are Thompson and Boeheim. Think about that for a second. John Thompson is one of the last of nine coaches to leave a press conference.

11

THE BIG EAST TOURNAMENT

MARCH 9, EVENING

It's the game of shame, the qualifying game between the two teams with the lowest records. In the stands sits Dave Gavitt, waiting for the start of what has become a tournament that in some ways is more fiercely fought than the NCAA, if only because the teams have already faced each other twice. Of course, Gavitt does more than Celebrity appearances. He has seen a great many games this season.

"I go to as many games as possible," he says. "That's what I like to do. I don't think any other commissioners go to as many games as I do. I probably go to 30 a year, not counting the tournament. The games are what makes this special.

"I do some of our TV games just for my own enjoyment. Certain media people criticize me for it, but I like doing them. And also it keeps me in touch with our coaches from a basketball standpoint. Also the players: by the time they are seniors I know all of them. Because the danger in this job is to get too removed from the kids. I don't even like the term 'commissioner.' It sounds like you're some kind of judge or arbitrator. That's not me. If that's what this job becomes, get someone else.

"My situation gets personalized too much. There are guys who are much better commissioners than I am, but the only two who were former coaches are me and Vic Bubas of the ACC. I don't resent that 'most powerful man in college basketball' stuff, but I don't much like it either. Nor do I think it's true. I have a purist's love for the game. I am continually fascinated by the game, enthused by it, have fun with it. That's my motivation. If it has to do with basketball, I'll do it. All my volunteer efforts have to do with the game. What was I? Someone from a small town in New Hampshire. The game has been very good to me, and every time I've been asked to do something for it, I've done it. I wouldn't get motivated to serve on some of the NCAA councils that have nothing to do with the game, nor would I be very good on them. Some people do volunteer work in their towns. Mine is all related to the game. I still love the game itself. It doesn't have to be a Big East game. I love the first round of the NCAA Tournament when all the games are on. It doesn't matter who they are. I watch and I coach both teams."

He got involved in international basketball in 1975, when he helped prepare the Pan-American team and took them all over Europe. His involvement with the NCAA Tournament started at the Final Four in 1977, when he was asked to be on the NABC board of directors. He was there for two years. When he stopped coaching at Providence in 1979, he was asked to be on the NCAA Selection Committee. He served on that for six years, eventually becoming its head.

He is asked if he ever worries that everything has gotten too big.

"I don't think the fact that our games are on television, or played in big arenas, change the way the game is played. But the one thing I think that's regrettable is that a Billy Packer or a Dick Vitale are now the ones that bring the game to us. And I don't mean to be disrespectful to either of them, because I think they're both good guys. And they certainly both have a real love for the game. But there's no balance to it. This is the electronic age, and Joe Fan is not being educated in the true beauty of the game—not in the purist sense of a Bobby Knight or a Pete Carril or a Ralph Miller. That's not what TV people want. They want controversy and excitement. And I don't blame a Packer or a Vitale. If they want to keep their jobs, they have to be entertaining. But the downside is we get the all-bubble-gum team, and all this stuff that takes away from the pure form of the game."

Is there too much pressure on the coaches?

"I don't believe coaches get fired in the best leagues in the country. They leave because they get burned out, or they can't handle the criticism. People get fired at places where they have administrators who expect them to go to the Final Four and they have no chance to do that. I look at the 10-year history of this league and the only coach who was fired was Gordon Chiesa last year at Providence. Billy Raftery quit at Seton Hall. Dom Perno quit at Connecticut. Chipman quit at Pittsburgh. So is there pressure? Yes and no. Here you can go 17–10 and still make the NCAA Tournament."

Does he worry about his schools?

"Not really. I used to worry about Seton Hall, because for a while there I didn't think they were going to be able to compete. Providence for a while. Boston College before they built the new building, because I wasn't sure they could stay competitive without it. But now I don't think there's any school in the league that can't compete. I worry a little about life at Georgetown after John Thompson, life at Villanova after Rollie, life after Looie. These places are not the Carrier Dome. All have been dominated by three very strong personalities."

Does he worry about the threat of scandal?

"I know one thing: if we were to have the types of problems that occur in some of the other conferences, we couldn't survive them because of the media markets we're in. I just don't think we could survive the publicity. The presidents would say it's not worth it, and that would be that. But I really don't worry about the schools because of their institutional controls. And I couldn't be the policeman for nine schools even if I wanted to. The presidents set the tone. The athletic directors reflect that tone. If you cheat at Boston College, you're gone. If you cheat at Villanova, you're gone. In some other conferences in the country, the fans and the booster clubs are running the programs. That's not happening here. John Thompson knows he can have a few bad years and survive at Georgetown. But if he gets caught cheating, he's gone. He knows that."

Gavitt pauses, weighing his words.

"Our schools are very fragile. The conference can provide the atmosphere, the forum, et cetera, but our schools don't have the support systems schools like Duke, North Carolina, and Maryland have. Our office handles all the TV for our schools. Presidents of the schools have called me to help them in putting together packages for coaches. In the beginning we wrote marketing programs for everyone. We promoted the Big East Tournament. We dealt with facilities, with game management. For instance, in 1975 Boston College sold less than 200 ticket packages for the Eastern Regionals 40 miles away. Now they sell 1500 ticket packages for a tournament they can be out of after the first day.

"In the beginning our goal was to be as good as we could be, and we can't stop striving for that. I don't worry about the coaches. They're into winning games and coaching their teams. I have a unique relationship with the coaches, because I was a coach. I like them all, and I want them all to be successful. They know that I'm not going to do anything for them that's going to give them an advantage over anyone else—for instance, I'm not going to tell a kid to go to a particular school— but they also know that I'm always looking out for their interests, that I will do everything to help them. It's some of the others I worry about. I have to lean on some of the ADs—even though I like them personally—but some have forgotten what it used to be like. Those are the ones I push. And sometimes I sense they're tired of being pushed and I understand that. And sometimes I get tired of pushing."

How tired?

Gavitt admits that for the first time in a while he's given thought to doing something else. This spring his son, Corey, who plays lacrosse at the University of North Carolina, will graduate. If once upon a time Gavitt never wanted to leave Rhode Island because of his family, now his kids are older. Throughout his career, Gavitt's important decisions have largely been based on family considerations. One of the reasons he gave up coaching is that he wanted to spend more time with his two sons. As he has said, "I had spent so much time helping to raise other people's children, and I wanted to spend more time with mine." He knew that with coaching he was always going to be a slave to the games and the practice schedule. Being an administrator is different; administrators have more control over their travel schedule. At the start of every year he took out his calendar and wrote in his sons' games, whether high school or college, then tried to work his schedule around theirs.

He's not sure just what he'd do if he ever walks out of the Big East office for good. Two years ago he turned down the chance to be the president of the New Jersey Nets. But the NBA still has some appeal to him—maybe the chance to run his own team. For despite all his administrative success, deep down Dave Gavitt is still a basketball coach. Old coaches never die, they just don't sit on the bench anymore.

Unlike most of the qualifying games, this one between St. John's and Boston College attracts a decent crowd, no doubt due to the presence of St. John's in the game. Not that anyone is used to having St. John's in the game. How bad has it gotten? The St. John's cheerleaders and the infamous Red Man have been suspended for lack of enthusiasm. Somehow it seems symbolic. Having the Redmen struggle takes getting used to.

Tonight, the Redmen go up by 9 after the first 12 minutes, Dana Barros has yet to score, and it appears the Eagles' season has only an hour and a half to go. O'Brien, concerned Barros is too pumped up for what could be his last game, even takes him out for a while to calm him down.

Then Barros scores 16 points in the next five and a half minutes and the game turns around. BC wins, 74–63. Barros finishes with 38, one of his all-time great performances, and the Eagles live to play another day. It is the Barros of legend: the quickness, the incredible balance, the deep jumper. It is also his message to the coaches who didn't vote for him for the conference's first team.

Ironically, the last time these two teams played each other, 10 days ago in Alumni Hall, Barros had two shots to either tie or win and missed them both. Afterward, St. John's Matt Brust, the Big East's version of Rambo, described Barros as a tiny bug he could step on. Of course, when asked who was the person he would least like to be guarded by, Brust said himself. Barros says he'd read those comments and used them to motivate himself. Tonight he has turned Brust every which way but loose. Carnesecca calls it one of the best performances he's ever seen and adds that Barros will play in the pros. "He'll need some picks, but he'll bury that jumper."

"It feels good to play well after everything that's happened in the last two weeks," says Barros.

St. John's has finished eighth, their lowest finish in the 10-year history of the Big East. It has had its lowest victory total in 25 years. It will not be invited to the NCAA Tournament for the first time in eight years. And now it's out of the Big East Tournament almost before it begins.

On the surface it seems like a lost year, but next week St. John's will get invited to the NIT and get another chance. It is one they make the most of. They eventually win the NIT, the second year in a row a Big East team has come out of the Big East qualifying game and gone on to win the NIT. Jayson Williams will be named the MVP, further evidence that he is on the threshold of Big East stardom.

Ironically, in the middle of the tournament Katha Quinn will die, on March 17, one day before her 35th birthday. Before St. John's plays Oklahoma State in a second-round NIT game there is a moment of silence. The team wears black swatches on their uniforms in her memory and they dedicate the rest of the season to her.

"The last time I saw her was the day before she died,"
Carnesecca tells the *New York Daily News*. "It was the first
time since her illness that she showed any sign of letting up.
Maybe it was just reality setting in. 'Coach,' she said, 'I
need a miracle.' "

After her death Carnesecca refuses to cheapen her memory by saying her death was a rallying cry for his team,
saying instead, "That's private."

Senior Matt Brust, though, expresses the emotion of his
teammates. All year he has been the leader of this young
team, the one link between Walter Berry, Mark Jackson,
and the good times of the past and this freshman class that's
supposed to one day put St. John's back among the Big East
leaders. Brust has always been a coach's player, the former
high-school football star turned loose on the basketball court.
There have been better players in the Big East. None have
ever played any harder.

"I am supposed to be the inspirational leader of this
team," he says. "But she is."

Maybe former Boston College coach Gary Williams best
described the Big East Tournament: "A guy once told me
you should want to coach where they give out big trophies
and play organ music."

And this is the place.

The Big East Tournament is more than just the games, of
course. It is a tribal ritual both for the fans and the media.
From the first year the tournament came to Madison Square
Garden in 1983, it's been one of the toughest tickets to get
in New York. Back in the early years the tournament headquarters was the Penta Hotel on Seventh Avenue, across
the street from the Garden, and it was a common sight to
see students in their school colors and painted faces in the
lobby, as if the entire hotel had become the setting for an
elaborate costume party. Nowadays the headquarters is the
Grand Hyatt, with its waterfalls and glitz: the look of expense-
account money. The tournament has gone uptown. Literally.

There are broadcasters who have been here for years:
Doug Logan, who does Syracuse; Rich Chvotkin, who does

the Georgetown games; Chuck Wilson, who does a talk show in Providence; Alan Segal, who broadcasts Boston College games; exbaseball player Dick Groat, the color man on the Pitt broadcasts.

There are many sportswriters who have covered the Big East Tournament for years: Bob Snyder of the *Syracuse Herald Journal;* Leigh Montville of the *Boston Globe;* Lesley Visser, once of the *Boston Globe,* now of CBS; Dick Weiss of the *Philadelphia Daily News;* the old guard of the Connecticut horde, Pat Drewry of Waterbury, Randy Smith and Phil Chardis of Manchester; Tom Luicci of the *Newark Star-Ledger;* Bill Parrillo of the *Providence Journal;* Happy Fine, one of the all-time cult figures in Eastern sports writing, someone who once spent a winter living in his car traveling to games around the East. In a sense the Big East Tournament is their convention, the games just an excuse to renew old friendships. Like soldiers who have been to war together, they have seen the same games, know the same people, share a common language. The players in the Big East come and go, but like the coaches, many of the sportswriters are here year after year.

They have also been witnesses not only to the Big East's growth but to the effect it's had on basketball both in the East and nationally.

One of them is Charlie Pierce of the *Boston Herald.* A short, rumpled man in his mid-30s, he always seems to look as if he thinks the counterculture has made a comeback. He came to the *Herald* after being the national political correspondent for the *Boston Phoenix,* a weekly paper that evolved out of the counterculture, and he is one of the few sportswriters in America who, in the course of a paragraph, can equate the Syracuse fast break with the Zapruder film on the Kennedy assassination and somehow make it make sense.

"Gavitt has always been two or three years ahead of everyone else," says Pierce. "He saw that college basketball was about to become a national sport, and he saw the role TV was going to play. He also saw, before a lot of people did, the impact of ESPN, how they could essentially put games on every night of the week and save the networks for the weekend games. So he created a league in which television markets replaced natural rivalries, and he was able to market it. How many times did Syracuse ever play Villanova, Connecticut play Georgetown, or Providence play Pittsburgh? These aren't traditional rivalries. They are television rivalries.

"But is it good for basketball in the East? I don't believe so. It's ruined the Big Five in Philadelphia. It's ruined Holy Cross. It's ruined every program in New York except St. John's. The Big East people will tell you there's a trickle-down effect. I don't believe it. I don't believe the Big East has helped anyone except the Big East. Should they feel guilty about it? No. Why should they feel guilty about doing something successfully which had been sitting there for years without anyone ever doing it?"

Pierce is also someone who has seen the evolution of the coaches.

"They've all become stars," he says, "and I despise the phenomenon. They make all this money and the kids get none of it. And now the kids don't even get the attention."

Pierce has long been critical of Thompson in print, calling him Grandmaster Clash. After the Olympics he wrote a scathing article on Thompson, ending it by saying the Large Father should take his medal, put it on his mantel for all the world to see, and have it *bronzed*. All the same he believes Thompson would have gained his enormous stature even without the Big East.

"He has made Georgetown the national sports team of the black community. You see black kids with Georgetown jackets everywhere. And that would have happened without the Big East. The Rollie monster, on the other hand, is a creation of the Big East. He's out of control. It's like after he won the title he became a legend in his own mind. If you beat him for a kid, you cheated. He's become everything I don't like about coaches. He's the star. It's always 'I never have enough players. It's me. It's my system.' But understand, I have a personal thing with him because he once chewed me out in front of my family and about a hundred people for something a colleague of mine wrote. That's just Rollie. 'I'm out of control.' And he's allowed to be. Evans

is going down the same road. He's unraveling. He spent his
first two years in the league always talking about what dogs
he had, then piling up technicals to the sky. But that's the
Big East. It's a big, loud TV show. It's not the chamber
music, the way the ACC likes to operate."

In the end, of course, Pierce says it all comes down to
Gavitt.

"I don't think there's ever been anyone more powerful in
college basketball," he says. "There has never been a Ken-
nesaw Mountain Landis in basketball. What you had was
certain coaches who had private duchies. It was like the
Balkans—no centralized authority. Then along comes this
guy whose hand seems to be everywhere: TV, the Olympics.
It's a classic example of empire building. And no one complains. TV doesn't complain. The fans don't complain. The
schools, which are making more money off this than they
ever dreamed of, certainly aren't going to complain. The
only people who complain are the ones on the outside, and
they are dismissed as sour grapes.

"But wherever Gavitt goes, there is innovation. And he is
the only coach who was ever able to get both Marvin Barnes
and Ernie DiGregorio to play the way they could. Why?
Because he was able to subordinate his ego, and he wasn't
afraid to take chances. He didn't try to play little Hitler and
control them. Think about it. He got Marvin Barnes, perhaps the ultimate head case in basketball history, to play for
him. So I guess what I'm saying is the reason the Big East is
successful is that Dave Gavitt once coached Marvin Barnes."

Several of the sportswriters here have been to all nine
previous tournaments. The first was held in Providence,
then Syracuse, then Hartford. Then a contract was signed
with Madison Square Garden. Interestingly, the tournament
almost ended up in the Meadowlands. Seton Hall voted for
the Meadowlands, because it was the nearby building they
hoped to play in some day. Syracuse voted for it because
they had a football association with the Meadowlands.
Villanova voted for it because the director of the Meadowlands was a Villanova alumnus. Others had had bad experi-
ences in the Garden, a building known for being run by the

unions, one not hospitable to visiting teams. In the end the Garden won out, but it had been close.

It didn't take long, though, for everyone to realize that the move to the Garden was another stroke of genius. For a new league seeking a national identity, what better place than Madison Square Garden? The first year the tournament was the cover story in *Sports Illustrated:* a picture of Billy Goodwin of St. John's sitting on a basket in celebration. Ever since that first year the tournament has dominated the back page of the New York tabloids for four days. It is treated as one of the big sports events in the city.

MARCH 10

Some sportswriters in the East consider this one of the greatest days in sports: the quarterfinals of the Big East Tournament. With two games in the afternoon and two in the evening, eight of the nine teams are on display. It is all here: the cheerleader pyramids, the mascots, the pep bands, all the pageantry of college basketball from noon until nearly midnight. All the NBA scouts are here, and the media contingent rivals the one for the Final Four, taking three rows of seats on one side of the court.

The first game of the afternoon is Seton Hall against Connecticut. The Hall is playing for a seeding in the NCAA Tournament. Connecticut is playing for its season. They are 16–11 and hoping that two wins this weekend might sneak them into the NCAA Tournament. With eight minutes left to play, the Huskies are only down by 4, but the Pirates take command in the final minutes as the Seton Hall student section behind the basket shout "NIT . . . NIT" at Connecticut. The Hall takes it, 74–66. Neither team shoots well— the Huskies shoot 28 percent for the game, and the Hall gets no points from their guards for the first 26 minutes. In a sense the game has been a microcosm of the season for both teams. The Pirates have had stretches where they struggled offensively but played great man-to-man defense, and they have found a way to win. Connecticut has played hard, stayed close, but hasn't won.

"Our kids all year have been finding a way to win," says Carlesimo afterward.

He is in the interview room, a large area in the bowels of the Garden. The ritual is always the same. The winning coach, along with a player or two, comes out first and sits at a long table in the front of the room. He is introduced by Chris Plonsky, who runs the press conference. The coach gives a short opening statement, in which he sums up the game in a few paragraphs, then takes questions from the reporters, which are first repeated by Plonsky.

"We didn't shoot fouls well, and I didn't think we played particularly well," Carlesimo says. "We got by on our defense and our character, like we have all year."

He has brought Ramon Ramos with him, still in his uniform. Ramos reiterates the same theme Carlesimo has stressed all year—namely, the Hall is a senior-dominated team that has much more balance than the Seton Hall teams of the past.

A few minutes later Carlesimo leaves and is replaced by Calhoun. The day before he was asked who his starters were going to be—not a bad question, considering that in 27 games he's used 13 different starting lineups. He had quipped he was going to put five uniforms in the locker room and send 10 players in after them, so "at least I'll know who my toughest players are." Not that it really matters. No one doubts his team is tough. How tough it is for them to score is another question. Calhoun describes the game as not something "Picasso would have been happy with," then becomes a lobbyist for the Huskies' slim chances of still getting into the NCAA Tournament, as if the constant discussion of the subject might make it a reality.

"I don't have any question that we belong in the NCAA Tournament," he says. "Unless everyone in there is Seton Hall, or Georgetown, or Syracuse. Seton Hall is more experienced than we are. That's the difference in the two teams. We entered the game 29th ranked in the power ratings, and we leave the game feeling pretty good about ourselves. So I actually should be celebrating now."

His voice seems to trail off. "But I can't find anything to celebrate about."

He is asked about Cliff Robinson's performance. Robinson was 3 of 17 from the field, one of his worst games of the year. In a sense, Robinson was again the basketball version of a tease.

"Cliff averaged 20 points and 8 rebounds a game for us this year," Calhoun says. "He didn't have a good basketball game today. He's not the first good player not to have a good basketball game."

The Connecticut press corps go into the press room adjacent to the interview area and start writing their Huskie postmortems. "It's like you can't spell 'Connecticut' without 'NIT,' " says Phil Chardis of the *Manchester Inquirer*. "Thank God I've written 'bubble' for the last time this year."

Later, Robinson is standing in the corner of a small locker room, trying to explain what went wrong. Somehow the scene seems symbolic. Sometimes when you think of Cliff Robinson's career at Connecticut, you think of someone who's always trying to explain why the results haven't been better. It's not really fair. Maybe it's the price tag for being 6-11 and always having to live under the curse of having great potential.

"You ended up 3 of 17," someone tells him.

Robinson looks at him. "What am I supposed to do?" he says. "Make an excuse? I can make an excuse, but there are no excuses."

Next week the Huskies will defend their title in the NIT. But if last year the NIT was a magical ride, this year it seems like some cruel joke. In the quarterfinals they lose to the University of Alabama-Birmingham. Not only that, they lose in their bandbox of a field house on the campus at Storrs, the place where, according to Carnesecca, even "Napoleon couldn't win."

Out on the court, the second half of the afternoon doubleheader pits Providence against Syracuse. After the Friars lost their second close game of the season to Syracuse, Barnes said he wanted to play Syracuse again. Now he has them again, with the same result. Syracuse wins by 3, 79–76, withstanding a furious Providence rally, for their 21st straight win over the Friars.

Syracuse had problems—Coleman was in foul trouble and Douglas was 5 of 14 from the field—until Billy Owens scored 15 points in the second half and turned it into his personal Garden party. For one of the few times all year he stamped his personal imprint all over a game. Not that he hasn't played well this year. He has averaged in double figures. He has rebounded. He has defended. He has done all the little things basketball purists love. But he's never taken over a game until today. This afternoon Billy Owens has shown the entire Big East what all the hype has been about and given a sneak preview of the future.

The other freshman who had a monster game is David Johnson. He is from Louisiana, another example of how Syracuse has become a national school. He spent last year prepping at Maine Central Institute and arrived at Syracuse with the reputation of being a great athlete. In the beginning of the year he seemed tentative, nowhere near ready to play. Recently he's had some great practices, to the point that Boeheim has labeled him the best pure athlete on the team. He also ends up with 18 points in the game.

Outside the Providence locker room is former coach Rick Pitino. The Friars have their 18 wins, but they have lost six of their last seven games. A few minutes earlier Pitino went into the room to tell Barnes and the Providence players not to be discouraged. They've had a great year already, and who knows what lies ahead when the NCAA Tournament starts next week? He reminded them that two years ago, when he and the Friars went to the Final Four by beating Georgetown, they had been blown out in the Big East Tournament by the Hoyas.

Now he stands in the corridor telling everyone who asks him that Barnes should be the coach of the year in the Big East. "I've been thrilled by what I've seen of the Friars all year." If a year and a half ago Pitino left Providence to go to the Knicks, in a sense he left a piece of his heart behind. These Friars are still his team in ways the current Knicks can never be. Soon Pitino will prove that college basketball

is his game. After losing to the Chicago Bulls in the second
round of the playoffs, Pitino will accept the coaching job at
Kentucky on June 1.

With 13 minutes to play in the first half, Alonzo Mourning has two fouls, and the score of the Georgetown-Boston
College game is tied. In comes Dikembe Mutombo. Playing
against a BC front line that features one guy at 6-9 and two
at 6-5, Mutombo immediately triggers an 18-2 run that nulli-
fies any suspense. Mutombo finishes the half with 12 points,
and the Hoyas ultimately win by 30, 82–52. Barros, played
box-and-one much of the game, is limited to just seven
shots.

Afterward, BC's Steve Benton is asked how tall Mutombo
is.

"Seven-nine."

"The way Georgetown is shaping up, they are a team that
can win the national championship," says O'Brien. "Their
only Achilles heel is their perimeter shooting. But they take
you out of the game with their defense and their shot-
blocking."

O'Brien is in the back of the building, on his way back to
the locker rooms. He says he's leaving tomorrow morning to
go recruiting. He knows now that his number-one priority is
to get some players. Every other team in the Big East will
be playing somewhere next week, either in the NCAAs or
the NIT, except the Eagles, where the balls have already
been put away for next year.

"I'm relieved it's over," says O'Brien as the sound of the
Pittsburgh-Villanova game is heard beyond the walls. "It's
really been hard. It's been the worst year of my coaching
life. One thing after another all year long. It's been tough
on the kids, too. Tough on everybody. The good thing is we
got some wins down the stretch, got some respect. I feel
really grateful for that. Cause the kids didn't quit, and they
could have. A couple of years ago I would have been all
over them, all the time, but after the Connecticut game
there—the lowest point of the season for us—we as a staff
made a conscious effort to lighten up. We became realistic.

And the kids responded favorably because we didn't bury them. But I'm very relieved it's done. I think we all are."

It's ironic that Massimino and Evans find themselves matched up against each other in the last game of the quarterfinals. Yes, they have patched up their feud from last year. They shake hands now and go out of their way not to say antagonistic things about each other. Still, one gets the feeling that all Pittsburgh has to do is beat out Villanova for another recruit and the feud will surface again. One also gets the feeling Massimino would rather lose to anyone else in the conference than Evans, unless maybe Jim Calhoun. In addition, the Cats, at 16–14, still cling to the hope that a victory tonight, and maybe an upset tomorrow, and they can sneak into the NCAA Tournament. Evans, on the other hand, needs a win tonight to ensure his Panthers of getting a bid. Pitt is 16–11. The consensus is that one more victory will put them in the tournament.

It's always a battle when these two teams play, and tonight is no exception. With 45 seconds to go and Pitt leading by 2, referee Joe Mingle calls an intentional foul on Villanova's Gary Massey for hitting Rod Brookins with an elbow out near centercourt. No matter that it's a strange time—and place—to be intentionally fouling anybody. Or that Massey certainly doesn't have the reputation of someone who intentionally elbows people. Or that it doesn't look like an intentional foul. Or even that Brookins afterward says he didn't think the elbow was intentional. A call is a call. Brookins cans both foul shots, and the Panthers win by 5, 71–66.

Massimino follows Evans to the front of the interview room. Evans has said all the predictable things: the victory should make it easier for the committee and how he's happy for his kids "because they deserve it." Massimino is wearing a white shirt and red tie. He is smoking his ever-present postgame cigar. He is asked about the intentional foul called on Gary Massey. After the game he had verbally blasted Joe Mingle in the runway, but now he's under control.

"I didn't think it was an intentional foul," he says, "but

let's get off the officials. I'm not the official, I'm the coach. I don't talk about the officials whether I win or lose. Never done it in 32 years and I'm not going to do it now. Anyone have any questions about the game?"

"What do you think are your chances of getting into the NCAAs right now?"

"I don't think they're very good right now," he says.

He hesitates, then mutters "unbelievable," almost to himself, and starts to get up.

He turns to Chris Plonsky. "I feel like I'm on trial," he says.

It has been a strange year for Massimino. Of all the coaches in the Big East, he may have now become the most controversial. Thompson has been so bizarre for so long now that he is like the eccentric relative that everyone takes for granted. Massimino now seems to generate the most emotional response.

Maybe that's only fitting. He is such an emotional man. You are either for him or against him. You are either part of the family or you are not. Yet you listen to his players talk about him, and they paint a portrait of a warm, caring person who will do anything for you and never ask for anything in return.

Then listen to someone who covers the Big East: "He's so damned cocky, and you know what bothers me most of all? He has more assistant coaches and guys in suits sitting on his bench than he does players, and you know all they're there for is to kiss his ass."

Which is the real Rollie?

They both are. Two sides of the same coin.

"Rollie is a very demonstrative coach," says Mike Tranghese, "and in the early years of the league people found that very entertaining. Now it's gotten more complicated. Rollie doesn't take losing very well, but you will never see him bad after a loss to John. Or Looie. A lot of it is just bark. It's just Rollie. Every year he calls me and complains about the schedule. He will go on and on, but before he hangs up he'll always ask how I'm doing personally."

Two days from now the Wildcats will not get an NCAA

bid. Instead they go to the NIT, where they lose at home in the quarterfinals to Michigan State.

MARCH 11

"People are always saying that Syracuse can't do this and can't do that," says Rod Baker, the Seton Hall assistant coach, "but I'll tell you what: they win games. They win a lot of games."

A few minutes earlier Syracuse beat Seton Hall by 3 points, 81–78, in a honey of a basketball game. With this game the Orangemen advance into their fourth successive Big East final and their seventh overall, the most of any Big East school. The Orangemen have been led by Douglas, who has scored 27.

"He's the player of the year as far as we're concerned," says Baker. "He got 28 and 25 against us this year. Charles Smith doesn't get 28 against us."

It's the 18th straight time that Syracuse has beaten Seton Hall. The perception might be that the Orangemen are just flash paper that disappears when the NCAA Tournament starts, but Baker is not convinced.

"They don't get respect because they don't do things conventionally," he says. "They don't run a lot of patterns. They don't seem to be conventionally disciplined. But when they know they got to play, they take it up a notch."

Once again Syracuse has made their free throws when they've had to, though they missed 10 in the first half. This inability to make free throws is one of their traditional failings, and Boeheim has brought in a guy named Ernie Hobby to work with his players. Ernie Hobby, the foul-shot doctor. Now, in the press conference, Boeheim is sitting in the front of the room, talking about how his team made those shots in the closing minutes of the game.

"In a timeout with eight minutes to go, we taught the team to make their free throws," he deadpans. "I have to take credit for that. I leaned over to them and said, 'The secret is to put the ball in the basket.' "

Boeheim says that since Sherman Douglas's sophomore year he's never put any reins on Douglas in the last few minutes of games. He has earned the freedom to take the game over. "In the last four or five minutes of a game he's the best I've seen in my time," says the coach.

"Derrick didn't seem tentative playing with four fouls," someone says, referring to Derrick Coleman. "Some players get very tentative."

"Derrick doesn't worry a whole lot," says Boeheim with a smile. Then he laughs, as if to himself.

"Jimmy, why did you go zone for a few minutes late in the game?"

"When we go zone and it doesn't work, I'm a bad coach," he says. "When it works I'm okay."

Back in the hallway Baker continues to talk about the perceptions surrounding Syracuse. "People keep putting Boeheim down," he says. "They say all he does is throw the ball out and they play. But he's a very good coach, because he gets them to win games. In this business that's the bottom line. There are a lot of other coaches with big-name talent who don't win as many games as he does."

The Georgetown-Pittsburgh game is a contest for the first seven minutes only. Then the Hoyas swarm all over the Pittsburgh guards, run off 20 unanswered points, and quickly snuff any potential drama, winning 85–62.

"The pace just got out of hand for us," Evans says afterward. "There was no way we were going to go 40 minutes at that pace. I think balance-wise and numbers-wise this is the best team I've seen them put on the floor. We have to play a near-perfect game to beat them. Syracuse, when they want to, can play very, very good defense, but they don't have that intensity all the time. If John has two guys who aren't playing defense, he'll pull them out and put in two other kids. And if they don't want to play defense, he'll sit them. This is a very good team. Mourning gets one field goal and they still beat us by 25. To beat them you have to have an awful lot of weapons."

He is asked who he likes better, Smith or Douglas.

"I like Smith better," he says. "He plays all the time with intensity, and he shoots it better."

A few minutes before, John Thompson had sat in the interview room with Charles Smith. Smith was asked about how he felt going up against Douglas again, maybe for the last time in their careers.

"We're not playing against Sherman," Smith said quickly. "We're playing against Syracuse."

"Did you notice the company line?" Thompson added, a large smile spreading across his face.

Once again, as he'd done so many times this year, Thompson has made fun of the old Hoya image.

If Mourning has been silent, Dikembe Mutombo has had 8 points. The day before he had 14 against Boston College. Afterward, he had said that in practice "I make all my hook shots. I don't know why they don't go in in the game. But my goal is to block as many shots as I can. I don't worry about scoring."

Mutombo continues to be a media delight. His personal story seems stranger than fiction. He learned the game in a Jesuit school called Boboto Institute in Kinshasa, Zaire. He played outdoors on a dirt court, where the games had to be played in the early evening because it was too hot earlier in the day. Ironically, a year ago Georgetown announced it had signed Dikembe Mutombo, a 5-10 guard. Now that seems like a cruel joke, so potentially dominating is Mutombo. There are even some people who think that Mutombo might some day be more intimidating than Mourning. Mutombo seems to block some shots without having to leave his feet, which is demoralizing to say the least.

Georgetown's awesome performance overall is reminiscent of the Hoyas' title team in 1984, when they not only beat teams, they dismantled them. Their performance against Pittsburgh sends a clear signal that they're going to be strong contenders for the national title. Patrick Ewing once noted that Thompson always used to say March was the time of year when the people who could play started playing. And everyone knows the Hoyas can play.

"Early in the year we said we were preparing for this time

of year," says Thompson. "People don't believe you when you say that. We try to learn by the mistakes we make. It doesn't seem easy to us. We don't walk off the court saying how great we are. We don't say we controlled and dominated. We try to find our mistakes before others find them. There's a tendency to find fault when you're trying to reach a level of perfection. But our kids know what time of the year it is."

John Thompson also knows what time of year it is.

MARCH 12

The years come and go. Wendell Alexis becomes Derrick Coleman, and the Pearl turns into Sherman Douglas, and still Syracuse reaches the finals of the Big East Tournament. If Georgetown has been the Big East's dominant team over the past decade, the Orangemen have made the biggest imprint on this tournament. Jim Boeheim is still standing on the sidelines looking like he just tasted something sour, the Garden is still a sea of orange-colored fans, and Syracuse is again turning the Big East Tournament into just another postseason Carrier Classic.

The only trouble is that this game is all Georgetown's. The Hoyas win, 88–79, but the score is deceiving. Syracuse plays with an injured Derrick Coleman, and at one point in the second half they trail by 19. For the third game in a row the Hoyas look invincible. Mourning is a monster the entire afternoon, finishing with 21 points and 4 blocked shots. The Hoyas are now 26–4, ranked third in the country behind Arizona and Oklahoma.

The game was billed as a showdown between Sherman Douglas and Charles Smith, and although they both finish with 16 points, Smith is voted the tournament's MVP, to go along with his selection as the conference's player of the year. "If Douglas is their general, then Smith is our commander-in-chief," says Thompson.

"I personally rated Georgetown first or second in the country all year long," says Boeheim. "But I don't know why I ever thought they were second. I must have temporarily lost my mind."

The bids to the NIT tournament are announced on CBS at six o'clock. As expected, Georgetown is the number-one seed in the East. They are sent to the Providence Civic Center, one of the first-round sites in the Eastern Regionals. Seton Hall, the third seed in the West Regionals, will play its first-round game in Tucson. Syracuse is sent to Dallas as the second seed in the Midwest Regionals. Pittsburgh is sent to Indianapolis in the Midwest Regionals as a midlevel seed. Providence is sent to Nashville, the 12th seed in the Southeast Regionals.

The Big East has sent five of its best teams to the NCAA and three to the NIT. Two will finish in the final eight, and out of nowhere Seton Hall will rocket into the Final Four. Once again, Dave Gavitt's "very own basketball league" is the beast of the East.

12

IN SEARCH OF THE FINAL FOUR

MARCH 17

Last week the Georgetown Hoyas swept through the Big
East Tournament like Sherman through Atlanta. Are they
the best team in the country? everyone asked. Tonight they
barely squeak by the last-ranked seed.

They find themselves in a time machine, transported back
to basketball of the 1950s, back when the game was played
below the rim and the emphasis was on fundamentals, not
athletic ability. In this type of basketball, players move
without the ball, go back door, do all the little things that
have been lost in this age of alley oops and slam dunks. It
resurrects memories of musty old gyms and cramped locker
rooms and two-hand set shots. This purist's vision is a type
of basketball that's rarely played anymore.

The irony is that the game figured to be a mismatch:
Georgetown, the Big East champ, versus Princeton, the Ivy
League champ. Scholarships against no scholarships. The
number-one seed in the East against the 16th.

Right from the tip-off, though, the Hoyas seem like extras
in a *Hoosiers* script. The game is controlled by Princeton

coach Pete Carril, long one of the grand old masters of the college game. Once his teams could play with anyone in the country, but that was before blue-chip players in the Ivy League dried up, and Carril became like a teacher without apt pupils, plying his trade in the obscurity of Hanover, New Hampshire, and Ithaca, New York, while the spotlight focused on others.

This game reaffirms the notion that the NCAA Tournament is all about magical nights like this, when the Davids of the basketball world have a chance to take on the Goliaths. For 40 minutes it doesn't matter what league you're in or how many times you're on television. This is one game, loser go home.

Princeton spreads the court. They run time off the clock. Then they go back door. Or they hit a three-pointer with the shot clock winding down. Out of sync, the Hoyas try to find their rhythm. Behind early, they are soon fighting for their season. Never in the history of the tournament has a 16th-seed knocked off the top seed, but Princeton comes as close as you can get. They lead for the first 30 minutes, and if not for Alonzo Mourning, the game would never be close. Too big for the Tigers underneath, Mourning is unstoppable whenever he gets the ball. He alone gets Georgetown the lead back in the closing seconds.

Even so, Princeton has the ball for the last possession only down by 1, 50–49. Then Mourning blocks Bob Scrabis's jumper from the top of the key. In the ensuing scramble for the ball Princeton gets it back. Princeton's Kit Mueller throws up a medium-range jumper at the buzzer that Mourning appears to block. Or did he foul Mueller? No foul is called, and the Hoyas have escaped.

Thompson is booed as he walks across the court to do a postgame interview with ESPN. Once again his Hoyas have become the villains. Charles Smith, who only had a single field goal, was called for an intentional foul with one second left in the first half when he threw an elbow at Scrabis. Mourning hit Princeton's Kit Mueller in the eye a few minutes before his last-second block. Both incidents drew the wrath of the crowd, who began rooting for Princeton as soon as they realized that an upset was in the making. The legacy of the Hoya past lingers, even though they are playing in the Providence Civic Center, a Big East building, and Thompson is a Providence College alumnus. The interview is conducted in a tight huddle in a vain attempt to muffle the noise. He is booed some more as he walks back across the floor to the tunnel that leads to the Georgetown locker room. He doesn't show a flicker of emotion.

"It's an understatement to say Princeton deserved to win this game," says Thompson. "I can't say enough about the kids at Princeton. Very possibly we could have been walking out of here today."

"Were you surprised the game was as close as it was?"

"No," he says. "Any coach in the country knows that when you chase Pete Carril, you're in trouble."

Thompson should know. His son, John, graduated from Princeton last year, after playing four years for Carril. Thompson goes on to say there is some consolation in being able to win a game you should have lost. He's right about that. His Hoyas have barely dodged a bullet.

This game ends the first round of games, and now there are three Big East teams still alive in the tournament: the Hoyas, Syracuse, and Seton Hall.

The night before, Pitt lost to Ball State in Indianapolis, 68–64.

The Panthers have finished the year at 17–13.

Before the tournament Evans said they were happy to be going anywhere. A month ago they were 11–10 and in danger of not getting into the tournament. Sean Miller said, "We had a nice year. We've been very up and down, but we did what we had to do—get enough wins to get to the NCAA Tournament."

Miller is right. Pitt has been very up and down, but it's also been a good year. Certainly it's been a transition year, a changing of the guard. No longer is Evans the new landlord inheriting someone else's tenants. This is now his team, his players, and he has seemed more comfortable. In a sense Evans has taken a few steps off center stage. There have been no controversies. His feud with Massimino appears to be over. He hasn't said anything particularly flamboyant all year. It's as if his transition period at Pittsburgh has ended.

All year Pittsburgh started five sophomores, so it was probably inevitable that it would be a team marked by inconsistency. It also was a team that didn't have any depth, a fact often overlooked. The Panthers essentially were a six-man team, the five sophomores and junior Rod Brookin. So one night the Panthers might be victims of their inexperience, on another their lack of depth. Yet there were nights when the Panthers could play with anyone in the country. They beat Georgetown. They beat Oklahoma. They beat Syracuse. They beat Seton Hall twice.

Most of all, Pittsburgh showed they are a team with its future all ahead of them. Brian Shorter has become a genuine Big East star. Posting the best scoring average of any first-year player in the 10-year history of the league, he was second only to Dana Barros in scoring in the league at 20 points a game. He has also been named the conference's rookie of the year, no small feat in a year that also included the more celebrated Alonzo Mourning and Billy Owens. Jason Matthews has become one of the conference's better young guards, a third-team All-Big East selection. He averaged just under 17 points a game, 11th in the league.

The Panthers have also had one of the best recruiting years in the country. In early February they signed Eric Mobley to go along with three others they signed in November. Mobley is a coup. Seton Hall wanted him. Providence wanted him. After seeing him play in an all-star game Looie Carnesecca will tell the Big East office that Mobley can have the same impact on the league that Mourning has had. Pitt is also supposedly leading in the recruiting hunt for Adrian Autrey, a junior guard at Tolentine in the Bronx, who promises to be one of the best guards in the country next year.

So sing no sad songs for the Panthers. Their season might have ended, but the future is mighty bright.

Also the night before, Providence lost to Virginia by 3 in Nashville, 100–97. Matt Palazzi got two three-point shots off in the final seconds, but both just missed, a heartbreaking way to end the season. They had thought they could beat Virginia. So had Barnes. When you have given Georgetown all they could handle in the Capital Centre and played Syracuse tough in the Dome—when you have survived a winter in the Big East—what's there to fear about Virginia? Once upon a time the Friars would play someone in the ACC and feel like they were tangling with giants. No more. That's the legacy of the Big East.

Afterward, Barnes thanked the seniors for the year, then he talked about the future.

"Every year this is the way it's going to be," he said. "Coming to play at Providence College is not just about playing in the Big East. It's about playing in the NCAA Tournament."

Later, he was asked if he would have taken this season back in November.

"Sure." He smiled. "But when we started out so well, we got greedy like everyone else. I'll tell you what: I don't know if this team would have wanted to play in the NIT. And I'll tell you something else: we got our confidence back this year. We brought some stability. These kids know we can play."

In other first-round games, Seton Hall gets by Southwest Missouri State, 60–51, in Tucson, but it's not easy. The Hall goes five minutes in the second half without scoring. The difference turns out to be foul shooting, especially in the last minutes of the game. Southwest Missouri State misses 8 foul shots in the final eight minutes, while the Hall makes 14 of its 16 foul shots. John Morton has 26 to lead the Hall.

"We were very fortunate," says Carlesimo. "In a close defensive game it's a struggle, and here you had two teams that played very good defense. But they missed a lot of free throws and we made ours."

In Dallas, Syracuse rolls over Bucknell, 104–81, without Derrick Coleman. Coleman is still bothered by the sore back that hindered him throughout the Big East Tournament last week, and it was Boeheim's plan to get by Bucknell without having to use Coleman. It works. Billy Owens takes up the offensive slack with 27 points.

"Billy made some great moves inside," says Douglas. "It was his best game of the season for sure."

"Owens showed what a big-time player he is," says Bucknell Coach Charlie Woollum. "Syracuse put the game on his shoulders and he came through."

Syracuse has another easy time in their second-round game against Colorado State, winning by 15, 65–50. The Orangemen lead by 10 at the half and coast home. Stephen Thompson has 21, and Coleman comes back and adds 12. Their next opponent is Missouri next week in the Midwest Regionals in the Hubert Humphrey Dome in Minneapolis.

Seton Hall's trip to the Western Regionals next week in Denver is a little more perilous. Up 19 at one time in the game against Evansville, the Hall goes through another second-half stretch when they have trouble scoring. Evansville comes back to within 1, 74–73, before the Hall holds them scoreless for the final 5:06 to reach the round of 16 for the first time in the school's history. The final score is 87–73.

"We're a confident team," says Carlesimo. "Sometimes that's bad. But the kids don't think they're going to lose. There aren't too many teams that can let a 19-point lead get away and be hanging from their fingernails and then come back. This team's been doing that all year."

After Georgetown beats Notre Dame by 7, 81–74, on Sunday afternoon to qualify for the Eastern Regionals next weekend in the Meadowlands, Thompson walks in to the interview room with Mourning and Smith. The two players have already showered and are wearing jackets and ties.

"I think they wear their suits under their uniforms," jokes Chris Plonsky, seated near the back of the large room.

"He's back." Thompson smiles, looking at Smith. "The little fella's got a big heart."

Friday night, after the Hoyas had nipped past Princeton, Thompson had made a late-night call to Smith's room. Thompson is not in the habit of making late-night phone calls to his players, but he wanted Smith to know that he needed to "make more mistakes mentally. I thought he was becoming too conservative."

But in the first half against Notre Dame Smith struggled again. Then he hit a three-pointer at the end of the half, a harbinger of things to come. Still, the Hoyas were down by 4, and before the second half had started, a fan behind the Georgetown bench began heckling him, telling him he was overrated. Smith went out and scored 28 points in the second half, including 17 of Georgetown's first 21 points of the half. Every time he scored, he pointed his finger at the fan who had heckled him, a rare display of emotion for the usually taciturn Smith. In your face.

Now as he sits alongside Thompson and Mourning, someone asks if hitting the three-pointer at the end of the half gave him confidence. Smith seems to go on remote control. On the court he always seems composed, within himself, his face a mask. It's the same when he's being interviewed. The words come out. The face reveals nothing.

"I always have confidence in myself," he says. "Even if I go 0 for 50 I'm going to keep shooting, because I think I'm a good shooter."

Then he is asked about his performance, and again he goes on remote control, saying how he owes everything to his teammates, blah, blah, blah.

"Charles really believes that stuff about his teammates setting good picks for him," Thompson interjects. "But basketball is not an equal opportunity game. He believes all that stuff I tell him about the company line, but we're a good team when he's not so democratic."

Again Thompson has played off the old Georgetown image. And when Mourning says he may have been conditioned to be excitable on the court, Thompson says with a laugh, "Not by me."

Smith is asked if he needed Thompson to tell him anything at halftime.

"I know what time of the year it is," he says. "I don't want to lose." He glances over at Thompson. "And I know he doesn't want to lose either."

As the press conference ends, Thompson and the two players start walking off the podium when they are met by a few reporters. Quickly Mary Fenlon comes to the rescue. "Alonzo, Charles," she says urgently. "Alonzo. Charles. Let's go."

Thompson trails behind, walking down the hallway behind the arena, still surrounded by a few reporters. He says he didn't think his team played particularly well this weekend and that they are going to have to play better to get to Seattle in two weeks. Then he starts talking about Smith. He has spent much of the year talking about Smith. One suspects Smith is one of Thompson's all-time favorites. He has taken great delight this year in telling how he miscalculated Smith's potential, how big Smith's heart is, what a great story he is.

"He really does believe that stuff about his teammates," he says. "It's not just all programmed. He doesn't have a star mentality. I think that comes from not being what he calls 'The Man' as a kid. And I respect that part of him, too. But now I tell him, 'You're the team.' "

Thompson continues walking, talking to a few reporters. In the hallway waits a large black man in a tan overcoat. It is Jim Hadnot, now a scout for the Sacramento Kings. Once they were teammates at Providence College, back when they were called the Twin Towers, two 6-10 black kids in a time in college basketball when that was rare. The old school chums embrace.

A few minutes later Thompson stops to do a TV interview. At that point Bill Shapland comes out of the Georgetown locker room in search of his coach.

"Where's Coach Thompson?" he asks.

"He's doing a TV interview," he is told.

"He's doing what?" asks Shapland in astonishment.

MARCH 26

It is Easter Sunday, a sunny spring afternoon, and Dave Gavitt is standing in the large press room on the ground floor of the Meadowlands. Yesterday he was in Denver to see Seton Hall beat UNLV and advance to the Final Four. They are the sixth different Big East team to reach the Final Four in the past decade.

He and Mike Tranghese were also in Denver on Thursday night when Seton Hall beat Indiana, 78–65, in McNichols Arena. It was Indiana's worst loss ever in NCAA play. The Hall blew open a close game in the final few minutes of the first half to go up 42–33 at halftime. The Hoosiers came with within 3, 54–51, with 8:16 left, but the Pirates dug in and regained control. In the final minutes, Tranghese, who was sitting a few rows behind the Seton Hall bench, stood up and high-fived Gavitt.

In a balanced attack, Morton had 17, with 6 free throws down the stretch. Gaze had 16, Greene 15, and Ramos 12.

Afterward, Indiana Coach Bob Knight said Seton Hall's defensive pressure from 12 feet was "the best I've seen all year. I think Seton Hall is a stronger team than we are. They deserved to win. They're strong, tough kids, smart kids, and they played that way all night."

"Our interior defense was excellent," Carlesimo said. "When you have good people who are willing to work, that's what happens. We have good defensive players inside. When you play good defense, you can hang in the game. There were a couple of times when Indiana had us stuck on a number, but we didn't let them gain much ground on us."

Carlesimo thinks people shouldn't be surprised by his team's success. "For some reason, people don't understand how good these kids are," he said. "They're good basketball players. All year they've found a way to win."

The next day Gavitt and Tranghese flew to Minneapolis for Syracuse's 83–80 victory over Missouri in the Hubert Humphrey Dome. Missouri, 29–8 and sixth ranked in the country, led at halftime, and with 18 minutes left in the game was in front by 7, 47–40. Then Coleman and Owens began controlling the boards against the taller Tigers, triggering the Orange fast break. As Missouri missed 11 straight shots, Sherman Douglas keyed a 16–0 spurt with 6 of his 27 points, and Syracuse went ahead 48–47 with 16 minutes left in the game. They were never behind again, and they iced the victory when Douglas, a 61-percent foul shooter during the season, made six straight in the final 1:08. Billy Owens added 23 points.

Then plane-happy Gavitt and Tranghese flew back to Denver to see Seton Hall beat UNLV, 84–61, in the finals of the Western Regionals. Like it did to Indiana, Seton Hall handed UNLV its worst tournament loss ever. They entered the game not only having won nine straight, but also bearing the distinction of having never lost an NCAA regional final. What does an upstart care? Leading by 1 with 14 minutes to play, the Hall scored 29 of the next 35 points to take control of the game.

Once again it was the Pirates' viselike defense that dominated the game, holding UNLV to a paltry 30 percent from the field. Gaze, who was named the tournament's MVP, had 19 points, and he also shut down UNLV's high-flying Stacey Augmon. Interestingly, Ramon Ramos only played 14 minutes and didn't score a single point. No matter. Anthony Avent and Franz Volcy came off the bench and combined for 20 points. Once again, the Hall's bench strength was a big advantage.

"We came up twice very big when it mattered," Carlesimo said afterward, standing in a hallway in McNichols Arena. "I don't think you can defend any harder than we did today. We're playing so well it's scary. At one point I looked out and we had more starters sitting than playing, but it just doesn't seem to matter with this team. I just want to get out of their way and not mess them up over the next five or six days.

"A lot of teams are good enough to get to the Final Four," he went on. "It takes luck besides talent. We feel very fortunate. I just want our guys to have a great time now."

Later that night, Tranghese stayed in Denver to celebrate with Seton Hall, while Gavitt took a red-eye east to be here today.

Now he is watching that game on the TV set in the corner of the press room. He already has one team in the Final

Four, which begins next weekend in Seattle. Now he has a chance to get two more in, which would equal the total in 1985, when the Final Four in Lexington was comprised of three Big East teams. It is nearing the end of the first half, and Syracuse is leading by 13.

"People across the country are paranoid about us already," says Gavitt with a sly grin. "Think what it will be like if we get two more today."

Two nights earlier Duke had danced all over Minnesota here in the Meadowlands, and Georgetown had edged North Carolina State, 69–61, squandering a 16-point lead in the second half. The Hoyas won even though Charles Smith played with the flu. Smith took only two shots and scored one point. Thompson likened him to "El Cid, where they propped him up, even though he was dead, and went out to fight the battle."

The day before at a press conference Thompson talked about how perceptions about his program have changed.

"We do things exactly the same way now," he said, "but the media has become a lot more familiar with us. In the beginning they were shocked when they found out they didn't have carte blanche coming through the door. Now, because we have been consistent, people aren't as offended or think we are attacking them personally."

Back in the press room with Gavitt, it does not look good for Syracuse. In the closing minutes Illinois has taken control of the game and go up by 3 with 15 seconds left. Stevie Thompson then comes down and takes a three-point shot. It misses. Syracuse loses, 89–86.

Once again Jim Boeheim's season has ended in frustration. Because Syracuse has not won the national championship, somehow they have failed. Earlier in the season, after he had won his 300th game quicker than all but two people in basketball history, he shrugged it off, saying, "If I win 3,000 games here and we lose a couple, there will be people who'll want to see me fired. People remember only the losses."

There's even been a rumor floating around the past month or so that Rick Pitino was all set to leave the Knicks and replace Boeheim, a rumor Pitino labeled as ridiculous.

From all accounts, Boeheim has been testy ever since the start of the tournament, defending everything from his record to his recruiting. Sitting at the podium in the Metrodome in Minneapolis after Syracuse's defeat, his mouth is turned down at the corners, and he rotates his head uncomfortably as if experiencing terrible neck pains. His answers are short and sour.

He is asked about Syracuse's inability to win the Big One.

"Some questions don't deserve an answer," he snaps. "That's one."

He also defends Sherman Douglas, who only scored one field goal in the second half and threw an errant pass with 33 seconds to play.

"Everyone's going to be disappointed," said Douglas afterward in a *New York Post* story titled "Orange Turn Bitter after Defeat." "There will only be one happy team at the end of this tournament. I think we had a productive season, we did everything we really wanted to do. But we missed out." Then he added, "It's been a great four years. I wouldn't trade it for anything. I think I accomplished more than any of you thought I could. So I'm proud of myself."

"We did not lose the game because Sherman did not score points," says Boeheim. "Your opinion may be different, and if it is, write it."

• Georgetown-Duke is one of those games made for TV. Two glamour schools. The ACC versus the Big East. Recognizable players in Mourning and Smith for the Hoyas and Danny Ferry for Duke. Two name coaches in Thompson and Mike Krzyzewski. Not only this, but the winner gains a trip to the Final Four.

For a while Georgetown looks like it is going to join Seton Hall in Seattle. After falling behind, they slice a 14-point Duke lead to 2 in just 1:45. They're charging back as only Georgetown can, turning up the defensive pressure, making Duke come unglued. Then, suddenly, Duke regains its poise. The comeback falls short.

As the last few seconds tick off the clock, Duke spreads the court. Then Phil Henderson is fouled, and the Duke bench erupts in celebration. Thompson, the omnipresent white towel over his shoulder, seems to slump a little. After a timeout he goes over and sits in the middle of the solemn Georgetown bench. There is no need to coach anymore. There are only 16 seconds left to play. It is over.

Georgetown loses, 85–77.

It seems like a game that's been waiting to happen for the Hoyas. Last week in Providence they had narrowly escaped a bullet against Princeton. Curiously enough, they never seemed to be the same after that. Either that, or they peaked too early at the Big East Tournament the week before. They got by Notre Dame thanks to a great second-half performance by Smith. They edged North Carolina State two days ago, but they were nowhere near as intimidating as they had been in New York two weeks earlier.

Strangely, Thompson plays Mourning for only 11 minutes in the second half against Duke, though Mourning is not in foul trouble. He ends up with 11 points and 5 rebounds and has been generally outplayed by Christian Laettner, the Duke freshman. He had played against Mourning in a few summer camps and practiced against him in the McDonald's high-school all-star game, but he "never did anything big." Until today, when he scores a game-high 24 points.

"It appeared to me Alonzo was getting very winded," says Thompson afterward.

Mourning is not one to second-guess Thompson.

"Why put someone in who's not contributing?" he says. "I made a lot of mistakes. I wouldn't call them freshman mistakes. I don't play like a freshman. It just was not my day. I was the big reason why we lost," he says. "I was moving in slow motion and couldn't get things clicking. The intensity I usually have wasn't there."

It has been a long year for Mourning. Not only did he go from high school to the Olympic training camp, and not only did he come into college as the most celebrated player since Patrick Ewing arrived eight years ago, he also joined Georgetown, perhaps the most controversial college basketball team in the country. Now he has ended his season with one of his worst performances. But he has had a great year.

He has led the country in blocks. He has been a dominant player in the country since the season began, living up to all the hype.

Thompson comes into the interview room on the ground floor of the Meadowlands. He sits on the podium in his dark suit. He is relaxed, cordial. He answers all the questions.

He says how Duke is a very seasoned team that didn't wilt when the Hoyas made their run at them. He praises Ferry. He praises the entire Duke team. He says Smith's ankle injury, while painful, did not affect the outcome of the game. He says all the right things.

Then he is asked about all the expectations that had surrounded the Hoyas in this tournament, especially after they had roared out of the Big East Tournament in New York two weeks ago as if it was their birthright to get to Seattle.

"Yes, there were a lot of expectations," he says. "But we earned those expectations. They weren't just given to us. And I like to think we fulfilled a lot of those expectations."

He seems ready to answer more questions. But he is informed his time is up. It is Duke's turn. So he walks off the podium and ducks through a blue curtain.

John Thompson's season is over.

The stage has been cleared for the fairytale team from South Orange, New Jersey.

13

ROOT FOR THE UNDERDOG!

MARCH 30

A Final Four always features more than just the games. It's the site of the NCAA coaches' convention, with all the attendant festivities. On Thursday night there is the senior all-star game. There is a slam-dunk competition on Sunday. It also is an end-of-the-year reunion, full of meetings and parties and hospitality rooms. Dave Gavitt has one meeting after another scheduled for four days before he flies to Munich for a meeting on international basketball in his role as the president of the USABA.

"When I first started coming to the Final Four, I used to come with Gerry Alaimo when he was at Brown," says Gavitt. "We were both young coaches then, and all we ever did was drink beer, go to the games, and drink more beer. Now all I do is go to meetings."

On Thursday night a Final Four salute dinner is held in the Westin Hotel. This is the formal kickoff to the weekend, complete with videos and a tribute to college basketball in the Northwest. One thousand people are on hand, and Brent Musberger of CBS is the master of ceremonies. Later, the lobby of the Westin is jammed. Off the lobby, in a bar called, appropriately enough, Shooters, Dick Vitale is playing one of those bar basketball games as a group of people crowd around. Vitale is the unofficial grand marshal of the All-Lobby team year after year. He is like a windup toy whose battery never runs down. He schmoozes with coaches, kibbitzes with fans, talks to whomever will listen. It doesn't matter if the TV light is on or not. Vitale is always on. Now he spots Tranghese, McElroy, and some of the Big East people at a nearby table.

"Seton Hall, baby," yells Vitale, a Seton Hall alumnus. "They've made me so proud."

The next morning the *Seattle Post-Intelligencer* runs a story about the fabled 1984 Georgetown team that won the national title here in the Kingdome. "With the possible exception of the John Tower nomination and Oliver North's unrestricted free agency, no executive decision in the nation's capital has been more fiercely debated in the last five years than Coach John Thompson's handling of his 1984 Georgetown basketball team," writes Dan Raley.

When the Hoyas played in the Western Regionals that year in Pullman, Washington, they stayed in Spokane, 90 miles north. Thompson's critics said his constant coddling of his players would not only hurt them on the court but also hurt them when they left their sheltered Georgetown lives and went to live in the real world.

"Thompson's legions of critics, however, are wrong," writes Raley. "His methods may not have been attractive or acceptable then, but the results are admirable now."

Of the 11 Hoyas who played here in Seattle that year, nine graduated. The two who didn't—Michael Graham and Victor Morris—left within a year of winning the title due to academic reasons. According to Raley, 53 of the 55 players who played four years for Thompson have Georgetown degrees.

"I learned the game from him, but I learned much more than basketball," says Patrick Ewing in the article. "He taught us how to act as human beings. He prepared us for life. If I had that choice again, I would go to Georgetown without thinking twice."

The Sheraton in downtown Seattle is the headquarters for the NCAA coaches' convention, and its lobby is the center of the action. Here some coaches spend the entire weekend, talking to people, listening to rumors, starting rumors, whatever. It is called the All-Lobby team, and if you are a coach looking for a job, being All-Lobby can be infinitely more important than being All-Tournament. So the lobby is always crowded with people drifting in and out. Here you can glimpse the biggest names in college basketball. Bobby Knight chats with Denny Crum. John Thompson and Mary Fenlon are having lunch in the coffee shop just off the lobby. A basketball goal, complete with backboard, has been placed in the center of the lobby, right there with the plants. Everywhere you look are people in warmup suits. Yell "Coach" and everyone would turn around expectantly.

"You could write a great novel just on what goes on in the lobby," says Gavitt.

One block away from the Sheraton is Convention Place, a cavernous new building with a lot of escalators, glass, and white walls that is a symbol of the new Seattle. This is the site of the coaches' clinics. You can hear one coach discuss "upward mobility in coaching" or someone else talk about computerized player evaluation. One coach discusses recruiting in a clinic called "Art, Science, or Hype?" In the Exhibition Hall, about the size of two football fields, might just be the world's largest basketball trade show. Innumerable booths sell everything from uniforms to balls to strength machines to brightly colored warmups to anything even peripherally involved with basketball.

Then there are the sneaker companies.

They are the new gods of the basketball world, and their banners hang from the ceilings like stained-glass windows in a new-fangled church: Reebok, Nike, Converse, Pony. They all have hospitality areas and give out freebies to coaches.

On Friday afternoon, all four teams have a public workout in the Kingdome, watched by several thousand people in the cavernous arena. Seton Hall comes out and the players,

in their blue and white warmups, start shooting around.
They have already practiced seriously at nearby Seattle University. This is just for show. Carlesimo stands near halfcourt
in his warmup suit. Nearby are his assistant coaches, John
Carroll, Rod Baker, Tom Sullivan, and Bruce Hamburger.

"Now I know how Dorothy felt," says Baker, looking
around. "The first thing I thought about after we won last
Saturday was: it's going to be me standing on the court at
the practices this Friday afternoon. I thought about how
many times I've come to the Friday practices and sat in the
stands and looked at other guys down on the floor, and now
it was going to be me."

He has been in coaching for 12 years at six schools, and
the Final Four has always been something that happened to
somebody else. "For someone like me, being in the Final
Four was unfathomable," he says. "It was like you always
knew someone in it. But it was never you, and you knew it
never was going to be you."

It's a funny thing about coaching. You mention college
coaches and everyone thinks of the ones with the big salaries and the huge sneaker contracts standing in the glare of
TV lights. But most people in coaching are just trying to
survive in the game. They make endless recruiting trips to
either look at kids who can't play or ones that they can't get
anyway. They spend their summer at countless summer
camps, doing all the grunt work, trying to make contacts, so
some day they won't have to be someplace where they are
never able to win enough. Most of all, they're trying to stay
in the game when everything around them says: "You should
get out and do something else, anything else."

"How many camps have I worked at?" he says rhetorically. "Hundreds of them. Zillions."

Baker first climbed onto the coaching carousel 12 years
ago. A former player at Holy Cross, his first job was as a
part-time assistant there. Then he wandered to Brown, then
Columbia, then St. Joe's. Six years ago he became the head
coach at Tufts, a small Division III school on the outside of
Boston, because he wanted to prove to himself that he could
actually coach a team, not just recruit for one. He was also

the assistant soccer coach, was in charge of the video equipment, and ran a dormitory. One summer he even worked as a mailman.

A few years ago he decided Division III wasn't enough for him and started applying for head coaching jobs. He came close at Yale. He came close at Columbia. Last year he came close to being Gordie Chiesa's assistant at Providence. He was distraught when he didn't get it. At the end of the year, Chiesa was fired. Sometimes you never know.

He knew Carlesimo from around the East, and he knew last spring that he was looking for an assistant coach. At the Final Four in Kansas City he bumped into him in the hotel lobby. "Should I be talking to you?" he asked him. Yes, said Carlesimo.

After the Hall won Saturday, Baker stood on the court carrying his infant son, Zachary. All around him were people hugging each other, players cutting down the nets, and he thought about how a year ago at the same time he had been distraught after getting beaten by Wesleyan in a regional Division III tournament.

"It's a strange business," he says, looking out at the Seton Hall players as they continue shooting.

"How's P. J. been?"

"The same," says Baker. "He's always the same. After Denver we went to Santa Monica for a few days before we came here. (It made no sense to go back home.) One night out there P. J. was on 'Sports Look,' the one with Roy Firestone. They sent a limo for him and everything. Afterward, he has the limo stop at Denny's for some burgers. That's P. J. He's just been on national television, and he stops at Denny's. You know what his biggest concern is? That we're getting behind in recruiting because we're in the Final Four. And you know what his second biggest concern is? That if we win, we'll have to go to the White House and that will blow another day of recruiting."

Nearby, Carlesimo is saying how he's known Duke's Mike Krzyzewski for years, ever since he was at Wagner and Krzyzewski was at Army.

"What first drew us together was the fact we were the

only two people in metropolitan New York who could spell and pronounce each other's names."

If the country is discovering Seton Hall, it is also discovering Carlesimo. If everyone in the Big East has known for years Carlesimo is truly one of the nice people in college athletics, now the nation's media is starting to learn it, too. The week before in Denver there had been numerous TV shots of his parents in the stands as the voice-over told how they have been loyal followers of the Seton Hall program through all the lean years. There had been much talk of how close the family was. After the season, Carlesimo will say how he thinks the family angle was overblown, that because he is single the TV cameras focused on his parents instead of his wife.

Nonetheless, in a profession in which many coaches seem stars in their own movies, Carlesimo always dismisses his own role in this team's success, implying that anyone could have coached this team merely by connecting the dots. You just have to watch his players to know that this is not true. Carlesimo has created a team that's extremely unselfish, a quality directly related to coaching. He never seems to miss an opportunity to boost both his players and his staff in the team's success and downplay his own contribution.

A few minutes later, as Andrew Gaze walks out of the interview room, he is immediately surrounded by reporters. What is the biggest adjustment you've had to make? What's the name of your club team? Are you coming back next year? The questions keep coming as he walks through the runway and back out into the Kingdome. Little kids hang over the railing asking for his autograph.

"Is this what you expected it to be?" he is asked.

Gaze looks around and smiles. "It is now."

He has become this Final Four's curiosity piece, the most bizarre story in a tournament that's always full of great stories. What other transfers from Footscray Institute in Melbourne have made it big in the Big East? If he needed some time to adjust his game, it's been apparent for a while now that Gaze has been the missing piece of the puzzle for Seton Hall. He's their best deep shooter, the best passer,

the most experienced player. Being the MVP of the Western Regionals was just the frosting.

"Without him we would not be here," says Carlesimo.
"It's that simple."

Gaze ducks into the Seton Hall dressing room, a large
room with blue walls, a green floor, and wooden stalls for
lockers. All year he has been a media delight. He is articulate, friendly, poised. All this and an Australian accent, too.

"What about next year?"

"As far as I'm concerned this is it," he says. "The way I
was brought up, the Olympic games and the world championships are supposed to be the ultimate. But I think this
will match it. That's something I never thought I'd be able
to say. Even if I was granted an extra year, after going this
far—reaching the Final Four—nothing could top this."

In a sense this has been his summer vacation, a six-month
hiatus from his real life. What did you do for the summer? I
played in the Big East and went to the Final Four. He says
how the scheduling just fell into place this year: because of
the Olympics his club schedule back home ended early.

"I do have the kind of attitude that I'm only here for a
visit," he says. "I've been doing tourist-type things. I'm not
really settling in and living here with the attitude that this is
my life and I have to develop a career."

"Why Seton Hall?"

"I didn't know the difference," Gaze laughs. "As far as I
knew, Seton Hall was renowned."

APRIL 1

Many people consider this the best day in sports. A basketball doubleheader on a Saturday afternoon. The Final
Four meet in the national semifinals.

A couple of hours before the first game, a carnival atmosphere reigns outside the Kingdome. The stadium is located
in an old warehouse district just a few blocks from Pioneer
Square, the city's refurbished waterfront area. The restaurants are jammed. The bars are full. There are booths

selling T-shirts and countless souvenirs. People in school colors walk the streets, even though it's drizzling. The new gimmick this year is several foul-shot booths. In them people play out their fantasies in the rain in the shadow of the Kingdome.

Interestingly, not a single conference champion is playing in today's semifinals. Seton Hall was second in the Big East. Duke was tied for second in the ACC. Illinois was second in the Big 10, Michigan third. Who says there's no parity in college basketball?

The Kingdome is huge. Built in 1976, it is the home of both the Seattle Mariners and the Seattle Seahawks. It seats 38,187 for basketball. Minutes before the game the feeling is electric.

Duke starts Danny Ferry, one of the leading candidates for the national player of the year, Christian Laettner, the Hoya killer, Robert Brickey, Phil Henderson, and Quin Snyder, who grew up in nearby Mercer Island, Washington. The Hall counters with what has been their starting lineup all year: Gaze, Ramos, Walker, Greene, and Morton.

Before the game gets underway, let's explore in more depth the latter trio. Walker, Greene, and Morton all played together while they were in high school for Riverside Church, the AAU team that's become one of the best in New York City. Run for nearly 30 years by Ernie Lorch, it has an alumni list that includes Mark Jackson, Kenny Smith, Rodney McCrae, Walter Berry, and Albert King, among others. Walker, Greene, and Morton were all from different slums of the city—Greene from Bedford-Stuyvesant in Brooklyn, Morton from the South Bronx, a few blocks away from Yankee Stadium, Walker from Harlem—brought together at a young age by their talent and basketball potential.

Their progress at Seton Hall did not follow a fairy-tale script, not in the beginning, anyway. Greene started as a freshman, before seeing his minutes cut as a sophomore. Last year he began the year on the bench and didn't become a starter again until the end of the year, when his insertion back into the lineup coincided with the Hall's turnaround.

Now he is the acknowledged oncourt leader who sets the tempo.

Morton's game always soared and dipped like a roller coaster. He had been a great high-school scorer, but that had been as a slasher, a one-on-one player. He played a little point guard, but he always seemed to be a turnover waiting to happen. He played a little off-guard. In the Big East he also needed a jumper, and he never had one. Then last summer he declined Carlesimo's support for a summer job and went to Seton Hall's Walsh Gym every day. He saw it as investing in his career. Hadn't he seen teammate Mark Bryant get drafted by Portland in the NBA?

"I figured if I improved my outside shooting, I'd have a great chance of making the NBA," he says. "And if I make the NBA, then I would get some cash."

As a freshman, Walker cut his hand climbing a fence and was out for a while. As a sophomore he chipped a bone in his foot and missed the end of the year. Last year he started coming into his own, living up to the promise he had shown as a senior in high school, when he had been named player of the year in New York State. He is 6-8, with thin shoulders and a head that seems too small for his body. His head is shaved and he plays without any expression. He is Seton Hall's "garbage player," scoring inside when no one is looking, fighting the continual battles under the boards that mean so much to the outcome of a game.

In the beginning against Duke, all five players seem nervous. Seton Hall gets off to a horrible start, down 20–8, and the game already seems to have gotten away from them. Afterward, Carlesimo will say he wasn't all that worried about the score, he just wanted his team to begin playing well. All year this team had come to play, and now in their biggest game of the season they start out in the middle of a nightmare.

Their experience, though, keeps them from panicking. The Hall comes back and narrows the Duke halftime lead to 38–33. The Pirates' marvelous comeback has been spurred, as many times before, by Gerald Greene. Then the Pirates come out in the second half and blow Duke away, 95–78.

Once again the Pirates have employed a tenacious man-to-man defense that totally takes Duke out of their offensive game plan. Their superior bench wears Duke down, especially after they lose Brickey in the first half with a bruised thigh and Laettner gets into foul trouble. The stats show balanced scoring, with Gaze getting 20, Walker 19, Greene 17, and Morton 13.

And after the Pirates send the Blue Devils back to the Carolina woodshed with a good ole-fashioned whipping, after the players celebrate on the Kingdome floor, after the obligatory television interviews, they realize that they are one game away from the national championship! This is a school that probably would be playing basketball in the Jersey State league if not for the Big East. This is a school that always seemed to be the dime-store team in the designer league.

The Hall.

Who would ever have believed it?

APRIL 2

On Sunday morning in a ballroom of the Westin, the last official press conference before tomorrow night's national championship game is held. In front of a few hundred reporters are Carlesimo, Gaze, and Ramos. Earlier Carlesimo was named the national coach of the year by a vote of the nation's coaches. For the second time in three years, the Big East has had the national coach of the year, Pitino having been honored two years ago in New Orleans.

"You might only get a team this special once," says Carlesimo. "I don't know that yet, but our staff talks a lot about it. This might be the best team we ever have. We're here because of the guys. If you lose sight of that, I think you're wrong. So you can be proud of what you accomplished, but you're just lucky."

He is asked about Gaze's future at Seton Hall. Though Linda Bruno of the Big East office has spent roughly the past month convincing the NCAA to allow Gaze one more year of eligibility, media snipers have been asking: Is Gaze any more than a hired gun?

"Because of the Olympic waiver Andrew didn't have to go to class the first semester," he says. "But he took a full academic load. I hope, obviously, for selfish reasons that he comes back. But I only represent basketball. I don't represent admissions. And if I can recruit two more like Andrew and Ramon, I'll be back here a couple of times."

He turns to his right to look at his star players. Ramos, with his bulk and his wide face with deep-set eyes, looks 30 years old. Gaze looks about the same, already bearing traces of gray in his light wavy hair.

"Ramon looks old, but he's just a kid. Jack's about 40 years old," Carlesimo quips, "Jack" being Gaze's Seton Hall nickname. "I don't think age is a factor. Experience is an enormous factor."

He is asked about his father's influence on his career. Back in the early years when P. J. struggled, critics often said he survived only because of his father's clout.

"Any success I've had is a direct result of my father's influence," he says, one more example that Carlesimo is secure enough not to feel defensive when people ask indelicate questions. "I think people have good feelings about my father, and that has carried over to me."

He says that, contrary to the popular mythology, this year's Hall team didn't just happen all of a sudden and rise from anonymity like a phoenix out of the ashes. He believes that every year the program got better. He says there are certain building blocks in the Big East: first you have to be competitive. Then you learn to win at home. Then you learn to win on the road. He thinks that the corner was turned two years ago, when the Pirates went to the NIT without a senior on the team.

Which brings him back to this year's team.

"I was a little concerned with the chemistry before the season," he says. "I wasn't worried about Andrew, but we had a close-knit, veteran team, and I was worried about them adjusting to him. Then in the first practice he makes four great assists. It took about 50 seconds. He blended in on the court right away. Andrew can fit into any basketball team. On the second day of practice we went to lift weights, and Andrew couldn't even lift the bar. He had never lifted before. So the kids started goofing on him and he started laughing and I knew then everything was going to be all right."

He goes on to say that he loved the Final Four in 1984 when Georgetown won it. Loved it in '85 in Kentucky when Massimino won. With others, such sentiment might be construed as traditional postgame patter. With Carlesimo it's genuine. He's forever saying how close the people are in the Big East, how everyone roots for the other conference teams in the tournament. In his particular view of the world the Big East is one big happy family who all genuflect to the conference banner.

"Seton Hall would not be here without being in the Big East," he says. "Our kids would not be here. There's no way you can separate our basketball success from the conference. When we started, we didn't have a recreation center. We used to do Nautilus in some place in South Orange. We lifted weights in Irvington. There was no training table. I don't think you can recruit without these things. You have to convince kids there's a commitment."

"If you loved those other Final Fours, what about this one?"

"This," he says, "is the best five or six days of my life."

Later that night is a party at a downtown Seattle lounge given by "The Retired Irish Bounce-Passers Association," the annual party given by Billy Raftery and Joe Healey, the owner of Runyon's in New York.

The so-called club came into existence four years ago in Lexington. Raftery and Healey were looking to rent a place and have their traditional Final Four party, when they were informed that Lexington was a dry town on Sundays. The only exception was a private club. Introducing "The Retired Irish Bounce-Passers Association."

Tonight it is jammed. It seems that everyone at the Final Four who has any connection to the East is here: Bobby

Cremins, the Georgia Tech coach whose roots are in New York; Tommy Penders, the Texas coach, who coached at Columbia and Fordham before becoming the Cinderella story of last year's tournament with Rhode Island; George Blaney of Holy Cross; Tom Brennan of Vermont; Al Skinner of Rhode Island; and various assistant coaches. Around midnight Gavitt and his wife, Julie, come in, along with Tranghese and McElroy. It's an unofficial Eastern reunion in downtown Seattle.

A few minutes later Carlesimo comes in. With him are his parents, one of his sisters, and his assistant coaches. He is the honored guest. He has long been one of the best-liked people in coaching, to the point that Calhoun supposedly has said the Big East coaches are made up of "eight assholes and P. J." Even in a business as cutthroat as coaching, the people here don't resent him for being successful. Not yet, anyway. That has become the new conference joke: next year Carlesimo will start to be disliked.

If tomorrow night he will play for the national championship, now he's going to party. He buys drinks for people. He makes small talk. He laughs.

"Do you think John and the Hoyas were here the night they played for the title in '84?" says someone, watching Carlesimo return from the bar with drinks for his family.

For he is the P. J. of old, staying up late, having a good time. Eat, drink, and be merry, for tomorrow we play for coaching immortality.

APRIL 3

It has all come down to this. All the practices, the recruiting, the weightlifting, the halftime speeches. All the film sessions. All the games themselves in this season that officially began with the first practice back on October 15. It has all come down to one game in the Kingdome. Seton Hall against Michigan for the national championship.

You couldn't ask for any better theater.

The *Melbourne Sun* has called Seton Hall "a little college from South Orange, New Jersey, unheard of much by Americans and all of Australia until Andrew Gaze showed up this year."

"I rang my girlfriend back home and she's very excited," Gaze says. "I play on the same club team with her brother back home, and she said he was over the moon in disbelief more than anything."

Gaze's buddy back home is not the only one over the moon. So is the Seton Hall campus. After the Duke win, the students celebrated in the streets in South Orange. The school no one ever heard of has become one of the great stories of this college basketball season, complete with a bearded coach who a year ago was going to get fired.

But every Final Four is full of great stories. The Hall is just one of them.

Michigan is being coached by Steve Fisher, the frog who dreamed of being a prince and became one. For years he was one of those faceless men on the bench, an assistant who was paying his dues, waiting for his chance. Then before the tournament started, Bill Frieder, the long-time Michigan coach, left to go to Arizona State. Fisher was named the interim coach. Now he is coaching for the national championship.

Michigan is led in the backcourt by Rumeal Robinson, a junior guard from Cambridge, Massachusetts, raised in the same neighborhood as Patrick Ewing. He too was born in Jamaica and came to America at an early age. When he was 10 his mother abandoned him. With nowhere to go, no money for food, he hung around the local elementary school, then snuck into the building when everyone else went home and slept in a back room. He did this for nearly three weeks before a woman who worked at the school as a crossing guard took him home. She later adopted him. Now she has come to see her adopted son play for the national championship, wearing a sweatshirt that says "Rumeal's Mom" on it.

Unlike Saturday's game in which the Hall had gotten off to an atrocious start, tonight they play their game. Afterward, several of the players will say that they weren't nervous, that they had played in too many games in too many places to be nervous. But the Pirates, who had gone through stretches throughout the tournament when the scoring did not come easily, again have trouble scoring, and they trail 37–32 at the half.

Michigan's Glen Rice, on his way to setting an NCAA Tournament scoring record, makes a three-point shot with 8:26 to go, giving Michigan a 10-point lead. The Hall comes back, though, sparked by Morton's one-on-one ability. With Michigan leading 66–61, Morton scores 6 straight points, and Seton Hall has its first lead of the second half with 2:14 to play. But Michigan comes back to go up by 3, before Morton makes a three-point shot to send the game into overtime. Throughout the second half Morton has been brilliant, turning the national championship game into his own personal playground. In scoring 22 of the Hall's last 28 points in regulation, he has given one of the most memorable performances in the history of the championship game.

And now the score is tied.

Five more minutes are put up on the clock.

The tension increases.

Both teams go to their benches for a timeout.

As the players are about to go back on the court for the overtime, Baker pulls Gaze back. Gaze has not made a field goal the entire game and taken few shots. "You think you can get us a fucking jumper now?" he says.

Gaze laughs.

With 1:17 to go in the overtime and the Hall up 79–76, Greene goes to the foul line with a one and one. He has been a 78-percent foul shooter throughout the season. If he makes 2 here, Michigan will be hard pressed to come back.

But he misses the first shot. Michigan comes back with the ball, and Terry Mills makes a turnaround jumper with 56 seconds to go, slicing the Hall lead to one. Seton Hall works the clock down, then Morton goes for the basket. But he forces his shot with just 11 seconds left and shoots an airball.

Michigan's Rumeal Robinson gets the ball and starts weaving down the court through the Seton Hall players, like water rolling downhill. As he gets into the right side of the lane, he has pentrated as far as he can go. With less than five seconds to go, he turns to his right in order to pass the ball back out. At that moment Greene bumps him. It's not a big bump, but there is some contact. Referee John Clougherty blows the whistle and calls Greene for a foul.

There are just three seconds remaining on the clock.

This is a highly questionable call. One of the unwritten rules of officiating is to never have a game decided on the foul line if it can possibly be avoided. Now Robinson goes to the foul line with a chance to win the national championship.

He sinks the two shots. Michigan now leads, 80–79.

Seton Hall calls a timeout. In the huddle Carlesimo sets up the last-second play. They must go the length of the court in just three seconds. But they have a play ready. All teams practice last-second situations all year long. The Hall is no exception. Just this morning they practiced a similar situation, and Greene had hit a shot at the buzzer. So Carlesimo is confident that they can still win.

Ramos takes the ball out of bounds and throws it downcourt. Walker catches it off balance, a little farther out than the play is designed for. With time running out, he throws up a desperation shot. It hits the backboard and bounds away as the buzzer sounds.

It is over.

Seton Hall has lost, 80–79.

As the Michigan players hug each other at center court, the Seton Hall players huddle in front of their bench with their hands joined over their heads. There is a couple of moments of silence. Then they walk out on the court to congratulate Michigan.

The Kingdome is in a frenzy. The Michigan pep band is playing their famous fight song, "Hail to the Victors Valiant," the one that has been reverberating through the building all night long. A few minutes later the Seton Hall players come back to their bench in their white uniforms with the blue trim and sit back down. For a few seconds they just sit there, faces blank, adjusting to the realization that their dream is over. Then Carlesimo comes over and motions everyone to follow him into the locker room. It is Michigan's time now.

* * *

An hour after the game, Carlesimo is sitting on a training table in the middle of the room. A few players and the assistant coaches are still there as well. None of them want to leave, because leaving this room means the season is really over. By staying they somehow hold on to the dream a little longer. All locker rooms have this bittersweet tinge on the last night of the season, like the last day of school when you know that come next year it will all be different.

Carlesimo has already done his postgame interview. He was the gracious loser, like always. He said he considers John Clougherty one of the best officials in the country, and he has no problem with the call; if he had to name one official in the country to make a call at that point in the game it would be Clougherty. It is the kind of class move Carlesimo is famous for within the Big East. Then he credited Michigan and Steve Fisher. He praised his own team. He is a good loser, talking as if losing the national title on a peculiar call in the dying seconds is no different than all those nights, through all those years, when he used to get pounded by the good teams in the Big East. He is the son of a coach, P. J. Carlesimo is, and he grew up with losing games. Afterward, he will say that one thing he learned from being around his father is that you're not going to win every game: "A loss isn't like death, or anything like that, and anyone who thinks it is doesn't begin to have a perspective on life."

Now he sits on the table in the middle of the room, his face drained of all expression.

"The other night at the coaches' dinner, I looked out at all those tables and I realized there were about 1,700 coaches in the room," he says. "Almost all of them are never going to have the remarkable experience I had. Maybe I won't have it again either. But there are much better coaches than me who have never been here, and if you don't realize that, you're missing the point."

He hesitates, searching for the right words.

"I'm disappointed for the six kids who will never again put on a Seton Hall uniform."

He stares at a stat sheet for a moment, then goes on.

"I'm the same coach I've always been," he says. "I just got better players. The difference in this profession is that you're judged by how a group of kids play. This group has made me look very, very good. You can always get good players. You can't always get good people like these kids."

He continues to sit and stare. Only a few people are left in the room now. The tears are all gone. Carlesimo has told the team to be proud of what they've achieved and to never look back. Now he is trying not to look back himself. He starts talking again about how special this team was, how they worked hard, came to play every day. He keeps talking. He doesn't want to leave this room behind, for once he leaves this room he will leave a piece of himself behind. He is only 39, but he has been a coach for 17 years already, and he knows he might never have a team like this again.

Eventually, John Paquette, the Seton Hall sports-information director, comes over and says it's time to go.

Carlesimo gets up to leave. Someone asks him what his plans are for the next few days.

"Well, I guess we won't be going to the White House."

EPILOGUE

The games are over, but the season never really ends. It just has its quiet periods.

• New developments in surprising Georgetown. The Hoyas have signed their first white player in seven years, a fact not lost on the *Washington Post,* which puts it right in their headline. He is Mike Sabol, a 6-7 forward from Gonzaga Prep in D.C.

John Thompson himself has been in the news, following his appearance on a special edition of "Nightline," where he said he had met with a District of Columbia drug dealer and told him that he didn't want any problems with his players.

"There was a hush when he got up to speak on 'Nightline,' " says Michael Wilbon of the *Washington Post.* "It was like Martin Luther King was going to speak, I kid you not."

Thompson later told Wilbon that when he returned from Seoul in the fall he had been told by people around town that Alonzo Mourning and John Turner had been seen with Rayful Edmond III, a reputed local drug dealer who had grown up with Turner in suburban Maryland. After his appearance on "Nightline," Thompson said he couldn't understand that some people would think it strange he would have a private meeting with a drug dealer.

"We cannot close ourselves off from the rest of society," he told the *Post*. "Anyone who experienced the Len Bias situation knows we cannot seal ourselves off from people. We'd better start confronting these problems. We'd better understand we're incorporated into these problems. This isn't *them* or *they*. The people involved with drugs and being killed are *our* children. It is not like somebody crawled out of some hole who is so different from us."

• Derrick Coleman, already Syracuse's all-time leading rebounder, has announced he is going to stay in school for his senior year. By staying at Syracuse he could become one of the top three players in next year's NBA draft. One of the reasons for his decision is supposedly the fact that J. R. Reid of North Carolina announced he was skipping his senior year to turn pro, and Reid's availability might push Coleman further down in the draft's first round.

• Seton Hall has signed three players: Jerry Walker, a 6-6 forward from St. Anthony's in Jersey City; Oliver Taylor, a point guard from Miami Dade North who went to high school in Queens; and Jim Dickinson, a seven-footer from Rhode Island who was also recruited by Providence. They are also heavily recruiting Phil Dixon, a 6-5 swingman from Toronto, as is Connecticut. In fact, the competition for Dixon has caused another spate of bad blood, this time between the Hall and Connecticut.

"They've been brutal," says Rod Baker, "especially Assistant Coach Howie Dickenman. I always thought he was a nice guy, but he kept telling Dixon we were going on probation because of the Gaze situation, and that P. J. was leaving. He killed us. All he did was negative recruit."

The Seton Hall staff is supposedly so upset at Connecticut that they are going to bring up the incident at the Big East coaches' meetings to be held a couple of weeks from now.

Before that happens, though, Dixon announces he is going to Connecticut.

*   *   *

There have been two national stories on Seton Hall. The weekend after the Pirates returned home, complete with a celebration in Walsh Gym where the students yelled for "one more year," Andrew Gaze went home to Melbourne. Before he did, he gave away all his Seton Hall memorabilia, supposedly even his Final Four ring.

He didn't leave without a certain backlash.

Phil Mushnick of the *New York Post* wrote, "Gaze seems like an awfully nice person, but let's face it . . . he's a two-semester hired gun for a college team."

The *New York Times* quoted the general manager of the Melbourne Tigers, Gaze's club team, as saying that $25,000 had been put into a trust fund for Gaze and his family during a six-month period in 1988. If it were determined that this was payment for playing, then Gaze could be declared a professional by the NCAA and declared ineligible. If this were to happen, Seton Hall would not only have to forfeit all its 31 victories this year but also return the $1.25 million it received by going to the championship game.

Larry Keating, the Seton Hall AD, said the story in the *Times* was incorrectly reported. "That's not a trust fund for Andrew," he told John Jackson of the *Bergen Record*. "There was a $25,000 general expense fund for all the players on the team. The fact of the matter is that most of the money has never been used and Andrew's father has kept it in case it's needed for operating expenses. It is my belief . . . that Andrew never received any compensation for athletic competition above the allowable expenses under NCAA rules."

At the end of April Keating said he had not heard anything from the NCAA and didn't expect to. Just in case, he was preparing a report to answer any question that might arise concerning the Gaze matter. He also said he was bothered by the insinuations Gaze was a hired gun and said Gaze had already completed three of his four courses before he left, and he is finishing the fourth by mail.

A couple of weeks later, one of the highlights of the Seton Hall basketball dinner was a phone hookup back to Melbourne, so everyone could talk to "Jack."

The big news, though, has been the courting of Carlesimo

by Kentucky. It's not entirely unexpected. Kentucky was once the most famous college basketball school in the country, back when Adolph Rupp was the baron of the bluegrass, and even now it's considered one of the true glamour jobs, where everything is first class, including the money. There is a 12,000-seat practice building, a plush athletic dorm just for the players, and a 23,000-seat arena in downtown Lexington that has hosted the Final Four. But after years of rumored illegal payoffs to players, they are now facing NCAA sanctions that could bar them from any postseason appearances for two years. The head coaching job opened when Eddie Sutton resigned in March, following an NCAA investigation that uncovered 18 violations. The school has already hired C. M. Newton to be its new athletic director, and he brings a clean image and the promise that things are going to be done differently in the future. After the Lakers' Pat Riley and the Knicks' Pitino expressed no interest in the job, Newton offered Carlesimo a salary in the vicinity of $650,000, about three times what he makes at Seton Hall. Carlesimo has four years remaining on the new contract he signed last spring but has a clause in it saying he's free to leave the school whenever he wants.

At the end of April, Carlesimo went to Lexington to meet with Newman and the seven-member search committee. While there he was supposedly asked what he needed to rebuild the Kentucky program and answered, "For you people to keep the cheaters out." This was quickly followed by a report that Kentucky had offered the job to Carlesimo and he had accepted. About the same time a Lexington writer said that the last thing Kentucky needed was an Italian coach from New York with a beard and a losing record.

So Carlesimo had come home to think about it. He was the guest speaker at the Georgetown basketball dinner. He talked to Keating. And he no doubt read the New York papers, all of which seemed to have an opinion on Carlesimo's future.

In the *Daily News*, Mike Lupica wrote, "P. J. Carlesimo is the best young college basketball coach in America. If he decides to shine his light on the Kentucky program, many of us around here will miss having him around. But I will cheer him for taking a shot at one of the storied jobs in his field. Clearly, coaching is Carlesimo's art. I'm sorry. His first loyalty is to that."

Also in the *Daily News,* Harvey Araton wrote, "The semester hasn't yet ended, the Final Four banner in the Robert E. Brennan Recreation Center still hangs, and already the Seton Hall Pirates appear to be nothing more than a team picture on the wall and a hefty check in the bank."

Araton quoted Joe Quinlan, Keating's assistant, as saying, "If you're here for the death watch you should have brought flowers."

But four days ago, on May 1, Carlesimo announced he was taking his name out of contention for the Kentucky job. He cited his ties to Seton Hall and to the East. "I really like it here. I've been treated well," he said in a prepared statement. "I am extremely comfortable living in the metropolitan area, competing in the Big East Conference, and I am certain no other environment would be as comfortable to me."

Now he is here in the Big East office to be interviewed by Mike Gorman for the Big East's 10-year video. The problem is that he's just finished playing golf with Gavitt and Tranghese, and all he has with him are his golf clothes.

"We are in the image-building business," says McElroy with a rueful smile. "We can't have him going before the camera in a cheap red golf sweater and green golf shirt. Not the guy who turned Kentucky down."

Someone eventually finds Carlesimo a yellow sweater.

"How has your life changed?" he's asked.

"After we lost in Seattle, someone asked me what I was going to do, and I joked that I was going to take a month off and find a wife. One of those morons wrote it and now I get letters from 65-year-old women saying they like the theater and going for walks on the beach. Unbelievable."

He is so swamped with correspondence and mail that he cancelled a spring trip to Greece and decided not to coach in Puerto Rico this summer.

"Are you going to Sawgrass for the coaches' meetings?"

Carlesimo smiles. "I wasn't sure for a while," he says. "I asked Dave if I go to Kentucky can I still go to Sawgrass and he said yes. But I still wasn't sure."

He goes into a room and sits down in front of the camera. In front of him is Mike Gorman, the voice of the Big East. The light goes on and Gorman starts to speak.

"When did you know this team was something special?"

"Our first exhibition game against Yugoslavia." Carlesimo laughs. "No, seriously, Alaska. After that we knew we were good. Then winning at St. John's. It also was a great schedule to prepare a team. Playing in a domed stadium in a Christmas tournament. The Big East Tournament in the Garden. All that makes you ready."

"At any point in the season did you start thinking about the Final Four?" Gorman asks.

"I never wasted a lot of time thinking about it," he says. "But the Tuesday after the Big East Tournament we told the kids that we as a staff thought we could win the national championship. I thought it was important the kids understand that. They needed to be reminded that we really thought they were that good. At that point, we felt that we weren't going to be playing anyone any better than Georgetown or Syracuse. And thus, potentially, there was not a game coming up we didn't think we couldn't win. It wasn't just rhetoric. They believed we could win every game."

"What did you learn from all of this?" Gorman asks.

Carlesimo ponders for a second.

"I don't know," he says finally. "That John Clougherty is not as good an official as I thought he was. That you have to stay with young players, that you can't give up on them. All of our kids struggled at different times, and those times helped them. Playing against Patrick and Chris and Walter Berry are the reasons they got better. It's the best preparation for the NCAA Tournament. So I guess I learned all those things."

He pauses for a second, and then he smiles. "But most of all, I think it reinforced what I always knew: that our league is the best."

Down the hall Gavitt sits in his office. One picture on the

wall depicts him with Jimmy Carter. Another has him with Ronald Reagan.

"By all the standards it's been a great year for the league," he says. "Maybe the best ever. Seton Hall. St. John's winning the NIT. Three teams in the final eight. These are the obvious things. But this year was by far the most competitive in the conference. Look at the caliber of play, so many close games, great young players, great attendance. Even BC, which came in last, had great attendance all year."

"Where do you think the Big East will be 10 years from now?"

Gavitt leans back in his chair. "The budgets, the staffs, the facilities, the support services, they're all there. That wasn't the case 10 years ago. But everything is in place now to be able to sustain the loss of the big personalities in the league: a Thompson, Massimino, Carnesecca, Boeheim. I think the biggest fear now is dismantling from the outside. Specifically, the football interests. Both regionally and nationally, that is the biggest risk."

He says that while football revenues have gone down nationally, basketball revenues have risen, and this does not always sit well with a lot of ADs across the country, many of whom have football backgrounds. So his biggest concern for the future is that "decisions that affect basketball will not be made for basketball reasons."

But all that is for the future.

For now Dave Gavitt is a happy man. Another successful season is over. P. J. Carlesimo, the hottest basketball coach in the country, is sitting in the next room, all set to return to Seton Hall. The Big East continues to be the most glamorous college basketball conference in the country. And so Gavitt looks out over the Providence River, here in the headquarters of his "very own basketball league," and smiles.

ON YOU HUSKIES
The 1989–90 Season

Every year some Big East team seems to jump into the middle of a basketball version of Cinderella.

In 1987, Providence jumped on that magic carpet that took them all the way to the Final Four in New Orleans. Last year it was Seton Hall. This year it was Connecticut.

Like Seton Hall, the Huskies have always been one of the forgotten teams in the Big East. The years have come and gone in the Big East, featuring showcase players from Patrick Ewing to Alonzo Mourning. Everything has changed, except that the University of Connecticut always seemed to be a team stuck on a treadmill to nowhere. It seemed forever trapped in a curious limbo between its past successes in the Yankee Conference and a glowing Big East future that always seemed off in the distance somewhere.

The season began with the usual expectations. Georgetown and Syracuse were picked to battle for first, with St. John's and maybe Pittsburgh challenging them. So what else was new?

Georgetown began the season as one of the top-ranked teams in the country. They had the twin towers of Alonzo Mourning and Dikembe Mutombo, potentially the most dominating inside game in the country. They also had Dwayne Bryant and Mark Tillmon, two guards who had played for three years. Syracuse had picked up LaRon Ellis, a Ken-

tucky transfer, adding him to the nucleus of Derrick Coleman, Billy Owens, and Stevie Thompson. On paper Syracuse
was as talented as any team in the country, even though the
only true point guard in the program was freshman Mike
Edwards. Boeheim began the season trying to get by with
Thompson at the point, but scrapped that shortly into the
Big East season. St. John's had a veteran team returning,
plus Boo Harvey, who had been an academic casualty the
year before. Pittsburgh had five starters back. Providence
had three starters back from a team that had gone to the
NCAA Tournament the year before, including the backcourt of Carlton Screen and Eric Murdock, called one of the
best in the country. Villanova was about to introduce a
great freshman class to go along with center Tom Greis and
a fine sophomore class.

Going into the season all these teams were expected to
challenge for an NCAA berth. The three others—Seton
Hall, Connecticut, and Boston College—had big questions
hovering over them. The Hall, last year's miracle team, had
lost all five starters. They were in transition as they waited
for Prop 48 freshman Jerry Walker to become eligible and
prize recruit Luther Wright to arrive. Boston College was
again caught in a talent gap, but had gotten a commitment
from Bill Curley, a 6-9 center from nearby Duxbury, considered to be the most symbolic basketball recruit in the school's
history.

The season didn't go the way anyone anticipated.

Pitt's Sean Miller missed the entire season with a stress
fracture of his foot, leaving the Panthers without a point
guard. They finished at 11–16. For St. John's, Jayson Williams went out midway through the year with a broken foot.
With Williams went St. John's hopes to make a big splash
nationally. The Redmen still made the NCAA Tournament,
where they beat Temple, then lost to Duke. Villanova was
inconsistent, a by-product of its youth, but finished 17–13.
They made the NCAA Tournament, but lost to LSU in the
first round. Providence went through a bad stretch midway
through the Big East season, but recovered in time to finish
17–10 and make the tournament for the second straight

year. They also lost in the first round, to Ohio State in overtime.

Syracuse not only spent the entire year searching for a point guard, but in a certain sense they always seemed to be a team whose whole never measured up to the sum of its parts. They shared the Big East regular season title with Connecticut, then lost in the finals of the Big East Tournament to the Huskies. They then lost to Minnesota by seven in New Orleans in the third round of the tournament.

The most disappointing team, though, was Georgetown.

After Alonzo Mourning's great freshman year, one in which he immediately became one of the top big men in the country, he seemed to plateau. At times he and Mutombo seemed to be in each other's way. At times he had trouble scoring. The perennial knock on Thompson's coaching is that big men don't seem to develop offensively. Mourning seemed an almost textbook example of that. The Hoyas got a great year out of Tillmon, but Thompson never really found anyone to give him solid production at the forward spot. In a curious sense, the Hoya team never really found its own identity. They came in third in the Big East, got beat in the semifinals of the Big East Tournament, and lost in the second round of the tournament to underdog Xavier.

As for individual honors, Coleman was named the Big East's player of the year. He also was a first-team All-Big East selection along with Mourning, Owens, Tillmon, Harvey, and Pitt's Brian Shorter. The all-conference second team was Thompson, Mutombo, Screen, Chris Smith of Connecticut, and Malik Sealy, the sophomore forward from St. John's. The third team was comprised of Bryant, Nadav Henefeld and Tate George of Connecticut, Jason Mathews of Pitt, and Marty Conlon of Providence. The all-rookie team included Henefeld, Edwards, guard Terry Dehere of Seton Hall, Villanova's Lance Miller, and Scott Burrell of Connecticut. Henefeld was named the rookie of the year.

Overall, though, the big story was Connecticut, the school that had always seemed not to count. Coach Jim Calhoun had arrived in 1986, and had been given a seven-year contract. The implication, of course, was that the resurrection of

the Connecticut program was no overnight job and that
Calhoun was in for a long haul. Maybe it was only fitting,
for Calhoun is a marathon runner and knows all about long
hauls. He has run ten marathons, five in Boston and four in
New York. He started running in 1975, partly to relieve the
pressures of coaching. Now he gets restless when he doesn't
run, and calls himself addicted. He says it's one of the few
times he's able to get away from recruiting and strategy and
alumni demands and the other hundred and one things that
go with being a Big East coach.

Calhoun is also someone who lost his father to a heart
attack when he was fifteen. But he's carried his father's
lessons of responsibility and hard work with him. These
were the values that Calhoun upheld through all the way
stations of his career, through all the high schools and all
the times when he must have thought that he would never
be anything but a high school coach. Calhoun has paid his
coaching dues.

In a sense, he is a throwback to the past. He is only
forty-seven, but his route to the big East and the media
spotlight has been carved out of small gyms and long bus
rides. Unlike so many of his contemporaries who have made
their reputations as recruiters, Calhoun built his career brick
by brick. He hadn't played at a prestigious college for a
prestigious coach. He hadn't gone to work at some glamour
school. He had never had a coaching "rabbi," the coaching
euphemism for someone who guides a young coach's career,
maps out the blueprint to the big time early, then gets his
protégé to follow it. He coached at a succession of high
schools in New England, then went to Northeastern when
nobody else wanted to coach there.

Even after he attained success at Northeastern, especially
with Reggie Lewis, he always had the look of a man who
had to prove himself. He always was the outsider, the face
in the window looking in at the party, knowing he belonged
but not getting invited. He had good teams at Northeastern,
but was always overshadowed in Boston by Boston College
and the Big East. And even during those winning seasons at

Northeastern, he must have wondered if Northeastern was going to be as far as he went.

In March, after the Huskies had won the Big East Tournament, Calhoun reflected on this: "I was thinking about all the other places," he told Charles Pierce of *The National*. "When you've played in the Pit, at Maine, you don't worry about places like Madison Square Garden. Here, they only yell at you to sit down. In the Pit, they pull you back into your seat. Or you think about New Hampshire, riding a bus for a couple of hours to play a game at three in the afternoon with about eleven people in the stands."

By the time he arrived at Connecticut, he already had built a winning program at Northeastern out of those ashes known as apathy and anonymity. Now he was being asked to do it again at a place where frustration and failed hopes all but had guaranteed spots on the team roster. It is also a place that might just be the toughest place to coach in the Big East, what with fourteen daily papers covering the team and a state that follows its basketball team religiously.

This year did not look promising. Though the Huskies had won the NIT two years earlier—arguably the school's greatest claim to basketball fame—even then it had finished eighth in the Big East. Last year they were tied for seventh, and many felt that the Huskies never were going to get out of the Big East's second division, Calhoun or no Calhoun. Before the season Connecticut was picked for eighth. Last year's stars, Cliff Robinson and Phil Gamble, were gone. Left were sophomore Chris Smith, the often maligned Tate George, and a bunch of no-names. The Huskies already seemed penciled in for the qualifying game in the Big East Tournament.

But Calhoun's teams always had played hard, even in the bad times. He liked to say that all his teams had three trademarks, whether the current ones at UConn or the ones back at Northeastern: "We'll outwork you," he said. "Number two, we're going to defend you every inch of the floor. Number three, we're going to play together."

Going into the season, Smith was the one player with star

quality. He had averaged a shade under 10 points a game as a freshman the year before, yet always seemed to be playing with shackles on. Smith said it was because he was a freshman playing in the shadow of seniors Robinson and Gamble. Calhoun was hoping it wasn't timidity. Either way, Smith had felt slighted when he did not make the Big East all-rookie team. He had spent part of the summer playing at the U.S. Olympic Festival, where he had played very well in the practices, not so well in the games. Everyone around the Connecticut program knew that for the Huskies to be significantly improved, Smith was going to have to start living up to the potential he had showed when he had come out of Kolbe-Cathedral High School in Bridgeport, back when Calhoun had said Smith could do more things with a basketball than anyone he had ever coached.

The other player with obvious big-time talent was freshman Scott Burrell from Hamden, Connecticut, whose older brother played football at UConn. The year before, as a high school senior, Burrell had been the best high school basketball player in the state. He also was a great pitching prospect, a first-round draft pick of the Seattle Mariners. He reportedly turned down a six-figure contract to play basketball and baseball at the University of Connecticut.

"Baseball is my future," Burrell said, "but right now basketball is more fun. It's a hobby."

For the third straight year Calhoun had gotten the best high school player in the state of Connecticut, Murray Williams from Torrington and Smith from Bridgeport being the other two. Keeping the best players home had been one of Calhoun's essential goals at a school that all too often had seen home-grown talent go elsewhere.

Sophomores Rod Sellers and Dan Cyrulik were the big men. Sellers was 6-9, from Florence, South Carolina. Cyrulik was a seven-footer from Williamsville, New York. The lone senior was George.

A complete unknown was Nadav Henefeld. He was a twenty-one-year-old freshman who the year before had been in the army in Israel and played for the Israeli national team. Growing up in the Tel Aviv suburb of Ramat-Hasharon, he had long wanted to play college basketball in the United States, but wasn't recruited. After he completed his three years of mandatory military service, he wrote letters to some twenty American schools, but drew little response. "I put in all my statistics," Henefeld said. "A few schools answered, but all they did was send information about their schools."

Calhoun heard about Henefeld from Marv Kessler, the former coach at Adelphi, who has coached in Israel. In April 1989 Henefeld visited both St. John's and UConn. When he saw the campus in Storrs he fell in love at first sight.

"After I talked with Coach Calhoun and the other coaches and saw the beautiful campus, I said to myself, 'This is the place for me,' " he said. "St. John's was nice, but if I went there, I would have had to live in an apartment and I wanted to live in a dormitory."

Calhoun, though, was not about to offer a scholarship to someone he hadn't seen play. So that summer he went to Tel Aviv to watch Henefeld play in the Maccabiah Games. Henefeld was the MVP. Nonetheless, Henefeld arrived at Connecticut as a question mark. Calhoun was not sure he would be able to contribute right away. He knew Henefeld had talent, but the adjustment to the Big East can be difficult for any new player, never mind one who had to adapt to both a new culture and English as a second language.

Nor did anyone really know if he was going to be eligible. Because he had served in the Israeli army and hadn't had time to take the SATs, the NCAA granted him a special waiver letting him take the test. In October he flew to Raleigh, North Carolina, at his own expense so he wouldn't have to wait longer to take the test. He missed the first two weeks of practice before learning he was eligible.

Sensitive to Andrew Gaze comparisons and changes that Henefeld was just another hired gun brought in for a year before returning home, Connecticut and the NCAA also looked into allegations that Henefeld had been paid to play in Israel. They found no evidence of it. Henefeld said he'd never been paid.

At the end of November, Henefeld left the Huskies and flew back to Tel Aviv for a key Israeli national team game against France in the World University Games. He scored 23 points in the six-point Israeli victory. Then he got on a plane to New York. In New York he changed planes to Seattle. In Seattle he changed planes to Anchorage, where he joined the Huskies in the Great Alaskan Shootout. It took him twenty-six hours. Then he went out and played in Connecticut's first-round loss to Texas A&M. In the next game he scored six of Connecticut's last eight points as the Huskies beat Florida State.

"Nadav does everything well," Calhoun said. "He's a great passer who moves the ball, and he's a very good shooter both inside and out. He also rebounds well and plays very good defense. And he's very versatile. His game, particularly his passing, is similar to that of Larry Bird's. Some of the kids call him Little Bird. He is an old-young player: young to our ways and old to the game of basketball because he has good instincts."

Henefeld is majoring in business and has insisted from the beginning that he was in this country for an education as well as playing basketball. "I liked it here from the first minute," he said. "I wanted to be part of college life. It's a beautiful place and everyone is nice."

By January he had become the story in the league, this year's Gaze. He scored. He led the league in steals. He played with unflappable poise. Better yet, he made his teammates better. He was called the Beast from the Mideast and the Gaza Stripper.

His nickname, though, was The Dove, and it came quite by accident. The first time Henefeld was introduced to Chris Smith, he said, in a thick Hebrew accent, that his name was Nadav Henefeld. Smith, thinking Henefeld had said his first name was The Dove, thought it was one of the coolest nicknames he had ever heard, and told everyone what a great nickname the new guy from Israel had. So The Dove it was.

Nadav was certainly different. At one point he went to see Calhoun with a problem: he thought he was receiving too much publicity, and that wasn't fair to his teammates. He also was surprised when, after one early season game, he saw his teammates joyfully celebrating. "But it's only a game," he said.

Before the season ended, he had become not only one of the great stories in all of college basketball, but also a cult hero in Israel. His accomplishments were chronicled almost daily by the Israeli media. A TV crew from Israel came to Storrs to film a day in the life of Nadav Henefeld. Four Israeli newspapers phoned the school's sports information office every game for an update of his accomplishments. O'Brien calls him the X factor. Boeheim calls him the most valuable player in the Big East.

As the season wound down, the big question, was, just how long would he stay in Storrs? The NCAA granted him two more years of eligibility, but Henefeld is under increasing pressure to return home and play professionally. He could earn as much as $200,000 a year to play in Israel.

Calhoun went into the season wanting to change the team's style of play. He wanted to run more. He wanted to press more.

"This team is so different from what we had when I first came here," he said. "Just think when I started. We had Jeff King at 6-10, Gary Besselink at 6-8, and Cliff Robinson at 6-10. We had Phil Gamble and Steve Pikiell with his injured shoulder. We didn't have any small forwards or perimeter players—that was my first year. We had no small forward on that team, really. So we've gone from a team with very heavy up-front emphasis to a team that is now, on the outside, much better."

But in December, in their first conference game of the season against Villanova in the Hartford Civic Center, they were so miserable they were booed off the floor at halftime. In early January they were blown out on the road at St. John's. Then things started to click.

After the regular season ended and the Huskies had a share of the Big East title, Calhoun sat in his office entertaining a sportswriter from the *New York Times*. The Huskies had become the first team in Big East history to have been picked as low as eighth in the pre-season and gone on to win the conference. They had been ranked as high as fourth in the country. Gampel Pavilion, the centerpiece of a new $28 million sports complex on campus, was finally open.

Calhoun was thinking about the annual luncheon to be held at the Grand Hyatt in New York City later in the week, the only time all nine teams are in the same place. His team had always seemed to be a Big East version of the poor boy at the party.

"You're sitting there nervous," he said, "getting ready for the 8–9 game, and you really didn't feel you were a part of the league. I don't think I checked the league standings at all. I never felt part of the Big East. I know we'd get publications and stuff sent to us from the Big East. . . . But the standings were the least of our concerns. Survival and building some respect were our major concerns. It has some symbolism for us, when you think about it. When you walk in, you're sitting at one table, and there's Georgetown, Syracuse, and Pitt, and when they look around at everyone in the league, guys look back at them with respect. We don't want to play for bragging rights. But respect is a nice thing to have."

By this time the Huskies had become a superb team. They didn't have any real stars. Nor did they shoot very well. They had little inside offense. They periodically had long stretches when they had trouble scoring. But oh how they played defense. They played zone. They pressed fullcourt. They trapped halfcourt. They played man-to-man. They even sometimes played triangle and two. They always seemed to be switching defenses, all called by Calhoun from the bench. The one contrast was they played them all with incredible intensity. In truth, the Huskies lived off their defense, stealing the ball time and time again. They scored off it. They got their momentum off it. Their defense became their juice.

Plus, they had great chemistry. If Syracuse seemed to be less than the sum of its parts, Connecticut was better than theirs. Maybe that was because there were no stars. Calhoun always preaches that when the team wins, everyone benefits and everyone gets recognition. Like Seton Hall the year before, this team played great defense and was very unselfish.

One case in point will suffice: when Chris Smith had been a high school senior, one of the people who helped recruit him was Tate George, even though Smith's presence might have meant reduced minutes for George. "I came in expecting I would have to beat Tate out," Smith said. "But I never felt that way after I met Tate. He made it clear we were on the same team and should work together. He helped me learn the system."

On Saturday afternoon of the Big East Tournament in Madison Square Garden, the Huskies played Georgetown in the semi-finals. In a sense, it was Connecticut's national coming-out party. The Huskies beat the Hoyas, and a strong case can be made that it was Connecticut's biggest basketball win ever. They had won in the Garden, on national network television. "This puts the rubber stamp on our program," Calhoun said.

He knew full well that being known in Connecticut and in Boston and in Providence and in small New England towns doesn't count. You have to win in New York. If the Huskies had come into the Big East Tournament and lost in the first round to Seton Hall, all the age-old perceptions about them would have been mouthed again. Beneath the gloss of this year's accomplishments, these really were the same old Huskies.

"New York is the mecca," he said after his team beat Seton Hall in the first round. "We had to prove we're legitimate. This is our chance to be showcased."

Calhoun was showcased as well. The day before he had been named the big East Coach of the year at the Grand Hyatt. His Huskies had ended the regular season 25–5, 12–4 in the Big East, co-champions. He was the hottest college coach in the country.

In his presentation of the trophy, Dave Gavitt said that to understand Calhoun's success it was necessary to go back to the 1986–87 season, Calhoun's first at UConn, when his two best players—Cliff Robinson and Phil Gamble—were declared academically ineligible midway through the season. "That was the key year for Jim," Gavitt said. "For a guy who had the success he had at Northeastern, to have the patience to get through the situation without overreacting and not be tempted to take shortcuts . . . without that patience and maturity he would not be enjoying the success he's enjoying today."

"It's probably one of the few times that it's not at a basketball game that the setting is very emotional for me," Calhoun said, standing in the bright lights of TV cameras, surrounded by notepads. He had waited a long time for a moment like this.

"You'd watch some other people getting the spotlight, and you'd say, 'I can do that,' " he said about the feelings he used to have when he was at Northeastern and all the coaching awards always went to someone else. "There's something in you that says, 'I want to show them.' I didn't think I couldn't coach when we were 9–19, but there is some satisfaction. What I am saying is that these lights are very nice."

Calhoun also knew though, that some of those who had come before had helped make this year a success. Earlier in the week he had gone to the Boston Garden to see Cliff Robinson, now a rookie with the Portland Trail Blazers. Phil Gamble was there also. He told them both that they had "set the table and now we're eating a great meal."

After Saturday's victory against Georgetown, Connecticut could no longer be dismissed. Moreover, Calhoun had to feel special satisfaction. Even if the Hoyas were not the intimidating team they once were, that much of their old Hoya Paranoia image is in the past, they are still the team the rest of the conference loves to hate. And they still are the Big East's measuring stick. Until you beat Georgetown, you really haven't proven anything.

They also have been Connecticut's alter image.

The Hoyas have a high-profile pedigree, complete with a national title in 1984. The only national success Connecticut ever had was winning the watered-down NIT in 1988. The Hoyas have an alumni list that includes Ewing and Reggie Williams and a host of others who have spent time on NBA rosters. The Huskies have a bunch of national no-names. The Hoyas had Alonzo Mourning, one of the marquee names in college basketball. The Huskies' best-known player was a former Israeli soldier. The Hoyas were coached by John Thompson, one of the most famous coaches in the country, a former Olympic coach. Calhoun, on the other hand, had thirsted for the bright lights for years.

Or as Randy Smith of the *Manchester Journal-Inquirer* said, "Everyone else in the state of Connecticut might be surprised this is happening, but Calhoun's not. He's been waiting for this for a long time."

The next day, Connecticut beat Syracuse on national television, winning their first Big East Tournament. They got a big spark off the bench from John Gwynne, who made six of seven field goal attempts. Ironically, John Gwynne grew up in the Washington, D.C., area dreaming of going to Georgetown. He went to John Thompson's summer camp. His father had season tickets to Georgetown games. But he went to DeMatha High School in Hyattsville, Maryland, and Thompson does not recruit DeMatha players because of his long-standing feud with their coach, Morgan Wootten. All this year Gwynne had been the Big East's version of the Piston's Vinne Johnson, explosive offense off the bench.

The win also gave the Huskies the first seed in the East in the NCAA Tournament, meaning they would play at the Hartford Civic Center, their home court for Big East games until this year when Gampel Pavilion opened on campus. In fact, this year they played eight of eighteen home games there, but the NCAA says that unless a team plays more than half their games at a particular site, it's not considered a home court.

The team returned to the campus Sunday night to a waiting crowd and a police escort. When Calhoun and his wife, Pat, walked into a local doughnut shop the next morning, they were cheered. Four thousand people watched the Huskies practice in the Hartford Civic Center the day before their opening round game against Boston University.

The Huskies struggled for a while against BU before blowing them out in the second half. Two days later they easily dismissed California to advance to the Eastern Regionals.

The site was Brendan Byrne Arena, the white monolith that rises hard by Giants Stadium in the Jersey Meadowlands. Because it is Seton Hall's home court, Connecticut had played there before.

Connecticut's opponent in the first round of the Eastern Regionals was Clemson. As the final minutes ticked down, it appeared their dream season was over. The Huskies were down by one after squandering a 19-point lead, and when Tate George missed an open jumper from just inside the top of the key with three seconds to play, the Huskies looked dead. But Clemson's Sean Tyson missed a free throw with 1.6 seconds to play, and Connecticut called timeout.

"Believe . . . believe," Calhoun shouted at his players.

In truth, they had little to believe in.

Calhoun called a play called Home Run. Scott Burrell was going to in-bound the ball and throw it all the way down court to George, who would try to get off a last-second desperation shot. The team often had worked on the play in practice, though they hoped they'd never have to use it. The only problem was, as Burrell would say later, it only worked about fifty percent of the time in practice, and that was with three seconds on the clock, not 1.6.

Burrell, who had been a high school quarterback good enough to be recruited by the likes of Miami and Notre Dame, threw a strike to George, who caught it along the right baseline. In real life the pass would have been too long or too hard or been batted away. Or else George would have caught the ball and not have had enough time to get a shot off. Or the shot would have been blocked. Or it would have missed.

But that's reality, and reality had very little to do with Connecticut's season. George caught the ball neatly, turned, and shot. Of course it went in. The Huskies erupted in pandemonium. Calhoun jumped off the bench, throwing his hand up over his head, heading in the direction of the Clemson bench for the obligatory post-game handshake with the opposing coach. He took one last jump into the air, then saw Clemson coach Cliff Ellis in front of him. He stopped short and shrugged as if to say, 'What can I say?' All coaches know that all too often the outcome of a game is out of their control.

When George made the shot, the entire audience watching the play *Chess* in the Bushnell Theatre in Hartford exploded in a hurricane of shouting and waving of transistor radios. The twelve hundred people who had gathered at Gampel Pavilion back on the campus at Storrs ran out on the court in delirious celebration, as though the game had been played there.

"My dream shot was the one I missed," said George. "That's the one I've worked on so much this season. When it rimmed out, I said, "Uh-oh, there goes our dream season.' "

It was only fitting that George made the shot. He was the senior, the link to the years of frustration. He had been maligned much of his first three years. He had talent, but was perceived as only a so-so shot, as being too soft. Other teams had marquee players in the backcourt. The Huskies had Tate George. He seemed to symbolize the plight of Connecticut in the Big East: good but not good enough.

When George had been a freshman he had showed up in the basketball office wearing a Yankees cap, shades, and a Walkman. Calhoun threw him out of the office. That set the tone of their relationship. Calhoun didn't think George worked hard enough or wanted it enough. He relied too much on his vast charm and too little on the work ethic. He seemed to have too many other interests that continually got in the way of his being a better basketball player.

George also had a disturbing tendency to stroll into practice a few minutes before it was to start, oblivious to his teammates who had arrived early for extra practice. Soon he became known as Late George. Several times in his first two years he was thrown out of practice. The penalty for being thrown out of a practice was reporting to Calhoun's office the next day.

"You dreaded those days," said George.

Because of his lackadaisical attitude, George became the vent for a lot of Calhoun's frustrations about his team. Only later did it become apparent that one of the reasons Calhoun singled out George for so much verbal abuse was because George could handle it.

In addition, George became the symbol of the Connecticut fans' frustration as well. Last year he struggled, losing his starting job to the freshman Smith. He was booed by the home crowd during last year's NIT. Only after that did George vow to work on his game and go out his senior year in style. He wanted to be a leader. He wanted to lend stability to what he knew was going to be a young team. He spent the summer in Storrs, launching a few thousand jump shots.

"I thought of transferring, especially after that 9–19 year," George said. He was from Newark, and at times he wondered what he was doing at a school in the Connecticut countryside playing for a coach who made his players run four miles three days a week before practice officially began in October.

"The key was my family," he said. "My mom wouldn't tolerate me jumping around. She reminded me the number one thing was to get out of the city, and number two was school. . . . We've been working damn hard for years. There have been a lot of laps and a lot of miles to get to where we are today. All them hills, that cemetery hill, those four-mile runs we felt were kind of ludicrous. A 'fun run,' that's what they call it."

Throughout this year George had become the glue that held the team together. The senior leader, he handled the ball against pressure. He ran the offense, allowing Chris

Smith to concentrate on scoring. He also was 6-5 and insturmental in Connecticut's trapping defenses. If Smith had the most talent and Henefeld got the most publicity, Tate George was the spiritual leader. Without him the Huskies would not have had their dream season.

Two days later they faced Duke in the Eastern final. Win and they went on to the Final Four in Denver. Lose and it was over.

Five times down the stretch the game was tied. Six times the lead changed hands. Duke was leading by three in the closing seconds, but Smith hit a three-pointer with eight seconds left, sending the game into overtime. The lead changed hands five more times in overtime, setting up the drama of the ending.

Connecticut was leading by one with two seconds on the clock. Duke had the ball out of bounds on the side of the court. Duke's Christian Laettner in-bounded the ball, then got it back. His double-clutch, lean-in jumper found the bottom of the net and Connecticut's fantasy had suddenly ended. Two nights before they had won on a last-second shot. Now they had lost on one.

"I hate to see Tate go out this way," Calhoun said. "But we went out the way we came in. We fought. We dug, we scratched."

"We're not better than Connecticut," said Duke coach Mike Krzyzewski. "They're not better than us. We just won."

A few minutes earlier Calhoun and Krzyzewski had hugged in the hallway of the Meadowlands, their emotion clearly visible for all to see. They both knew that either team could have won the game, that either team could now be going on to Denver and the Final Four, instead of going home, the dream over.

In the tearful Connecticut locker room the players were trying to put the loss into perspective after a magical season. The room was hot and small. Too many people were crammed into it, all wanting answers when there were none.

"They should all cry," said Calhoun. "Not for what they

did badly, because of what they did so well. We did won-
drous things."

"Now there aren't any more trips." said John Gwynne.
"There aren't any more practices. There isn't any more
being together. The season is over and it hurts so much. We
were one game away, and we may never get this far again.
Duke has been to four Final Fours in the last five years.
They've already had their chance. We felt this was our
chance."

Henefeld stood across the room. Minutes before, he had
cried openly. "It's very painful," he said, "but I'll never
forget this experience. People will say it's only a sport, but
it's painful because we were so close, like a family."

He was asked if he could describe to his friends back home
in Israel what it meant to have come so far, yet still come up
short of the Final Four.

"I could go home and describe it, but they wouldn't
understand," he said. "Even the people who came to this
game might not understand. You'd have to have followed us
from the first day of practice until now. What we gave. The
hard work and sacrifice. The hard times. The better times."

Throughout the year Calhoun had been asked about Tate
George, and had said little. At first he had said that every
time he praised George, he seemed to go out and play
poorly. But there was more than that. Calhoun and George
always had a unique relationship, equal parts tension and
affection. As the season wound down, and George's career
at Connecticut with it, it was apparent their relationship had
also become laced with emotion. After George had made
the dramatic shot to beat Clemson and Calhoun was pep-
pered with countless questions concerning his senior guard,
he had said he would speak about Tate George when the
season was over. Now it was.

"He epitomizes what we want UConn basketball to represent," Calhoun said. "I've been waiting for four years to say
that. Tate George is as good a player as you're going to see.
He's everything you could ever want in a player. And as
good a player as he is, he's an even better person.

"I'm just so damned proud of these kids. I've always said

it's been a dream to coach in the Final Four, but I wouldn't trade a hundred Final Fours for the privilege of coaching these kids. You can't always write your own script. We can't write all our own endings, even though we'd like to."

No, you can't always write your own endings.

But the Huskies of Connecticut certainly wrote a great script.

REGULAR SEASON STANDINGS

	BIG EAST			All Games		
	W	L	PCT	W	L	PCT
Georgetown	13	3	.813	23	4	.852
Seton Hall	11	5	.688	25	5	.833
Syracuse	10	6	.625	25	6	.806
Pittsburgh	9	7	.563	16	11	.593
Villanova	7	9	.438	16	14	.533
Providence	7	9	.438	18	9	.667
Connecticut	6	10	.375	16	11	.593
St. John's	6	10	.375	15	12	.556
Boston College	3	13	.188	11	16	.407

BIG EAST ALL-STAR SELECTIONS

Player of the Year: Charles Smith (Georgetown)
Defensive Player of the Year: Alonzo Mourning (Georgetown)
Rookie of the Year: Brian Shorter (Pittsburgh)

All-Conference Selections
(*unanimous choice)
First Team

G	Charles Smith, 6-1, Sr. (Georgetown)
G*	Sherman Douglas, 6-0, Sr. (Syracuse)
C	Ramon Ramos, 6-8, Sr. (Seton Hall)
F*	Derrick Coleman, 6-9, Jr. (Syracuse)
F	Brian Shorter, 6-7, So. (Pittsburgh)

Second Team

G	Dana Barros, 5-11, Sr. (Boston College)
G	Stephen Thompson, 6-4, Jr. (Syracuse)
C	Alonzo Mourning, 6-10, Fr. (Georgetown)
F	Jayson Williams, 6-9, Jr. (St. John's)
F	Cliff Robinson, 6-11, Sr. (Connecticut)

INDIVIDUAL SCORING

			G	FG FGA	PCT	3FG FGA	PCT	FT FTA	PCT	PTS	AVG
1.	Barros, Dana	Boston College	27	215-453	0.475	103-241	0.427	110-130	0.846	643	23.8
2.	Shorter, Brian	Pittsburgh	27	190-318	0.597	1- 2	0.500	160-229	0.699	541	20.0
3.	Robinson, Cliff	Connecticut	27	202-429	0.471	4- 10	0.400	129-187	0.690	537	19.9
4.	Smith, Charles	Georgetown	26	178-361	0.493	22- 57	0.386	113-141	0.801	491	18.9
5.	Williams, Jayson	St. John's	25	183-322	0.568	0- 2	0.000	105-147	0.714	471	18.8
6.	West, Doug	Villanova	29	198-431	0.459	61-155	0.394	84-114	0.737	541	18.7
7.	Thompson, Stephen	Syracuse	31	251-389	0.645	6- 20	0.300	59-126	0.468	567	18.3
8.	Douglas, Sherman	Syracuse	31	229-415	0.552	31- 87	0.356	73-125	0.584	562	18.1
9.	Coleman, Derrick	Syracuse	31	200-337	0.593	0- 8	0.000	153-212	0.722	553	17.8
10.	Morton, John	Seton Hall	30	168-374	0.449	66-154	0.429	111-133	0.835	513	17.1

FIELD GOAL PERCENTAGE

1.	Thompson, Stephen	Syracuse
2.	Shorter, Brian	Pittsburgh
3.	Coleman, Derrick	Syracuse
4.	Williams, Jayson	St. John's
5.	Douglas, Sherman	Syracuse
6.	Greis, Tom	Villanova
7.	Conlon, Marty	Providence
8.	Smith, Charles	Georgetown
9.	Sealy, Malik	St. John's
10.	Barros, Dana	Boston College

FREE THROW PERCENTAGE

			G	FT FTA	PCT
1.	Miller, Sean	Pittsburgh	27	71- 78	0.910
2.	Matthews, Jason	Pittsburgh	27	132-146	0.904
3.	Barros, Dana	Boston College	27	110-130	0.846
4.	Morton, John	Seton Hall	30	111-133	0.835
5.	Ramos, Ramon	Seton Hall	29	98-119	0.824
6.	Brust, Matt	St. John's	27	90-110	0.818
7.	Smith, Charles	Georgetown	26	113-141	0.801
8.	Singleton, Billy	St. John's	27	75- 95	0.789
9.	Walker, Daryll	Seton Hall	30	127-162	0.784
10.	Massey, Gary	Villanova	30	82-105	0.781

REBOUNDING

			G	ORB DRB	TOT	AVG	HI
1.	Coleman, Derrick	Syracuse	31	117–245	362	11.7	19
2.	Shorter, Brian	Pittsburgh	27	103-163	266	9.9	20
3.	Ramos, Ramon	Seton Hall	29	78-147	225	7.8	13
4.	Martin, Bobby	Pittsburgh	27	80-122	202	7.5	13
5.	Robinson, Cliff	Connecticut	27	73-127	200	7.4	14
	Williams, Jayson	St. John's	25	63-121	184	7.4	14
	Mourning, Alonzo	Georgetown	27	72-129	201	7.4	17
8.	Conlon, Marty	Providence	27	75-114	189	7.0	16
	Turner, John	Georgetown	25	62-114	176	7.0	11
10.	Sealy, Malik	St. John's	25	72- 95	167	6.7	13

ASSISTS

			G	AST	AVG	HI
1.	Douglas, Sherman	Syracuse	31	277	8.9	22
2.	Screen, Carlton	Providence	27	188	7.0	12
3.	Miller, Sean	Pittsburgh	27	169	6.3	13
4.	Greene, Gerald	Seton Hall	30	155	5.2	10
5.	Smith, Charles	Georgetown	26	135	5.2	16
6.	George, Tate	Connecticut	27	131	4.9	10
7.	Buchanan, Jason	St. John's	27	130	4.8	10
8.	Wilson, Kenny	Villanova	30	145	4.8	10
9.	Murdock, Eric	Providence	27	127	4.7	9
10.	Porter, Darelle	Pittsburgh	27	125	4.6	12

STEALS

OVERALL		G	STL	AVG	HI
1. Screen, Carlton	Providence	27	97	3.6	7
2. Murdock, Eric	Providence	27	90	3.3	6
3. Thompson, Stephen	Syracuse	31	64	2.1	5
4. Smith, Charles	Georgetown	26	51	2.0	5
5. Robinson, Cliff	Connecticut	27	50	1.9	5
6. Douglas, Sherman	Syracuse	31	56	1.8	5
7. Owens, Billy	Syracuse	31	56	1.8	5
8. George, Tate	Connecticut	27	45	1.7	7
9. Buchanan, Jason	St. John's	27	46	1.7	4
10. Jackson, Jaren	Georgetown	27	46	1.7	4
11. Massey, Gary	Villanova	30	51	1.7	5

BLOCKED SHOTS

OVERALL		G	BLK	AVG	HI
1. Mourning, Alonzo	Georgetown	27	135	5.0	11
2. Coleman, Derrick	Syracuse	31	116	3.7	8
3. Mutombo, Dikembe	Georgetown	27	65	2.4	12
4. Greis, Tom	Villanova	30	50	1.7	5
5. Robinson, Cliff	Connecticut	27	39	1.4	4
6. Ramos, Ramon	Seton Hall	29	40	1.4	7
7. Shamsid-Deen, Ab	Providence	27	35	1.3	4
8. Foster, Cal	Providence	27	30	1.1	4
9. Owens, Billy	Syracuse	31	33	1.1	3
10. Werdann, Robert	St. John's	23	25	1.1	3

BOSTON COLLEGE

PLAYER	G	FG FGA	PCT	FT FTA	PCT	OR DR	TOT	AVG	A	BLK	S	MIN	AVG	PTS	AVG
Barros, Dana	27	215-453	0.475	110-130	0.846	13-83	96	3.6	89	3	43	1021	37.8	643	23.8
BIG EAST	16	116-273	0.425	85-99	0.859	7-52	59	3.7	55	1	16	618	38.6	371	23.2
Benton, Steve	27	141-314	0.449	97-129	0.752	54-92	146	5.4	87	2	22	947	35.1	394	14.6
BIG EAST	16	70-176	0.398	54-78	0.692	25-57	82	5.1	51	1	11	551	34.4	207	12.9
Able, Doug	26	93-175	0.531	42-68	0.618	62-79	141	5.4	12	26	21	590	22.7	228	8.8
BIG EAST	15	50-103	0.485	17-28	0.607	37-40	77	5.1	4	15	8	329	21.9	117	7.8
Beasley, Corey	27	82-187	0.439	33-61	0.541	56-68	124	4.6	16	13	14	669	24.8	197	7.3
BIG EAST	16	54-114	0.474	22-39	0.564	37-35	72	4.5	9	4	8	408	25.5	130	8.1
Moran, Bobby	26	46-116	0.397	34-41	0.829	25-55	80	3.1	73	5	42	638	24.5	150	5.8
BIG EAST	15	22-64	0.344	18-22	0.818	12-26	38	2.5	31	3	21	360	24.0	76	5.1
Edwards, Bryan	26	45-138	0.326	30-48	0.625	16-34	50	1.9	44	0	16	415	16.0	130	5.0
BIG EAST	15	29-91	0.319	22-32	0.688	10-24	34	2.3	27	0	8	291	19.4	88	5.9
Stovall, John	12	16-41	0.390	6-8	0.750	6-16	22	1.8	6	2	9	143	11.9	40	3.3
BIG EAST	6	3-14	0.214	3-4	0.750	4-8	12	2.0	1	0	2	57	9.5	10	1.7
Jackson, Corey	15	16-46	0.348	10-22	0.455	19-17	36	2.4	7	0	6	179	11.9	42	2.8
BIG EAST	8	12-31	0.387	9-17	0.529	13-9	22	2.8	3	0	3	114	14.3	33	4.1
Hjerpe, Tom	21	11-31	0.355	27-34	0.794	15-19	34	1.6	5	5	2	200	9.5	49	2.3
BIG EAST	13	4-17	0.235	16-18	0.889	8-7	15	1.2	4	2	1	119	9.2	24	1.8
Pruitt, Reggie	25	19-39	0.487	6-14	0.429	14-31	45	1.8	4	8	10	292	11.7	44	1.8
BIG EAST	16	11-25	0.440	4-8	0.500	9-10	19	1.2	4	3	5	187	11.7	26	1.6

CONNECTICUT

PLAYER	G	FG FGA	PCT	FT FTA	PCT	OR DR	TOT	AVG	A	BLK	S	MIN	AVG	PTS	AVG
Robinson, Cliff	27	202-429	0.471	129-187	0.690	73-127	200	7.4	43	39	50	847	31.4	537	19.9
BIG EAST	16	121-264	0.458	65-92	0.707	44-71	115	7.2	22	17	26	516	32.3	311	19.4
Gamble, Phil	27	119-290	0.410	46-63	0.730	32-54	86	3.2	41	5	28	806	29.9	326	12.1
BIG EAST	16	67-179	0.374	28-40	0.700	21-30	51	3.2	20	4	21	496	31.0	183	11.4
Smith, Chris	25	92-218	0.422	21-36	0.583	32-36	66	2.7	72	6	35	680	27.2	236	9.4
BIG EAST	14	57-144	0.396	16-20	0.800	21-23	44	3.1	33	2	19	404	28.9	150	10.7
George, Tate	27	70-159	0.440	56-74	0.757	35-58	93	3.4	131	5	45	767	28.4	198	7.3
BIG EAST	16	37-89	0.416	35-47	0.745	16-30	46	2.9	76	2	25	474	29.6	109	6.8
Williams, Murray	27	63-152	0.414	45-66	0.682	43-49	92	3.4	41	6	27	555	20.6	171	6.3
BIG EAST	16	35-82	0.427	25-38	0.658	20-28	48	3.0	17	2	15	341	21.3	95	5.9
Gwynn, John	24	59-122	0.484	21-27	0.778	14-13	27	1.1	12	1	7	273	11.4	148	6.2
BIG EAST	13	29-59	0.492	10-12	0.833	9-5	14	1.1	4	0	3	134	10.3	72	5.5
McCloud, Willie	26	50-103	0.485	32-42	0.762	54-44	98	3.8	13	10	29	509	19.6	132	5.1
BIG EAST	16	36-78	0.462	18-21	0.857	41-27	68	4.3	13	7	21	361	22.6	90	5.6
Sellers, Rod	27	36-81	0.444	25-49	0.510	48-65	113	4.2	5	9	7	453	16.8	97	3.6
BIG EAST	16	16-35	0.457	12-25	0.480	24-29	53	3.3	2	4	5	254	15.9	44	2.8
DePriest, Lyman	27	28-66	0.424	7-17	0.412	23-34	57	2.1	20	4	25	340	12.6	63	2.3
BIG EAST	16	12-26	0.462	3-9	0.333	12-18	30	1.9	8	3	6	182	11.4	27	1.7
Cyrulik, Dan	20	18-35	0.514	5-8	0.625	12-24	36	1.8	0	3	2	144	7.2	41	2.1
BIG EAST	11	5-11	0.455	2-2	1.000	4-7	11	1.0	0	1	1	55	5.0	12	1.1

GEORGETOWN

PLAYER	G	FG FGA	PCT	FT FTA	PCT	OR DR	TOT	AVG	A	BLK	S	MIN	AVG	PTS	AVG
Smith, Charles	26	176-361	0.493	113-141	0.801	19- 77	96	3.7	135	4	51	864	33.2	491	18.9
BIG EAST	15	89-203	0.438	67- 87	0.770	12- 45	57	3.8	69	3	21	537	35.8	258	17.2
Jackson, Jaren	27	139-304	0.457	51- 74	0.689	60- 81	141	5.2	54	10	46	711	26.3	360	13.3
BIG EAST	16	71-168	0.423	33- 43	0.767	34- 47	81	4.1	31	3	23	450	28.1	192	12.0
Mourning, Alonzo	27	125-209	0.598	96-152	0.632	72-129	201	7.4	22	135	12	750	27.8	347	12.9
BIG EAST	16	72-124	0.581	53- 84	0.631	37- 66	103	6.4	12	71	5	463	28.9	197	12.3
Tillmon, Mark	25	75-169	0.444	33- 50	0.660	20- 37	57	2.3	27	4	19	464	18.6	203	8.1
BIG EAST	16	56-109	0.514	15- 25	0.600	12- 21	33	2.1	18	2	10	303	18.9	146	9.1
Turner, John	25	63-135	0.467	56-100	0.560	62-114	176	7.0	29	15	15	564	22.6	182	7.3
BIG EAST	14	35- 64	0.547	31- 55	0.564	32- 72	104	7.4	9	7	8	356	25.4	101	7.2
Bryant, Dwayne	27	68-132	0.515	42- 62	0.677	18- 52	70	2.6	94	3	41	642	23.8	193	7.1
BIG EAST	16	38- 79	0.481	32- 47	0.681	12- 33	45	2.8	54	0	21	388	24.3	116	7.3
Winston, Bobby	27	49- 96	0.510	21- 43	0.488	35- 51	86	3.2	85	5	36	459	17.0	119	4.4
BIG EAST	16	29- 58	0.500	12- 25	0.480	22- 26	48	3.0	40	3	21	277	17.3	70	4.4
Bell, Milton	19	29- 52	0.558	12- 18	0.667	18- 23	41	2.2	10	10	7	177	9.3	71	3.7
BIG EAST	8	7- 14	0.500	4- 6	0.667	5- 5	10	1.3	2	2	1	59	7.4	18	2.3
Mutombo, Dikembe	27	40- 58	0.690	20- 41	0.488	32- 62	94	3.5	5	65	9	314	11.6	100	3.7
BIG EAST	16	15- 26	0.577	7- 13	0.538	16- 36	52	3.3	1	42	5	197	12.3	37	2.3
Thompson, Ronnie	22	17- 35	0.486	5- 6	0.833	1- 8	9	0.4	16	0	5	123	5.6	42	1.9
BIG EAST	12	9- 19	0.474	2- 2	1.000	1- 5	6	0.5	3	0	1	49	4.1	22	1.8

PITTSBURGH

PLAYER	G	FG FGA	PCT	FT FTA	PCT	OR DR	TOT	AVG	A	BLK	S	MIN	AVG	PTS	AVG
Shorter, Brian	27	190-318	0.597	160-229	0.699	103-163	266	9.9	47	15	15	955	35.4	541	20.0
BIG EAST	16	109-182	0.599	104-155	0.671	48- 88	136	8.5	27	10	7	576	36.0	322	20.1
Matthews, Jason	27	131-265	0.494	132-146	0.904	30- 45	75	2.8	34	7	25	793	29.4	452	16.7
BIG EAST	16	74-150	0.493	80- 87	0.920	15- 31	46	2.9	19	3	16	479	29.9	254	16.5
Martin, Bobby	27	104-217	0.479	125-191	0.654	80-122	202	7.5	18	25	23	898	33.3	333	12.3
BIG EAST	16	52-115	0.452	71-110	0.645	48- 69	117	7.3	6	17	13	540	33.8	175	10.9
Brookin, Rod	26	93-206	0.451	50- 77	0.649	24- 53	77	3.0	25	5	37	607	23.3	267	10.3
BIG EAST	15	55-116	0.474	32- 43	0.744	13- 25	38	2.5	16	2	21	366	24.4	164	10.9
Miller, Sean	27	77-184	0.418	71- 78	0.910	7- 46	53	2.0	69	0	27	957	35.4	278	10.3
BIG EAST	16	44-104	0.423	45- 50	0.900	5- 27	32	2.0	04	0	18	578	36.1	163	10.2
Porter, Darelle	27	80-196	0.408	48- 66	0.727	36- 87	123	4.6	25	13	31	790	29.3	213	7.9
BIG EAST	16	47-123	0.382	32- 43	0.744	22- 52	74	4.6	72	9	20	513	32.1	130	8.1
Johnson, Gilbert	17	9- 18	0.500	10- 13	0.769	7- 12	19	1.1	2	1	1	90	5.3	28	1.6
BIG EAST	8	5- 9	0.556	3- 4	0.750	3- 9	12	1.5	0	0	0	43	5.4	13	1.6
Cavanaugh, Pat	25	12- 44	0.273	11- 22	0.500	3- 11	14	0.6	25	0	11	192	7.7	37	1.5
BIG EAST	15	5- 16	0.313	6- 10	0.600	1- 4	5	0.3	10	0	4	81	5.4	16	1.1
Bailey, Nate	17	3- 15	0.200	8- 10	0.800	5- 10	15	0.9	9	1	0	94	5.5	14	0.8
BIG EAST	7	1- 5	0.200	0- 0	0.000	2- 2	4	0.6	3	0	0	27	3.9	2	0.3
Maslek, Steve	15	1- 8	0.125	4- 6	0.667	5- 8	13	0.9	1	0	0	64	4.3	6	0.4
BIG EAST	6	0- 2	0.000	0- 0	0.000	2- 2	4	0.7	1	0	0	18	3.0	0	0.0

PROVIDENCE

PLAYER	G	FG	FGA	PCT	FT	FTA	PCT	OR	DR	TOT	AVG	A	BLK	S	MIN	AVG	PTS	AVG
Murdock, Eric	27	154-	334	0.461	93-	123	0.756	34-	95	129	4.8	127	9	90	874	32.4	442	16.4
BIG EAST	16	98-	223	0.439	53-	75	0.707	20-	43	73	4.6	62	2	54	555	34.7	276	17.3
Conlon, Marty	27	142-	274	0.518	82-	115	0.713	75-	114	189	7.0	57	13	28	833	30.9	380	14.1
BIG EAST	16	74-	156	0.474	57-	80	0.713	46-	68	114	7.1	32	6	9	513	32.1	217	13.6
Pallazi, Matt	27	133-	272	0.489	30-	35	0.857	28-	33	61	2.3	48	2	26	674	25.0	348	12.9
BIG EAST	16	68-	149	0.456	27-	30	0.900	15-	21	36	2.3	30	1	14	415	25.9	187	11.7
Screen, Carlton	27	119-	245	0.486	72-	96	0.750	13-	38	51	1.9	188	0	97	883	32.7	317	11.7
BIG EAST	16	65-	142	0.458	47-	60	0.783	4-	18	22	1.4	100	0	53	537	33.6	181	11.3
Foster, Cal	27	68-	121	0.562	61-	88	0.693	39-	62	101	3.7	9	30	10	428	15.9	197	7.3
BIG EAST	16	44-	87	0.506	48-	64	0.750	23-	40	63	3.9	7	13	6	288	18.0	136	8.5
Shamsid-Deen, Ab	27	64-	110	0.582	45-	63	0.714	40-	54	94	3.5	10	35	10	447	16.6	173	6.4
BIG EAST	16	41-	67	0.612	28-	40	0.700	23-	28	51	3.2	8	20	3	270	16.9	110	6.9
Bent, Greg	20	47-	83	0.566	10-	15	0.667	12-	33	45	2.3	4	7	7	239	12.0	105	5.3
BIG EAST	12	27-	44	0.614	4-	8	0.500	10-	13	23	1.9	0	1	3	142	11.8	58	4.8
Wright, Darryl	27	44-	97	0.454	36-	45	0.800	18-	47	65	2.4	39	3	9	357	13.2	136	5.0
BIG EAST	16	26-	63	0.413	27-	32	0.844	11-	29	40	2.5	24	3	6	247	15.4	87	5.4
Watts, Chris	25	24-	67	0.358	2-	3	0.667	6-	16	22	0.9	23	4	7	270	10.8	72	2.9
BIG EAST	14	7-	21	0.333	0-	0	0.000	3-	5	8	0.6	10	0	2	111	7.9	20	1.4
Bragg, Marques	14	13-	28	0.464	6-	15	0.400	10-	7	17	1.2	4	3	1	78	5.6	32	2.3
BIG EAST	4	1-	1	1.000	0-	0	0.000	0-	1	1	0.2	0	1	0	8	2.0	2	0.5

ST. JOHN'S

PLAYER	G	FG	FGA	PCT	FT	FTA	PCT	OR	DR	TOT	AVG	A	BLK	S	MIN	AVG	PTS	AVG
Williams, Jayson	25	183-	322	0.568	105-	147	0.714	63-	121	184	7.4	14	21	9	825	33.0	471	18.8
BIG EAST	15	112-	200	0.560	63-	89	0.708	39-	76	115	7.7	9	13	2	520	34.7	287	19.1
Sealy, Malik	25	128-	263	0.487	48-	86	0.558	72-	95	167	6.7	52	20	28	928	37.1	310	12.4
BIG EAST	14	57-	134	0.425	32-	53	0.604	42-	46	88	6.3	22	6	12	510	36.4	147	10.5
Brust, Matt	27	93-	222	0.419	90-	110	0.818	25-	93	118	4.4	81	3	38	986	36.5	310	11.5
BIG EAST	16	54-	137	0.394	57-	71	0.803	12-	60	72	4.5	54	2	24	613	38.3	189	11.8
Buchanan, Jason	27	85-	177	0.480	57-	70	0.814	19-	38	57	2.1	130	2	46	838	31.0	235	8.7
BIG EAST	16	49-	110	0.445	35-	43	0.814	10-	22	32	2.0	74	1	24	535	33.4	137	8.6
Werdann, Robert	23	78-	158	0.494	30-	49	0.612	43-	104	147	6.4	34	25	22	614	26.7	186	8.1
BIG EAST	13	40-	92	0.435	22-	35	0.629	24-	58	82	6.3	17	9	11	335	25.8	102	7.8
Singleton, Billy	27	70-	150	0.467	75-	95	0.789	28-	79	107	4.0	25	6	18	521	19.3	215	8.0
BIG EAST	16	42-	95	0.442	46-	57	0.807	22-	45	67	4.2	15	2	13	339	21.2	130	8.1
Aiken, Darrell	18	13-	29	0.448	13-	17	0.765	4-	4	8	0.4	11	0	2	134	7.4	41	2.3
BIG EAST	11	10-	20	0.500	5-	9	0.556	2-	3	5	0.5	8	0	2	75	6.8	27	2.5
Mullin, Terence	22	13-	25	0.520	17-	19	0.895	2-	8	10	0.5	21	0	7	172	7.8	48	2.2
BIG EAST	14	10-	19	0.526	11-	12	0.917	2-	7	9	0.6	13	0	3	123	8.8	35	2.5
Milhaven, Barry	16	8-	27	0.296	11-	23	0.478	11-	14	25	1.6	6	1	6	117	7.3	28	1.8
BIG EAST	10	7-	20	0.350	9-	19	0.474	10-	10	20	2.0	3	1	5	87	8.7	24	2.4
Muto, Sean	24	1-	30	0.433	5-	10	0.500	14-	36	50	2.1	6	10	2	224	9.3	31	1.3
BIG EAST	14	5-	14	0.357	2-	2	1.000	8-	15	23	1.6	2	3	1	107	7.6	12	0.9

SETON HALL

PLAYER	G	FG FGA	PCT	FT FTA	PCT	OR DR	TOT	AVG	A	BLK	S	MIN	AVG	PTS	AVG
Morton, John	30	168-374	0.449	111-133	0.835	28-79	107	3.6	81	14	43	856	28.5	513	17.1
BIG EAST	16	88-204	0.431	75-91	0.824	14-38	52	3.3	40	4	20	476	29.8	281	17.6
Gaze, Andrew	30	134-261	0.513	65-91	0.714	39-96	135	4.5	87	14	28	953	31.8	408	13.6
BIG EAST	16	80-151	0.530	39-57	0.684	19-65	84	5.3	51	12	16	568	35.5	238	14.9
Ramos, Ramon	29	137-242	0.566	98-119	0.824	78-147	225	7.8	37	40	19	798	27.5	372	12.8
BIG EAST	15	80-143	0.559	64-77	0.831	43-75	118	7.9	20	17	10	453	30.2	224	14.9
Walker, Daryll	30	108-218	0.495	127-162	0.784	81-116	197	6.6	34	11	29	795	26.5	343	11.4
BIG EAST	16	45-105	0.429	80-99	0.808	43-60	103	6.4	20	5	14	441	27.6	170	10.6
Greene, Gerald	30	66-160	0.413	96-126	0.762	12-70	82	2.7	155	4	30	914	30.5	254	8.5
BIG EAST	16	31-83	0.373	65-87	0.747	7-37	44	2.8	89	2	14	545	34.1	139	8.7
Volcy, Frantz	30	60-107	0.561	42-58	0.724	32-49	81	2.7	8	15	6	375	12.5	162	5.4
BIG EAST	16	30-55	0.545	21-29	0.724	16-28	44	2.8	6	8	4	187	11.7	81	5.1
Cooper, Michael	29	60-110	0.545	26-42	0.619	33-55	88	3.0	26	14	11	452	15.6	146	5.0
BIG EAST	16	28-53	0.528	5-10	0.500	13-25	38	2.4	14	8	3	234	14.6	61	3.8
Avent, Anthony	30	54-120	0.450	24-40	0.600	34-55	89	3.0	9	20	6	314	10.5	132	4.4
BIG EAST	16	20-50	0.400	10-15	0.667	14-25	39	2.4	3	8	0	152	9.5	50	3.1
Wigington, Lelan	24	8-29	0.276	25-30	0.833	2-15	17	0.7	45	1	12	212	8.8	41	1.7
BIG EAST	11	2-10	0.200	3-7	0.429	0-1	1	0.1	7	0	1	60	5.5	7	0.6
Katsikis, Nick	25	14-31	0.452	2-3	0.667	4-11	15	0.6	13	2	4	124	5.0	37	1.5
BIG EAST	14	6-10	0.600	0-1	0.000	2-6	8	0.6	3	1	2	42	3.0	15	1.1

SYRACUSE

PLAYER	G	FG FGA	PCT	FT FTA	PCT	OR DR	TOT	AVG	A	BLK	S	MIN	AVG	PTS	AVG
Thompson, Stephen	31	251-389	0.645	59-126	0.468	76-79	155	5.0	58	14	64	1007	32.5	567	18.3
BIG EAST	16	112-184	0.609	29-72	0.403	40-48	88	5.5	37	5	38	568	35.5	255	15.9
Douglas, Sherman	31	229-415	0.552	73-125	0.584	28-48	76	2.5	277	1	56	1076	34.7	562	18.1
BIG EAST	16	108-213	0.507	53-84	0.631	13-22	35	2.2	137	1	23	577	36.1	262	17.6
Coleman, Derrick	32	200-337	0.593	153-212	0.722	117-245	362	11.7	95	116	40	1042	33.6	553	17.8
BIG EAST	16	92-173	0.532	99-132	0.750	71-113	184	11.5	38	57	27	581	36.3	283	17.7
Owens, Billy	31	147-272	0.540	72-113	0.637	86-117	203	6.5	97	33	56	987	31.5	372	12.0
BIG EAST	16	75-157	0.478	41-63	0.651	41-50	91	5.7	39	15	31	537	33.6	195	12.2
Roe, Matt	31	125-249	0.502	36-53	0.679	12-67	79	2.5	57	1	32	816	26.3	356	11.5
BIG EAST	16	60-128	0.469	11-18	0.611	7-21	28	1.8	13	0	10	455	28.4	164	10.3
Johnson, David	30	44-97	0.454	23-50	0.460	19-40	59	2.0	29	3	13	404	13.5	113	3.8
BIG EAST	15	17-37	0.459	6-13	0.462	10-16	26	1.7	12	1	5	179	11.9	41	2.7
Manning, Richard	30	44-83	0.530	27-35	0.771	15-36	51	1.7	4	9	3	286	9.5	115	3.8
BIG EAST	15	13-24	0.542	7-10	0.700	4-9	13	0.9	1	2	1	103	6.9	33	2.2
Harried, Herman	30	44-80	0.550	16-35	0.457	35-53	88	2.9	13	2	12	317	10.6	104	3.5
BIG EAST	16	13-28	0.464	7-15	0.467	11-14	25	1.6	3	2	5	156	9.8	33	2.1
Scott, Anthony	18	16-40	0.450	6-10	0.600	6-12	18	1.1	11	6	7	132	8.3	44	2.8
BIG EAST	5	5-8	0.625	0-2	0.000	2-2	4	0.8	1	0	0	24	4.8	10	2.0
Rogers, Erik	14	7-20	0.350	6-12	0.500	8-15	23	1.6	3	2	3	56	4.0	21	1.5
BIG EAST	4	3-7	0.429	0-0	0.000	4-4	8	2.0	2	0	1	13	3.3	6	1.5

VILLANOVA

PLAYER	G	FG FGA	PCT	FT FTA	PCT	OR DR	TOT	AVG	A	BLK	S	MIN	AVG	PTS	AVG
West, Doug	29	198-431	0.459	84-114	0.737	33-107	140	4.8	75	14	38	995	34.3	541	18.7
BIG EAST	15	90-208	0.433	40-58	0.690	12-54	66	4.4	41	9	21	536	35.7	244	16.3
Greis, Tom	30	174-326	0.534	79-110	0.718	73-115	188	6.3	42	50	19	844	28.1	427	14.2
BIG EAST	16	97-183	0.530	44-59	0.746	47-59	106	6.6	28	27	9	456	28.5	238	14.9
Taylor, Rodney	30	92-187	0.492	91-119	0.765	79-110	189	6.3	14	5	19	733	24.4	275	9.2
BIG EAST	16	45-93	0.484	64-82	0.780	40-50	90	5.6	8	3	10	368	23.0	154	9.6
Wilson, Kenny	30	90-203	0.443	69-86	0.802	8-54	62	2.1	145	1	24	894	29.8	276	9.2
BIG EAST	16	48-105	0.457	28-37	0.757	5-28	33	2.1	74	0	11	485	30.3	138	8.6
Massey, Gary	30	86-153	0.562	82-105	0.781	57-77	134	4.5	57	8	51	959	32.0	254	8.5
BIG EAST	16	50-90	0.556	40-48	0.833	26-41	67	4.2	29	4	21	540	33.8	140	8.8
Dowdell, Marc	30	66-145	0.455	46-77	0.597	51-111	162	5.4	21	16	10	684	22.8	179	6.0
BIG EAST	16	38-90	0.422	26-41	0.634	28-66	94	5.9	13	6	6	412	25.8	102	6.4
Walker, Chris	29	27-81	0.333	16-23	0.696	4-18	22	0.8	40	1	18	366	12.6	80	2.8
BIG EAST	15	18-52	0.346	2-4	0.500	4-7	11	0.7	14	1	9	196	13.1	45	3.0
Woodard, Greg	30	20-77	0.260	25-32	0.781	12-19	31	1.0	18	2	4	272	9.1	74	2.5
BIG EAST	16	11-35	0.314	13-17	0.765	7-6	13	0.8	4	2	4	125	7.8	40	2.5
Bekkedam, Barry	13	4-14	0.286	5-7	0.714	2-17	19	1.5	4	3	2	81	6.2	13	1.0
BIG EAST	4	0-0	0.000	0-0	0.000	0-2	2	0.5	0	0	0	11	2.8	0	0.0
Miller, David	22	7-18	0.389	5-9	0.556	3-10	13	0.6	10	0	9	138	6.3	21	1.0
BIG EAST	12	2-10	0.200	0-3	0.000	2-6	8	0.7	6	0	4	82	6.8	4	0.3

GAME TIME!

Revised and updated with over 75 all
new sports records and photographs!

THE ILLUSTRATED
SPORTS RECORD BOOK
Zander Hollander and David Schulz

Here, in a single book, are more than 350
all-time sports records with stories and
photos so vivid it's like "being there." All the
sports classics are here: Babe Ruth, Wilt
Chamberlain, Muhammad Ali ... plus the
stories of such active stars as Dwight Gooden
and Wayne Gretzky. This is the authoritative
book on what the great records are, and
who set them—an engrossing, fun-filled
reference guide filled with anecdotes of
hundreds of renowned athletes whose
remarkable records remain as fresh as when
they were set.

There's an epidemic with 27 million victims. And no visible symptoms.

It's an epidemic of people who can't read.

Believe it or not, 27 million Americans are functionally illiterate, about one adult in five.

The solution to this problem is you... when you join the fight against illiteracy. So call the Coalition for Literacy at toll-free **1-800-228-8813** and volunteer.

Volunteer Against Illiteracy. The only degree you need is a degree of caring.